For Jim from Doug,
with a brother's love, and
51 years of friendship
and admiration.

August 1989

Street of Dreams

Street of Dreams

The Nature and Legacy of the 1960s

Douglas M. Knight

Duke University Press Durham and London 1989

Library of Congress Cataloging-in-Publication Data
Knight, Douglas M., 1921–
Street of dreams: the nature and legacy of the 1960s / Douglas M.
Knight.
Bibliography: p.
Includes index.
ISBN 0-8223-0902-5
1. United States—History—1961–1969.   2. United States—Social
conditions—1960–1980.   3. Universities and colleges—United States—
History—20th century.   4. Duke University—History—20th century.
I. Title.
E841.K58   1989
973.922—dc 19   88-36420

For Chris, Doug, Tom, Steve

Filiis Fratribusque

Always in the deep core of history there seems to preside an invisible presence, a sort of extraterritorial power of which the traditional historian is largely unaware. It is as if below the opaque field on which events crowd, like black iron filings on a table in an experimental laboratory of physics, an unseen force moves from time to time like a magnet, concentrating and compelling the metal units about it into a vital magnetic pattern. History describes faithfully what happens on the surface of the table, but what goes on underneath remains often beneath its notice.—Laurens Van der Post, *The Dark Eye in Africa*

Contents

Preface   xi
Acknowledgments   xv

The Antecedents   1
  A View from the Bridge   1
  Years of Angst and Plenty   8
  The Prophets and the Mountebanks   17
  Voices in the Wilderness   22
  The Rhythms of Time   30

Decade of the Dream   36
  In the Beginning   36
  The Curve of Action and the Common Bond   45
  A Special Strength   53
  The Corridors of Power   60
  Poets, Playwrights, Prophets   70
  Force and Insight: The Dynamics of the Decade   78

Looking-Glass Land   95
  Duke in the 1960s: A Web of Purposes   96
  Duke: Money and the Governance of the University   102
  Paul Gross: The Dilemma of Power   104
  The Ford Grant   106
  Loyalty Oath in North Carolina: A Classic Issue   108
  Jesse Helms: Politician in the Making   110
  Reason in Madness: The Special Case of Berkeley   111

Duke and the Fine Arts: More Than Meets the Eye   114
Two Campuses or One?   117
The Duke Student Body in the 1960s   118
The Visitors: Dissent in Many Voices   124
The Road Not Taken   127
Universities Under Fire: The Dancer and the Dance   132
A Quiet Day in Dixie   134
Duke Faculty: Where Angels Fear to Tread   140
Yale: Oh, Brave New World   143
Administration: The Necessary Evil   146
The San Francisco State of Mind   151
Duke at the End of the Decade   153
The Curve of Power: University Style   156
To Push Back the Walls   158

Continuums of Change: From the Sixties into the Eighties   161

Index   201

Preface

This book grows from a good deal of personal experience in the decade of the sixties. Essential to it, however, are the reflection and analysis allowed by the last twenty years. The eruptions of the time have been distanced. They can now be recollected with fair tranquility, and they call for several kinds of exploration.

I see the period in a dual historical context—both through the events which brought it into being, and those which it has influenced in surprising and often half-hidden ways. There are major historic parallels to it, and one decade of the nineteenth century in particular may help us understand its driving eccentricities and urgencies. At the same time a whole cluster of today's cultural patterns owe it their style and stance. Positively or negatively, the decade is still thoroughly alive for us.

I shall not be concerned with a detailed chronology of the time, except as certain events have a causal sequence, and as they reveal a double life which deserves our attention—with one meaning for us as we lived them day by day and another as we now see them whole and to a degree external to us. I concentrate on the inner life of the decade as we saw it in the universities, in the world of artists and publicists, in the almost mythic perception of people, events, and movements which many shared, and in the emergence of certain major and permanent changes in our society which are the enduring legacy of the time. Changes in everything from religious form to administrative structure show us the lines of stress and response which grew from the sixties.

The reinforcement, the support which major movements gave to one another is one of the decade's most compelling aspects. It is possible indeed to see the structure of the period as a Buckminster Fuller dome, with each element supporting the others; the mutual support is there only in flashes, of course, but its effects are powerful —so powerful at times that they seem highly coordinated, seem to be the result of common planning. In fact, they result from urgent but disparate concerns which, to the amazement of most of us caught up in them, flowed together for a while and took their strength in part from one another. There was a brief, vivid coherence of emotion and purpose alive within a great diversity of causes. The antecedents and consequences of those singular years are not secondary, however; they are essential to my interpretation of what went on. Indeed, the usefulness of this book will result, I hope, from its sense of the long continuity of major events fully as much as from an intimate sense of their uniqueness at the time.

At the same time there are unique experiences which should be recorded. W. H. Auden's "images that hurt and connect" are the stuff of history as well as the inner life. Duke and the university experience will form one of the two central sections of the book; I shall consider Duke in particular, not just in its response to the major issues and movements but as an institution which moved ahead in its growth, often despite the events raging around it. As a result, we shall be dealing with Siamese twins—Duke in the sixties and Duke in itself.

Duke will serve, along with a group of sister institutions, as a mirror for large and stormy realities brought to a focus within them. The universities are vital for our understanding of the issues; but like the established churches (whose reactions are also deeply revealing) they are not the issues they mirror. Those issues are well known in a general way. I shall give my chief attention to the inner force of each, the passion which gave it a certain trajectory during the decade and brought it to rest at a point not predicted by and often alien to the first intent of those who urged each movement along its fateful path. Whether the military, the liberal politicians, the radical left, the black nationalists, or the varied women's movements—all were driven by their dreams, and all found their dreams reshaped as they issued in action. I shall ask where the dreams came from, what happened to them during the decade, and what came of it all.

October 1988

Acknowledgments

It is hard indeed to do justice to the help I have received in writing this book. I owe a debt, not only to the individuals whose names follow, but to places and experiences long past: to Exeter which first set my mind on the path of learning; to Yale for a superb education in literature and criticism, as well as for the discovery of my teaching vocation; to Lawrence and Duke Universities for the hard lessons and great rewards of the President's job; and to the Questar Corporation for a unique encounter with American industry. All of them have contributed greatly to my perception of the nineteen sixties.

My debt to individuals is far more specific: criticism of a first outline or of certain completed sections; help with the production of the manuscript, with its styling, its consistency. The staff of Duke University Press must come first; I do not know whether to praise more their courtesy or their judgment. Neither they nor the friends whose names follow are responsible for the limitations of this book, but they can take credit for improving it: James Armsey, Laura Bornholdt, Marguerite Braymer, Debra Egner, Eleanor Elliott, William Griffith, Judith Hancock, Constance Kenderdine, Clark Kerr, Ethan Knight, Grace Nichols Knight, Maynard Mack, Nancy Weiss Malkiel, Joseph Martin, Deirdre Mullane, Charles Muscatine, Doris Parrish, James Perkins, John Schaff, Mary Semans, Jerry Sherwood, John Summerskill, Mariella Sundstrom, Alan Williams, Margaret Wimsatt.

The Antecedents

A View from the Bridge

In November 1960 the Rockefeller Brothers Fund released *Prospect for America*, the result of four years of study and discussion by some of the ablest men and women in the country. Many of them were to become our common property in the next decade—Dean Rusk, Henry Kissinger, John Gardner, Charles Percy. Many were already dominant figures in the thought and action of post-war America—Edward Teller, James Killian, David Sarnoff, Henry Luce, Nelson Rockefeller. There were roughly a hundred of them supported throughout by an unusually able staff; their six reports brought us to the living edge of our most turbulent decade, and there may be no better voices than theirs to tell us what we *thought* we thought. Certainly, there were no voices so highly structured, so well-coordinated, and yet so diverse.

As I use them to introduce the decade, then, I pay them my deepest respect for a valiant effort. The senior panel put the issues in their first paragraphs:

> We who have taken part in this project have done so in the conviction that the United States has come to a crucial point in its history.
>
> The signs are all around us. Probably never have these signs—of growth and change, of danger and dilemma—so abounded in all spheres of our national life. From the security of our nation to the renewal of our cities, from the education of our young to

the well-being of our old, from the facts of military might to the subtle substance of spiritual strength—everything seems touched by challenge. (p. xix)

The panel then developed the challenge from six perspectives that raised—or should have raised—the major options available to us in foreign and domestic policy. As I comment on what was left unsaid and unperceived, I am painfully aware of the peril which all prophets face; it is impossible to know the future and often trivial to indulge one's hindsight as though it were wisdom. At the same time the issues not perceived in 1960 determined the course of the coming decade as relentlessly as those which were seen. And that fact is worth our serious attention. Much of the shock and tragedy of the time resulted from those forces we did not see. They are spelled out equally by the omissions as by the analytical thrust of the Rockefeller panel reports, so that the texts come through to us now with a very special urgency of meaning. They carry the burden of all that has happened since.

The panels issued their six reports at various times in the late 1950s: Report I, *The Mid-Century Challenge to U.S. Foreign Policy*; Report II, *International Security: The Military Aspect*; Report III, *Foreign Economic Policy for the Twentieth Century*; Report IV, *The Challenge to America: Its Economic and Social Aspects*; Report V, *The Pursuit of Excellence: Education and the Future of America*; Report VI, *The Power of the Democratic Idea*. Clearly, the whole study is directed equally toward our own society and toward our world commitments. In each report a position is developed—often brilliantly —which does intimate what was to come to pass—but intimates it obliquely, in a mist for all the clarity of statement. (I am reminded of Tolstoy's dazzling description of the start of the battle of Borodino, where the armies march down into a fog-shrouded valley, invisible to one another.) Panel I, for example, bases its view of American foreign policy on the twin assumptions of an enormously powerful enemy and a fluid world political situation within which positive actions must be taken. "But when the international order is in flux, or when a new order waits to be created, responsibilities are thrust on some nations that call them to undertakings far beyond anything suggested by their own immediate interests" (p. 20). When these concerns coalesce, or if they seem to coalesce in some quarter of the world, then it will be the obligation of the United States to meet that supposed challenge.

> This brief and necessarily limited review of the nature and dimensions of the Communist threat should not obscure what is one of the most important facts about the cold war; namely that it is being waged by Communists as one conflict. (p. 48)

> Our policies must be shaped to specific cases, but with the broad principles outlined above continually operative. (p. 52)

Once we have said this much, a political trap is set for the 1960s, that trap of involvement in Southeast Asia, all the more dangerous because it marked our altruistic desire to help the new nations of the world in their self-determination. With supreme irony the panel identified this stance at the start of its analysis. "The attempt to be 'realistic' in French Indochina—supporting a colonial power so as to contain communism—was a faltering effort partly because of the realization that we were going against our natural respect for national independence" (p. 15). As a result, the real nature of the French failure in Vietnam was concealed from us; we could not believe that a "communist" government in Vietnam might be basically nationalistic in its resistance to all intruders. Still less could we recognize that Soviet and Chinese purposes in the area were at profound variance with one another. The menace was perceived to be monolithic, with any local government called communist automatically regarded as the puppet of outside powers. The millennial antagonism of Vietnam and China was ignored—if indeed it was even known. There is no need to labor the point; we would move step by step into a situation whose true nature we did not recognize and whose tactical character we failed utterly to understand. A guerrilla war of national liberation—as the French example had just demonstrated—is virtually impossible to combat by conventional military means. The road would be long, the steps often plausible, but the necessary preconditions for disaster are described for us here by Panel I. The report was issued on December 8, 1959.

Panel II provides the appropriate technical support for the theoretical position developed by Panel I. I hesitate to comment too caus-
tically on the devotion of one whole report to *International Security:
The Military Aspect*. With its cold war preoccupation—tempered by
an equal horror of nuclear weaponry—it is a highly detailed evo-
cation of attitudes which were current coin in Washington of the
1980s. "Ever since our unilateral disarmament at the end of World
War II failed to produce the peace we desired so earnestly, the
United States has been forced to engage in a military effort unprece-
dented in our history in peacetime. Even so, it has still proved inadequate to the challenge we confront" (p. 99). Of more than casual
interest is the fact that the report was drafted by Henry Kissinger.
Perceptions which were to inform in many ways the foreign policy
of the 1960s perhaps found their clearest early expression in it. Like
Panel I, Panel II believes that the Soviet Union and China constitute
one menace. It is insensitive (or inimical) to the radical expression
of nationalist hopes, so that it will be equally opposed to Castro and
Ho Chi Min. It is pious in its avowals of horror at nuclear weaponry
but analyzes its many forms and possibilities and concludes far from
its cautious origin: "The willingness to engage in nuclear war, when
necessary, is the price of our freedom" (p. 117).

I do not wish to shoot fish in a barrel, though the temptation
is great. There is an overwhelming sadness to these two reports,
however. They provide a mirror image of the military and political
disasters of the 1960s; their ignorance of the real scenario is so great
that I can almost call it innocence. And it is vital for us to recognize
that such innocence was *in itself* one great contributing cause of the
disasters to come—disasters which would mark in the deepest sense
a loss of American innocence, and a loss of pious superiority in world
affairs as well. Already in 1958 the path out of Eden showed, white
in the moonlight of the future.

There were other roadways also to be walked, leading to the other
great hidden mysteries of the world economic/social order on the
one hand, and on the other to the inner life of American democracy as embodied in American educational hopes and dreams. In
these two major areas of the report there is not the haunting déjà
vu which we get from the military section. Panels III and IV ad-

dress, instead, the brave new world of postcolonial economics and the events in American economy and society which should accompany this massive international liberation. Panel III tries to remedy the sterile militarism of Panel II by recognizing the legitimate aspirations of the new nations—including their extreme nationalism—and by affirming (with valiant optimism) that "the challenge before the free world is to bring about a new international order" (p. 174).

This is set against the Sino-Soviet techniques of economic subversion and political penetration. From the perspective of 1958 it seemed to a committee of highly thoughtful and experienced men (there were no women on this panel) that Soviet aid and trade relationships had "assumed proportions that indicate a continuing degree of dependence rather than a casual or transient bargaining incident" (p. 178). Cuba had not yet emerged as a prime example for the 1960s, and of the twenty or so others listed only Syria, Yemen, Afghanistan, and Ethiopia have had a significant relationship with the Soviet Union. The other African ventures were still to come, of course, but sober hindsight shows that during the 1960s the Soviet effort would be far less effective than the panel feared. Its reservation about the effectiveness of the free world effort, on the other hand, was all too accurate.

> The Soviet effort is impressive primarily because the free world has failed to develop a workable structure within which the industrialized and newly developing regions can co-operate in fulfilling the aspirations of their peoples. We must contribute to the growth and cohesiveness of the community of free nations, not merely because we wish to prevent an expansion of the Soviet sphere, but because we want to co-operate in bringing about a new international system dedicated to peace, to human dignity, and to respect for national independence. (p. 180)

There is no field, perhaps, where prophecy has such a poor record as in international economic planning. A major American war triggering massive inflation, the growing dilemmas of food overproduction on the one hand and famine on the other, the emergence of major economic power centers (Japan chief among them), the redistribution of capital through massive lending to the Third World—

all of these would be taking their present shape during the 1970s—
and in part because of the 1950s as well as the sixties. Virtually none
of this was anticipated by the panel, which may well have made the
mistake of believing that far more of our economic destiny was in
our own hands than the facts would support. We can perhaps say
only one thing in explanation—that the preoccupation with Soviet
economic subversion was, like the fear of Sino-Soviet military adventures, an effective red herring. It kept us from looking with steady
eyes at our own policy; we were too simply responsive, and as a result the voices of alienation and dissent already had a text ready to
hand as the 1960s began.

One brief paragraph is tragically prophetic of our national difficulties as Vietnam overtook us: "A widening disparity between the
industrialized and the less developed nations would make the attainment of a peaceful community of nations increasingly difficult. A
great deal depends therefore on the ability to speed up the rate of
growth of the less developed regions" (p. 237). As our resources
burned away in Vietnam we had little energy left for attention to
Africa and Latin America, the areas which would move into disas-
trous economic and social difficulty during the 1960s. Nor would it
be any easier to give proper attention to the concern of Panel IV for
our national health in economic and social matters. The ambition
displayed by this panel has in any case a touch of the Utopian about
it, since it takes as its mandate the discovery of ways in which economic and social growth can sustain the needs articulated by the
other panels.

The concluding panels dealt with matters which undergird all the
rest: appropriate concepts and perceptions of education, and a basic
grasp of the democratic idea itself. Here we are confronting our
systems of values and the best ways of bringing them to life in one
complex society. Here we do not have the burdensome retrospective
irony of the earlier reports; the extreme positions toward education
and democracy taken by the major activist groups will stand, not as
a repudiation of our basic tenets, but as judgments on our failure to
live up to what we profess. Where earlier panel reports foreshadow
violence, the blurring of our vision, Dante's dark wood where the
straight way is lost, these last reports tell us clearly and eloquently

what the vision is. There is no need to rehearse them here; they will be constant subjects of anguished discussion and action throughout the sixties and will be alive throughout this book. The sixties would not have had such power to disturb our society, after all, if every major group had not been so concerned—so compulsively involved —with the root questions of value. We shall also find that these sections of the overall report have great significance when we come to look at the 1980s, with their particular reshaping of the basic issues of education and the democratic idea. They are fine enough to serve as text and benchmark for appraising the somber changes which were to come.

A final word about the participants: taken singly, they are as distinguished an array as one could assemble. What is missing? Women are very largely absent; it is startling, for example, to find that the one woman on the education panel is Marguerite Hickey, at the time an editor of *The Ladies' Home Journal*. (And the result of the panel's work shows this lack. Only one brief section is devoted to the education of women, and it is commonplace by comparison to the rest of the report.) There are virtually no black members of the various panels, although the head of the Urban League is a member of one. There is no extended consideration in the report of the problems of integrating minorities into the mainstream community. I find no novelists, no poets, no painters, no composers. I must assume that they were not made part of this discussion because they, like blacks and women, did not have access to the sources of power.

All of this might seem irrelevant, except that much of the thrust of the various movements of the 1960s was devoted to exactly these questions of participation which must be asked of any group in power. What have they failed to understand? How does one reconcile the privileges of the powerful with the needs of the unenfranchised? Is politically motivated, doctrinaire warfare a valid use of that power? Whatever the "right" answers to these questions, they and many others like them were posed more vigorously in the 1960s than they had been for a century. So far as such questions were raised by the Rockefeller panel (and some certainly were), they were subject to aggressive challenge and scrutiny by many people, young and old, who felt that the pious professions of virtue in the power centers of the country were sadly out of contact with the reality of the country's action and its need.

We have in the Rockefeller Report a fascinating commentary in prospect, then, a curtain raiser through its contrasts with the actual 1960s. It helps us greatly to understand one aspect of the decade to come—its power to surprise and bewilder us, its constant shock to our previous perceptions and patterns of thought. For the true *antecedents* of the 1960s, however, we must look elsewhere. Above all, we must understand the long, often hidden development of movements and attitudes which were part of the basic structure of our society but were seldom understood in their true fierce natures. In the 1960s no one could avoid their insistence or mitigate their savagery.

Years of Angst and Plenty

If the Rockefeller Report captured—often unwittingly—certain of the issues which would be aflame in the 1960s, it was not a time-oriented analysis of that United States which emerged from the Second World War to find itself *the* world power—with all the rights, privileges, and responsibilities of that position. Steps had been taken which seemed to make for stability—the United Nations and the Marshall Plan, for example—and the patterns of the cold war had been all too clearly established. Vigorous acts of containment in Greece and Iran had seemed effective, the Korean War had been limited at a critical moment, and those inevitable postwar yearnings for familiar and domestic life-styles had been well satisfied. What then threatened to disrupt those hopes and patterns which were dominant in the explicit aspects of our national life between 1945 and 1960? The answers were blowing in the wind long before Bob Dylan wrote the words for them. The Rockefeller Report, as we have seen, reveals them but without scrutiny.

The world political situation, seen from the U.S. perspective as we approached the 1960s, had for us a paranoid quality which we did not call by its right name. We were more uneasy than we chose to articulate; cold war doctrine did not lay itself open to serious question, and that very reticence strengthened our anxiety. Soviet paranoia was matched by our own sense of a brooding, monolithic danger. We did not have room in our thinking for a sophisticated or multiple view of world politics. The Soviet Union and China were one adversary, for the old, specious China doctrine still dominated our official thinking. In this constantly polarized stance (us or them) we were bound to feel a primal unease for which Korea had become a clear signal. When would it happen again?

The most ominous aspect of this position was its rigidity, which kept us from exploiting many opportunities for political maneuver in the highly fluid postcolonial world of the 1950s and 1960s. That world was one of great hope and high expectation, not only for the nations soon to be born, but for many groups worldwide who felt a profound resonance with aspirations so long denied and (as time would show) so romantically exaggerated. As we shall see, the realities—and the myths—of colonial exploitation were to provide a major theme for the rhetoric of the 1960s in both the black and women's movements. More ominously for future U.S. foreign policy, the postcolonial turmoil was seen as a battleground for East and West. The driving power of the new nationalisms was obscured by our preoccupation with their formal structure. We were victims of the labels; a new socialist nation was too easily accepted as a pawn for the other side; the chance for shrewd political maneuver was often foreclosed. The results would be tragic in Cuba and Vietnam, to pick only two. The official mentality of the 1948–60 years made our later misjudgments almost inevitable.

Beneath this movement of the new nations there were still larger and often less formed movements and changes of attitude which contributed to our deep sense of unease. Brutal Soviet actions in Central and Eastern Europe were less significant than the destabilizing force of the upheaval which was World War II. The Soviet motives were clear and could be confronted and resisted. The great ground swell of change, initiated by the precursors of World War II in Africa and Spain, was harder to understand because it was so varied, so enormous in its implications for further change, so laden with the sufferings which had spread worldwide. This ground swell was hardly felt in the United States at a level of daily concern. The efforts of the later 1940s were designed to put the world together again, and for the defeated Axis powers events certainly lived up to the plan. Outside that bright circle, however, we were only half-conscious of countries coming into being, of countries planned in ways that guaranteed conflict. Most of us did not know enough about ethnic and religious alignments in the unborn countries of Africa and Southeast Asia to judge the consequences when they acquired some kind of official boundary and status. But along with the postcolonial hopes there were darker plans being nurtured by a hundred sects and subnations, hoping now for an identity long denied but fiercely cherished. Taken together, they created a sense of international unease, precisely at a time when our conscious effort was directed to stability and order, to a sense that the world could become a perfected version of its old self.

One element in this half-seen, half-heard tsunami of change was the technical legacy of violence left us by World War II—a legacy we are still struggling with in its highly perfected terrorist forms today. During World War II the means of subversion were developed far beyond anything we had seen before. Since the ends were patently good, we felt that we were in no position to temporize with the means. Instead, we elaborated them brilliantly—particularly in Europe—and created a body of experience and procedure still being drawn on today in twenty "small" wars throughout the world. (These wars are in fact the pattern that world conflict has assumed; it is a daily curse of the late twentieth century, but its roots were established in World War II and its first elaborations were felt during the 1950s. The struggles which led to the founding of Israel, with all its hidden consequences, form a particular case of this violent worldwide realignment of social structures. It is a paradigm of all that was not clearly seen in the 1950s, though the discomfort was already in place. We set out to right a terrible wrong; the consequence was a seemingly endless and insoluble pattern of conflict.)

We can see a clear duality in the emerging political structures of the 1950s, and in both aspects it would have a compelling influence on the rhetoric and the action of the 1960s. The first is a yearning for some intimate identity with the political/social structure, so that it becomes almost a projection of the individual or the tribe. The second is the orthodox hope (which so many of us shared without giving it much critical analysis) that the United Nations would, with normal reverses and stalemates, be in reality one major world force for stability and mutual understanding. Its aims were so patently virtuous that it would have been churlish not to give it our allegiance.

As that hope came to seem less and less certain, and as the newly emergent Third World turned the UN into an organization vastly different in its thrust from that projected for it in 1945, the hopes for world order became steadily stronger but often turned in other directions. As a result, the high dreams were kept alive in new and unfamiliar forms—sometimes wonderful forms like *Hair*, for example —and they would show themselves in odd new religions, Utopian poetry, drug cults, and the other phenomena of the sixties. Here it is most important to recognize that they stood as a counterforce to the increasing ugliness of the international order which began to develop in the decade of the fifties.

That ugliness, in turn, owed much of its substance to the new nations themselves, which were incidentally transforming the shape of the UN but much more centrally transforming themselves in the blood and horror of civil struggle. The vague discomfort of the 1950s, the sense that the sea was moving in restless ways, became the full storm of the 1960s. And these struggles for identity, for self-realization—often monstrous in themselves—would serve as major provocations both to the Soviet Union and to the United States.

These provocations were to be given their full force by an intricate net of issues and decisions which we shall see in the second chapter of this book. One aspect of the 1950s world deserves special mention here, however. There were great military organizations in place; despite the clamor of the radical right they had not in fact been weakened nor lost any of their emphatic influence on our national economic and political life. When President Eisenhower delivered his startling valedictory attack on the military-industrial complex in 1960 he was drawing on a lifetime of experience as well as conviction. (One will not find any hint of that warning in the Rockefeller reports, by the way.) For our purposes it is crucial to realize, not only that we had such a massive force in being, but that it was oriented to the kinds of conflict for which both the military and industrial support systems had originally been developed and toward which they were directed.

The implications of this military-industrial position were twofold. First, the mere fact of having such an organization in place meant that it would be likely to respond to provocation. To put the matter another way, as a country we were likely to respond with this particular kind of force because we had it in place. If it had not been so vigorous, we might well have considered other approaches to the Southeast Asian situation. Second, the nature of this available force made it singularly inappropriate for use in the type of conflict which the French had already met in Vietnam and which we were to meet there and elsewhere. The saddest spectacle of the Vietnam War was our use of heavy bombing, helicopter gunship attacks, and the "liberation" of territory at whatever cost to the inhabitants and the agriculture. None of these techniques was destined to weaken, contain, or even limit the effectiveness of a mobile guerrilla force.

The large texture of the 1950s showed these and other elements of deep unease in international relationships, together with a good deal of hopeful complacency. What can we say of the major political, cultural, and intellectual institutions within our own country? How did the churches or the colleges and universities see their world, for example? What was most important to them about it? The answers may seem simple, or they *might* have seemed so to the casual eye and heart at the time. There was in our religious and educational stance a clear desire to return to a comfortable and familiar version of American life. (We see the same wish reflected everywhere: in advertising, in the cozy definitions of the place of women in society, in the lavish concepts of auto design which are always a fascinating barometer of the country's weather.) Both Harry Truman and Dwight Eisenhower were father figures; and while neither was in fact a comfortable or simple man, both projected images of homely virtue. Middlewestern and middle class, they reassured us even while they made complex decisions about global violence.

In fact, however, this is only part of the truth. The same dual or ambivalent quality was abroad in education, politics, and religion that we saw in our troubled international relationships. There were vigorous explorations of the bases for and the relevance of religious conviction, and there were major changes under way in American higher education. The New Frontier and the Great Society were still to come, but there was a clear perception that the senior politicians of one generation had played out their game. There would soon be room for a new one; its members were already sharpening their minds and their claws. At the start of the fifties we had no national wish to accept the wit and brilliance of Adlai Stevenson; by the end of it we were ready for Camelot.

This complexity of political attitude found a clear parallel in the religious life of the decade. Interest in formal religious activity was very high; the established churches were both an antidote to the dislocations of the war and an affirmation that the old values stood firm.

The intellectual and critical aspects of religion in the 1950s were not as predictable, however, as the reassertion of traditional religious forms and structures suggests. The emphasis on new definitions of the social gospel given by the penetrating minds of men like Reinhold Niebuhr was carried forward, both in this country and internationally, as the "successor of choice" to nineteenth-century missionary activity. This emphasis on the social gospel matched very well, of course, with the hopes for infant nations and for their Christian minorities which were shared by many established churches; it was present also (though in a more subdued form) as a constant critique of government military policy. This subtheme, tied to the short-lived World Federalist movement, as well as to the more formal pacifist elements in the Christian churches, would assume some remarkable forms during the 1960s.

The university-related aspects of religious commitment took a direction which foreshadowed the sixties in quite another way. A significant concern with the religious dimensions of intellectual activity showed itself in a good deal of writing and earnest discussion. A particular thrust of those most involved in such exploration was the insistence on rigorous critical thought as a foundation for any bridge-building between patterns of religious belief and some specific learned discipline. The integrity of that secular discipline was respected fully; this was not an attempt to "capture" the intellectual world for sectarian purposes (like many campaigns which we see in the 1980s). Instead, it was an energetic reinterpretation of basic intellectual assumptions in a variety of fields. As such, it inevi-

tably raised questions about uncriticized positions, as well as directions and conclusions too easily taken for granted in many fields of
academic scholarship and teaching. Both implicitly and explicitly
the concept of relevance was raised in these discussions; a major
thrust of this intellectual/religious movement was its questioning of
scholarship for scholarship's sake. In its concern for significance, for
scholarship and teaching as *illumination* of one form or another, it
was preparing a major rallying cry for the decade to come. (And of
course those of us involved in these explorations were totally uncon-
scious of the particular fire we were feeding.)

These concerns ran counter to much that was developing in
American colleges and universities between 1945 and 1960. American higher education was in the fast lane after World War II; there
was little interest in a return to the simpler days before the war.
Where we were attempting to design the most comfortable and re-
warding consumer culture ever seen in mass form, the colleges and
universities were moving to even more seductive music. They were
not less materialistic than society at large; rather more so, in fact.
But it was not the materialism of comfort and domestic prosperity;
it was the heady substance of power, which higher education had
never experienced in this form.

Colleges and universities have always had certain kinds of power
in our society. The men whom they educated were a dominant part
of the power elite, and through a great variety of changes they maintained this special service to our society. Their research functions
become steadily more important, but their major contribution was
the production of educated men—and, finally, women. The numbers
of these college graduates had grown, but they were still a small fraction of those who graduated from secondary school—a fact which
concentrated one kind of power in a small number of institutions.

World War II had an astonishing impact on this pattern and on the
assumptions which underlay it. College enrollments increased radically; the GI Bill made it possible for men and women who formerly
never would have thought of college to obtain a higher education.
As they seized the opportunity, they changed the attitude of their
society; what had been the good fortune of few became the prerogative of many. And women were not left behind; as the change

of attitude took place, they accepted it and enrolled in steadily increasing numbers. We had, in fact, a crosscurrent of attitudes in the 1950s. With all the emphasis on consumer domesticity as the feminine ideal, more and more young women decided that they would have education as well. Out of that decision would come a variety of tensions, and they would find their analyst in Betty Friedan. But all of that was still to come, and meanwhile higher education was every year a more customary part of life.

Strains were put on the system by these changes, strains which would go far beyond the mere logistics of large numbers. The attitude toward these increases would be at the heart of the trouble to come; we talked then about a silent college generation, but perhaps we did not ask what might stimulate them and bring an end to their silence. That seeming complacency was often indifference; students were increasingly separate from those issues which animated their academic elders.

Of course, we cannot carry this judgment too far. A great many skilled and conscientious teachers continued to be just that; but the greater (in conventional terms) the institution, the more its policymakers had issues other than student matters to absorb their time and energy. Among the legacies of World War II was an explosion of research in fields first explored under the stress of wartime need. Many of these research projects led back, in turn, not only to expanded industrial development, but to new military technologies. The universities came quickly to an essential role in the weaving together of government, industrial, and military interests—at the levels of both policy and execution. The voice of the consultant was heard in the land; surprisingly often he was Professor Catchpole, off to fulfill his contract in Washington. Just as often, of course, the contract would come to him; grantsmanship became a major measure of academic success, and one could even hope to capture a major laboratory, certainly some long-standing research support. Promotion, and all the good things that follow, depended on it.

If this was gratifying to Catchpole, think what it meant to Dean Boysenberry and President Hardscrabble. It was a time of growth, of excitement, of heady competition. There were unusually stimulating developments in the foundation world as in government—new programs, new goals, and some major infusions of capital for the lucky ones. We made jokes about it ("The Edifice Complex"), but we enjoyed it. As one of the Hardscrabbles I can testify that a period of rising *and realized* expectations year after year is true elixir for a college president. He is in fact riding an updraft, but he begins after a while to think that his own talent must have a good deal to do with such repeated success.

There were two major hazards for higher education in the expansionist fifties. The first came from our participation in the power structures of the nation, the second from successes which dulled our self-critical senses. As a result, we moved dramatically in new directions but without much awareness of the move. Physical plant construction had to make up for the long arrears of the Depression and the war years. The hard sciences demanded money and sophisticated space; and the soft sciences felt the most acute pressure to outdo their fellows in rigor and elaborate "scientism." Both found significant and rapidly growing relationships with the world of daily action, decision, and influence over events. We accepted our part in these new enterprises without planning them, and inevitably we modified and diminished old enterprises without giving them serious thought. We were surfing, and while we did talk a good deal about liberal education (particularly in the undergraduate colleges), we were in hot pursuit of our new goals and new rewards.

The most significant aspect of this stance was not the flawed nature of the goals. One could make a sound case for them as significant for the new life of the universities. But to adopt goals uncritically laid us open to criticism, and indeed bred weaknesses which many movements in the sixties would find it easy to exploit. And this would be true above all because our espousal of the liberal and liberating studies had such a strong smell of conventionality about it. This was particularly clear in humanistic studies where the genteel tradition had faded under the impact of great numbers and widely diverse student backgrounds. At the same time the humanities found themselves in an embattled position, particularly in their relationships with the social scientists. The result was that, a generation after the studies of society made their bid to be called "scientific," the humanities moved grudgingly—and destructively—in the same direction.

There has been for the last hundred years or so a great deal of nonsense spoken and published about the sciences and the application of their method to other fields of study. First came their ascendancy, and then the desire to claim that other fields were "just as scientific" in their methodologies. German linguistic scholarship was a prime and widely imitated example, but in nearly every field of humanistic studies there was a movement toward rigorous neutral scholarship and a movement away from valuation—which was designated as subjective and therefore of no solid use. Valuing was taken to be soft and personal, where nonvaluing studies were taken to be hard and objective. The large and obvious metaphysical questions posed by this dichotomy were generally ignored in the academic world of the fifties. There were bitter arguments, but they did not address the central problem—the fact that *all* intellectual analysis is based on a value system, a set of suppositions or acts of faith. To fail to understand this is in fact to be quite unscientific because unrigorous in the use of the mind.

The importance of this muddled situation in the house of intellect was that it weakened the heart of college and university life just at the time when all the powerful distractions of money, government, and industrial power were making themselves felt most vigorously. As we look toward the sixties, we can already hear the cries of irrelevance. It would be one of the talisman words; I have alluded to it before and it will return along with its companions when we discuss the sixties in detail. At this point we need to recognize simply that once again we were moving toward a conflict which we neither anticipated nor understood.

The Prophets and the Mountebanks

Social revolutions, like countercultures, come in many shapes and sizes. In the 1950s there was action in each arena; and though the two seemed far apart, they would come together a decade later in their sense of a shared human urgency. The overt social revolution concerned the rights of all men in our society to educational and social access in all public institutions. And this right was dramatically affirmed in a great Supreme Court decision of 1954. Its impact was immediate as well as far-reaching. As president of Lawrence College, I was visited one afternoon in 1955 by three trustees—all of them staunch fraternity men, two of them violently agitated, and the third there, as he told me later, "to see that there is fair play and that they don't try to run all over you." Their message was in fact a lament rather than a tirade, and I heard the clichés about social change in their basic, classic form. "I know," said the elder of the two mourners, "that there will be, must be change. But why here and why now?" Intriguingly enough, the change *had* already started, on a college campus in Wisconsin which had not had black students since the 1890s. The fears of my friends were fully justified; that decision released more energy, more long pent-up and yet urgent frustration, than any of us had thought possible—or even thought about in any sustained way.

We must be honest in retrospect. It would be pleasant to write that the American academic community was aware of a great need to educate blacks in the country's universities and that we were busily devising programs to that end. Of course, such was not the case and never had been, even in the first flush of enthusiasm seen so briefly and partially after the Civil War. Most of us in northern colleges were not opposed to black students—if they appeared in the normal course of things and were qualified. We were not blocking anyone's entry; we felt comfortable about our racial attitudes and the way we implemented them—or not, as was the case for most of us.

What we did not see, did not understand, was exactly what events showed us in the mid-1950s. There had not in fact been access, and there was a tremendous desire for it. There was not adequate preparation; there were serious—sometimes horrendous—social problems: there were issues of money. But none of these mattered in the face of the single explosive issue of access—guaranteed and to be pursued. That pursuit was often as naive as our white ignorance of it and of the force behind it. The legal decisions of the fifties were really only the trigger; we shall see much more of the long-standing passion behind them which made the explosion possible.

There have been countercultures for as long as there have been cultures to dissent from. The word became fashionable and pretentious in the sixties, yet the fact of them is almost immemorial whenever an artistic and intellectual community confronts its society. A distinction has to be made among three kinds of dissent, however: the merely trivial, the "different" in art (pop art in the sixties) which is as transient as a mayfly; the major artistic venture (Joyce's *Ulysses*) which embodies its culture, uses it in an essential way as part of the organic structure of the work, but transcends it in a final worldview which is a commentary on that culture; and the explicit, formalized dissent which is chiefly concerned with an alternative to the dominant social pattern. In this third case the dominant culture is in an adversary relationship to the dissenting one; but both participate in creating the counterculture.

It is quite possible for the dissent of one decade to be the conforming standard of another. Certainly, in a fifties' novel like *On the Road*, in the early Presley or Buddy Holly just before his death, we see an extremely rapid shift from dissenting voice to trendsetter to pillar of the new orthodoxy. Most striking is the fact that when it first appeared each work seemed to belong to a cult, a group set apart from the mainstream. Then in short order Kerouac's book became a metaphor for a whole style of behavior, a guide which went far to define the outward shape of the Beat Generation. Presley and Holly hit the sticky, teenybopper conventions of the fifties with the tremendous shock of four-letter perception and action. "Are you going to play it, or are you going to do it?" the voice and the intoxicating beat ask us. The world evoked is in bourgeois bad taste—urban-country hustle, blue suede shoes and all. But it comes through as electrical, as high passion, as dissent which does not even bother to be antagonistic because it is pushing on so fast to something else.

The impact of this was release, freedom, saying the unspoken and acting the unacted. These forerunners of the sixties were not urgently concerned with the intellectual issues which would come to dominate; they were the setters of a style, a way of encountering society, an attitude toward personal relationships, and a musical platform on which many singular houses of performance would be built. By the end of the fifties the very young heard all this in their bones, while their elders could hardly hear it at all. A music was available, ready to be the vehicle of thought, indictment, anger, and political action. Like the literature, the music provided a basic set of statements, a stance, and a language which could be used for many purposes.

Not all of these purposes were still hidden in the womb of time, nor were the newest styles of music and literature the only signposts. Their impact was enhanced by changes in social expectation which included many groups at many levels of privilege. For all of us the tempo of the period was steadily increasing. The saturation of our world by the electronic media was just beginning, but already our expectations were quickened and our demands for experience of every kind—vicarious and direct—were moving to a more and more frenzied tempo. This meant in turn that we used up our artists, our musicians, our magazines at a steadily faster rate and—most important for the decade to come—that we expected there would always be more available to take their places.

Such expectations made it easy in the sixties to demand rapid answers to problems, and also made it seem logical and "natural" to move from position to position, cause to cause, at a violent pace. Much of this tempo which made the sixties hard to cope with had its beginnings here in the accelerating cultural drumbeat of the post-war period. At the same time, however, there was a far more somber side to these heightened expectations. The long-standing hopes and frustrations of major groups in our society were intensified by the very complacencies and attempts at serenity which colored so much of the period from 1945 to 1960. The black and women's movements (not to mention the special case of a coherent student movement) only seemed in abeyance during these years. The restless black migration from the South grew from a deep frustration as well as a desperate hope. And there was an equal countercurrent for women in their steadily increasing numbers employed outside the home. (This latter shift is fascinating because it occurred in the face of a massive campaign to get women back into their domestic boxes after the heady employment experiences of the war years.) In both cases we had a time of gestation for the major and overt actions of the sixties.

It is a truism to say that students were apathetic in the 1950s, but (as we have seen) they were being prepared for some very different roles by the privilege of their position, which gave many of them a good deal of security and ease while it made them seem at times relatively unimportant in contrast to the events taking place around them in the college and university world. They often questioned this apathy themselves, since they were not so much apathetic as unsure where they fitted into the larger meaning of events. I remember a good deal of discussion and a fair amount of soul-searching and purpose-seeking on the part of serious students. They were not being called on for much that was significant, and as a result they were the last student generation for whom that dismal cliché "preparation for life" had some elements of truth. They were in a holding pattern, but as I look back I can see that this had far more to do with their situation than it did with their inner natures. But they provided the legends of apathy and indifference against which successor college generations could react.

One final aspect of the expectation patterns which run through the fifties is the complex nature of the official and by now highly bureaucratic liberalism of government at many levels—liberalism expressed in long-standing public programs rather than in any passionate conviction about human rights or the responsibilities of affluence. To a significant degree we expected less of our bureaucracy than it was theoretically equipped to deliver. The urgency of the 1930s which led to so many bold steps of social assistance was naturally enough obscured by the war and then almost obliterated by the prosperous years afterward. We did not *want* those problems to exist in any insistent way; it is almost as though we legislated them away in our hearts and minds. As a result, we continued our sense (inherited from the thirties) that we were responsible through formal programs to aid the needy, the unenfranchised, the lost; while at the same time we persuaded ourselves that the problems addressed by these programs were no longer acute. Like some in the 1980s, we said that the old needs were no longer there.

We were half-right; the needs had changed, and they now stemmed above all from those migrations into the cities. To ignore their significance almost guaranteed that the hope which motivated them would be largely unfulfilled. The country despair of the South would become the urban despair of the black ghettos in the North, and we would be on the way to Newark and Watts. Like so many other events I have described in these last pages, our decisions—and equally our failure to make certain decisions—in the fifties would exacerbate the major problems of the 1960s. To say this is not to give in to an easy determinism, but a great impetus toward disruption would be provided by attitudes whose consequences we did not foresee—and indeed did not choose to consider in any depth. The 1950s were not a reflective decade; we hoped that many of our problems were on the way to resolution; and while the concept of benign neglect was articulated far later, we were already busy practicing it. The challenges which we chose to take seriously were the exciting and in many ways adolescent ones of growth, power, acquisitiveness. Our education in maturity was still to come.

Voices in the Wilderness

We have been considering the postwar period, but there were other and more substantial dimensions to American life which created a context for the 1960s. The aspirations of women and blacks have roots which go back to the beginnings of the country. There was, further, a far more pervasive interaction between the problems of these two groups than most of us understood in the 1960s. Some of the strident mutual identification would have seemed much less fanciful if we had understood the aspirations and severe frustrations of both groups.

A customary reaction to this statement would be one of patronizing disagreement. About blacks, our solid northern bourgeois (who had survived the Depression and the war) would say in 1955, "*I* certainly have nothing against blacks" (only he would have called them Negroes). "Sure it's been rough at times, and we know how bad it can be in the South. But opportunities are getting better all the time, and anyway we all have to make our way in this world. No one made it easy for me, and I'm not about to vote a handout to anyone else." About the frustrations of women, he would have been even more bemused. "What do you mean, aspirations and frustrations? Don't I give my wife everything she wants? Doesn't she spend most of our income? She isn't stuck in an office all day. She has her freedom and her friends, once the housework is done. She has a pretty easy time of it, and if we're going to talk about frustration, I have my share. What are you trying to do, stir up trouble?"

This amalgam of attitudes is one which almost all of us shared to one degree or another. These are Eliot's "certain certainties," the given attitudes which save us the trouble of vigorous thought. If it seems that I am indicting my neighbor, let me make it perfectly clear that I am indicting myself. An event from my early twenties will make the point about blacks abundantly clear, while my attitude toward the aspirations of women will be just as evident from a comment on the university administrative years.

At the start of World War II I found myself in New Haven, looking with delight at the remarkable preflight unit then quartered at Yale. For their mealtime music and weekly parades they—and the rest of us, fortunately—had the stimulus of Glenn Miller's Air Force Band. One platoon of the unit was black, and for them the "St. Louis Blues March" was created. The rest of the unit was impressive in its precision, but at one point in the parade the music would change, and we were treated to the only dance-march drill I have ever seen. Those of us who looked on were like the other platoons, earthbound clods by comparison. I remember almost saying it aloud. The point of the story, however, lies in what I did *not* say, or think, or even consider—that this was a segregated unit, and that it stood, not only for the segregated nature of the armed forces, but for the normal, segregated thought of the time. It seemed eminently proper and thoroughly delightful. I was not capable of seeing that these men were taking their segregation as a sign of honor. I saw that they were putting the rest of us down by their style, but that they were not simply rejoicing in it—this I could not see. I felt myself thoroughly emancipated in the matter of color, while in fact I was merely blind to all it meant in barriers and limitations. And so, of course, I could not see in the 1950s how deep the resentment at their treatment during World War II would run among blacks. I saw—or believed I saw—that opportunities for improvement in status had come from their wartime experience, but I did not look beyond that. Nor did I see that the experience of life in northern cities would be so bitter and cramping for southern blacks; but of course they did not see that either. We were all the dupes of our hope.

Our blindness about the position of women in our society was, if anything, even deeper because it involved all of us so directly. I mentioned the neglect of women in the Rockefeller Report, but the imperception strikes much nearer home. I use my own experience, because the job I accepted in 1953 put such grave demands on my wife. These would persist for seventeen years, and by the end of the time I understood all too well what the frustrations of such a career were. Today, of course, a college president's wife is no longer expected to be both minion and duenna of the place, but until the fierce realignments of the sixties her service was taken for granted and without question by the whole community—and most of all by the university president himself.

I mention women in this particular professional situation not only because I know it so well, but because in extreme form women represented the anomalous position of many others. At the heart of their difficulty was the fact that so much was accomplished, but most of the time in someone else's shadow—and often *as* someone else's shadow. I cringe even now when I think of the speeches my wife listened to so uncomplainingly, but of course her deprivations went far deeper than boredom. She and those like her were not recognized and compensated for what they did. Two men doing a similar amount of skilled work would never have been expected to accept one salary for it. Nor would one of them have been asked to give up most of the legitimate recognition, the ego satisfaction, which was his right. And what the university president's wife put up with in a highly public situation millions of women put up with in their more private lives. The overt guidelines of the 1950s all pointed this way, no matter how the work patterns and the college enrollments were shifting toward that assertion of women's rightful place and role which came so abruptly a few years later.

These personal, yet symbolic, reminiscences are only prelude to the acknowledgment of the long labors of both blacks and women. I have to recognize for a whole generation of us that we knew amazingly little about the real effort which had for more than a century

gone into both movements. (Of course, the anguish and the yearning went back a great deal further, to the beginning of slavery and
the first demands of a new world which forced American women to
be a little different from their English forebears.)

A major reason for this ignorance, of course, was the relative obscurity which had overtaken both movements in the postwar years.
One logical outcome of the society which I have sketched was its
indifference to urgent social programs of all sorts. Just as there were
virtually no student movements to parallel those which I knew as an
undergraduate just before the war, so there was little of the outer
urgency which had launched the NAACP and lent such strength and
style to black culture in the twenties and thirties. Equally, there was
none of the battling spirit which had made the suffragist movement
possible, none of the "race apart" attitude which was so remarkable
an aspect of womens' higher education in the late nineteenth and
early twentieth centuries, none of the flapper independence which
had created a brief but vivid subculture in the years just after World
War I.

Indeed, the two postwar periods are in striking contrast because
the two major movements were positioned so differently. Black
America was having its first great impact on a wider culture in the
1920s—and in small part for a wonderfully comic reason. The secretary of the navy in his wisdom had worked with some success to close
down New Orleans as a liberty port. The black musicians in the great
sporting houses had to look for work; they looked up the river and
west—to St. Louis, Kansas City, Chicago. Jazz was liberated from
its regional boundaries, with an immediate impact on the culture
of the twenties and a steadily widening and deepening influence on
American music as a whole. Black culture was given a great push;
the brilliant life of Harlem in the thirties would not have assumed
its stature without the excitement and liberation of the twenties. In
the 1950s few such stirrings were evident to the larger society.

Similarly, in the culture of women in the fifties there was none
of that self-assured assertiveness which had succeeded the struggle
for the vote. The young women of the twenties evidently took the
blood and ridicule of the suffragist movement for granted, while
they borrowed its assertiveness and transferred it to a new style of

personal life. By contrast, women in the fifties seemed almost to
be manipulated into a submissive, conformist, and domestic stance.
Such at least was the role insistently displayed in the media and
preached by the orthodox. In those years the phrase *culture of women*
would have been laughed at with scorn. There was a position for
women, all kinds of expectations and duties, but nothing that would
allow us to talk about their common culture. That would change,
but in the fifties the ambivalence in women's position was at one of
its periodic highs; with a multitude of roles assigned, she was too
occupied to seek out the fulfilling major ones. She was busy, in short,
creating case studies for Betty Friedan.

What we must understand, however, if we are to make sense of the
explosive development of both movements in the 1960s, is that in
obscurity or notoriety they had a long, remarkable history of determined effort to establish positions of honor and dignity in a society
which loudly asserted its disparagement of their pretensions. The
result was a tenacity which outlasted the good times as well as the
bad. When Faulkner dedicates a book to a black servant, he puts his
finger on the heart of it: "She endured."

But for blacks, as for women, endurance was by no means enough.
There was, from the 1860s on, constant pressure within the black
community to accomplish two things: first, to assert a cultural meaning within that community, growing from its past and at the same
time establishing its current significance, its vitality; and second, to
demonstrate black competence in those arenas of effort and achievement which were automatically assumed to be the unique posses-
sions of whites—and most probably of Anglo-Saxon whites at that.
These two distinct strands of black effort moved together, sometimes
twining in mutual support but much more often in conflict or at
least in disagreement over the best direction for black energy and
enterprise to take.

The argument between Booker T. Washington and W. E. B. Du
Bois was the most famous of these running debates, but they were
—and still are—characteristic of the unresolved issues of direction
and significance which hamper black life in the larger community.
(As we shall see in the final chapter, they are poignant aspects of the

1980s, even with the emergent inner-city political power of blacks and the dramatic economic successes of a relatively small black sub-society which has co-opted white values and given them some subtle and ironic shapes.) During the 1950s a generation of black men and women were preparing themselves for a massive series of assaults on the problem of their own significance. We would all learn.

Women had been—and had seen themselves as—quite another kind of subculture. Blacks were in a sense all too visible, too easy to identify; white women, on the other hand, were in a constant and often covert struggle to make an identity for themselves. This effort lends a double emotional charge to the place of black women, who had to cope with a special form of the general problem. It is well known but not well understood that black women have always pro-vided the greatest hope for stability in black families. In the slave years it was commonly felt that one could be sure of a child's mother, and to that responsibility was often added the responsibility for white children as well. For these and several other major reasons (the mo-bility of black men as they looked for work, as one example), black women after emancipation had to try to lend order to the disorder that succeeded the first Utopian dreams of equality.

The push for self-education by these women is one of the most remarkable aspects of the black experience. They saw very quickly that unless they could change themselves, the freedom they had gained would mean little. They would all still be in servitude; only the rhetoric would be different. By the most heroic efforts a sur-prising number of black women acquired a basic education, and—so far as the economic rigors of life would allow—they passed on to their children both the desire for and the means of learning. It would be hard to move beyond the tradition of service in their em-ployment, but when they broke through the servitude of ignorance they increased their options substantially.

White women had to fight for education just as stubbornly, though usually in far more genteel ways. It is possible, in fact, to see the struggle for equality in its many forms as a struggle for equity in education. The control exercised by men over women for so long was more than a legal construct; it was law sanctioned by several major power structures. And these structures depended in turn on particular kinds of education which were by common (masculine) consent regarded as improper for women.

Improper in this context is a highly loaded word. The first women to assert their religious awareness publicly were attacked as unnatural, as doing violence to the order of things. Samuel Johnson's notorious remark about women preachers was mild by comparison with the animosity shown on this side of the Atlantic. Even the first "Female Academies" at the turn of the nineteenth century were directed to the circumscribed and predetermined needs of women. Abigail Adams was a rare figure indeed, and when she asked John to "remember the ladies" she was speaking for the host of her silent sisters as she urged that women in the new order deserved special recognition and understanding. Certainly, they did not enjoy much of either, and the nineteenth century would show how stony the road to understanding could be.

The first opportunities for assertion outside the home came through the church. Clerics needed the energy and persuasive power of their female parishioners, and the opportunities for Christian charity through the church became many and varied in the earlier part of the 1800s. The changing nature of our society was already clear; and the growing cities were creating serious problems of many social and individual kinds. There were no agencies to meet these needs, so women created them, administered them, and found for the first time that they were effective in public affairs. It is easy to overstate this new freedom, but it was clearly a major step beyond the constraints of the seventeenth and eighteenth centuries. And of course a special push was lent to this activity by the growing abolition movement. As thinking Christians realized more and more clearly, slavery posed problems which had to be resolved not only for the country's sake but for individual peace of mind. Such a situation was tailor-made for the sensibility and energy which women could provide, and the impetus it gave to the nascent women's movement was substantial. By the time abolition had run its course, women were aware of their effectiveness as a group in influencing the direction of major events.

It was a remarkable discovery, and it highlighted all that women did not yet have available to them in public life and in the professions. Beneath and beyond the founding of the great women's clubs, and the firm establishment of the movement for universal suffrage, there was a deep concern for education. It was a concern that once again tied the emerging hopes of women to the struggle of blacks. The level was different, but the desire was the same; the bond was at times fully recognized, often only half-glimpsed, and by some women it was feared and resisted. But it would continue, and in the 1960s it would receive its most dramatic and overt expression.

The story of the struggle for higher education for women is an intensely moving one. The effort to block it took such singular forms, while the even greater effort to establish it was so rigorous, that it is painful to revisit the whole saga. The pronouncements of educational pundits make the nature of the problem repellently clear. Women became a threat as soon as they began to show how effectively they could handle the demands of higher education. Their whole effort was directed toward the establishment of some reasonable equity in education—and of course beyond that lay the unthinkable, the idea that once women had access to higher education they would expect to make use of it. The denying maneuvers of trustees, deans, and college presidents would have been high comedy if the purposes behind them had not been so malicious.

The fierce, at times messianic quality of the women's colleges seems out of balance only until one recognizes what they were opposing and being opposed by. That resistance forced the growth of some remarkable institutions, which drew their strength from their separateness, their determination to prove what could be done quite apart from the will or wish of the masculine society around them. And that determination expressed itself, not only in an insistence on education of the highest quality but in a push toward the great professions for which liberal learning had always been the preparation. The acceptable feminine callings were not enough, and the push for the vote was paralleled in energy by a push for admission to all the professional graduate schools.

An interesting distinction emerges here. Education has always been pulled in two opposed directions. The love of learning for its own sake is counterposed to the use of learning for some other purpose. The precise form of these opposed views varies enormously, as do the reconciliations between them which we are constantly attempting. The "education of gentlemen," as practiced at Oxford and Cambridge, and to an extent in privileged American colleges of the late nineteenth and early twentieth centuries, is a debased form of the pursuit of learning for its own sake. The hundreds of "how-to" courses in trivial subjects are a debased form of purposeful education. But the meaning of this opposition of values was extended in a very special way by women; the utility of education was to reside not in its surface value but in its power to give independence. It was a means and not just an end, but it was a means of progress toward a great end—the establishment of a new position for women in the social structure.

Progress was never steady and never assured. As we have seen, there was an exuberant independence in the 1920s which drew little of its strength from the ideals of Smith and Bryn Mawr. In the 1950s, too, the mores of the moment did not *seem* to further this independence. But taken over the long period from the Revolution to 1960, the movement of the Movement was in this direction. The extreme assertions of the 1960s were completely consistent with a long history of self-discovery.

The Rhythms of Time

Historians—and then the rest of us—have long puzzled over the patterns which the passage of time seems to summon forth from events. Theories and arguments have ranged from the most structured to the least: from pattern as illusion in a random world to pattern as tyrant and master over our individual lives and wills. The danger of excess seems to lie with this second group; the temptation to make fact fit theory is seductive. Without giving way to Spengler or even Toynbee, however, there are recurrences in certain types of event, rhythms which seem to grow from the interaction of unusual social tension, a pattern of potential change in dealing with it, and the mysterious shaping power of a relatively small number of individuals. To put it so is to speak ponderously, but the claim that there are such periods is substantial, though not easy or even comfortable to consider. These periods depend on a critical mass of people and actions; and when that mass assumes a volatile form and is then triggered—often by a seemingly small or trivial event—we get a nova explosion. Circumstances change with extreme speed—often violence—and we seem to move into a new society.

The change may be transitory, or once in a while it may truly lead to a new order. But the period which gives it being is always fascinating and sometimes of great significance even if outward events do not go as the participants had hoped. Successful change, in fact, is not the hallmark of these nova periods. They are marked by high intensity of emotion, great joy and great anger mingled, and the quality of dream—dream understood as a sequence of events which cannot hold their shape even though they are real in many significant ways. For the most part the beginnings of major wars are not the events I speak of; they have predictable patterns and long shadows thrown before them as they come upon us. These great moments of discovery are dazzling and defined by what they are not at least as clearly as by their own unique markings. Classic examples in our recent European/American past might be the 1789–93 period in France, the late 1840s in many countries of Europe, the 1880s in the United States, the 1920s, and the 1960s. Widely variant in their dreams, they are kindred in their passionate involvements and flamboyant hopes.

These particular moments in time are only examples of an aspect of human dynamics that may well be as old as society itself. They are close enough to us, however, so that they may show us some important and specific characteristics shared with the 1960s. As they were experienced by those alive at the time, they were certainly sudden, dramatically active years but with long and often hidden historical roots. In each case there emerged abruptly styles of behavior quite at odds with the mores immediately preceding—or still present— in the parts of society *not involved* in the new action. In several cases there was an enthusiasm for the brave new world which was not realistic (as we look back at events) but which may still have altered the future in important, unforeseen ways. In every case there was conflict between conservative and radical ideas, traditional and eccentric behavior, conventional and experimental morality, and a sense of the stable past clashing with a highly volatile present and future.

One of the most fascinating and surprising periods is that of the 1870s and 1880s. I am deeply indebted to Page Smith for treating in his distinguished history of the United States many aspects of that time in ways which stirred me to ask how its hopes and its anguish might illuminate the 1960s. On the surface and at first view it seemed an unlikely period to contemplate; our conventional view of late Victorian America did not allow much room for free spirits and freer behavior. There emerged to my surprise a turbulent, many-sided American society, determined to explore—and exploit —its own assumptions and aided in this drive by the urgencies of both industrial and frontier life. Naturally, these explorations were present for many decades in American life, but they fused with certain other unique concerns of the 1880s to give a special intensity to events.

The texture of the period was compounded of extremes. There was the obvious one of great wealth rapidly acquired by means which often kept workers in poverty. There was great technical progress and sophistication set beside the rudest kinds of frontier and urban life. Political thought of the most laissez faire sort was set off against a substructure of European radical and anarchist theory. Aberrant sexual mores and the assertiveness of organized women's activity were flamboyantly contrasted with the familiar stereotypes of sanctified homes and subordinated wives. Blacks moved to the North in some numbers, partly because the contrast between the dream of freedom and the reality of oppression was so extreme as to be intolerable. And underlying all of these were some remarkable interactions among widely divergent groups who superficially had little to draw them together.

The legendary inequities of the time were fueled by the simultaneous emergence of major industrial advances, a frontier which could be opened and exploited by that new technology (the railroad, for instance), and an immigrant population which was in no position to embody Jefferson's mythic yeoman-citizen. This great explosion of activity (without the impetus of a major war) has no equal in our history. It was a particular kind of nova; the raw materials, the people, the capital, and the technical skills all came together to give the country an economic and social shock that worked for a few years like a violently stimulating drug.

Even the inequities were not static. Employment might be available one month and be lacking a month or two later. In a pure market economy the hardships of this pattern are obvious. For the entrepreneurs fortunes could be made and lost with giddy abruptness, but for a worker the question of food for tomorrow was often a major issue. Suddenly, we have a fertile ground, not only for the first great period of industrial labor unrest, but even more for a reaching out to other members of society wrestling with an unstable world.

Unlike movements of the 1960s, however, most of these major groups never found a full voice. Blacks, for example, migrated if they could to escape their new and extralegal slavery; they added pressure to life in the northern cities, already beginning to show their immigrant congestion and competition, but they also fed the general distress of the time. They were too new to their own freedom to make use of it or to respond to the currents of radical political thought which European immigrants had brought with them. Here, there was a substantial philosophic base for questioning the present state of society—and not just one base but a spectrum of them, with black, red, white, and blue cards marking the varieties of radical doctrine and the degrees of competence at exploring and expounding them. The apparatus was sometimes elaborate, while its effectiveness was sporadic and ephemeral.

But those organized groups, small as they were, added to the fears of social disorder to which the shifting black population and the intermittent but violent workingmen's protests lent so much seeming substance. This fear is a major aspect of the establishment view in all of the periods which bear a family kinship to the 1960s. A messianic hope or a desperate assertion on one side seems always to lead to an irrational and panic fear on the other. Those who have a good deal to lose in a volatile time tend to jump to conclusions. The china rattles and we cry earthquake, while our poor neighbors wish that the earth would move a little, but fear that it never will.

In these periods of climactic turmoil, we see two major kinds of motivation which do not ordinarily run together. Some dissenters shake society out of despair, but some do it for fun (one might almost say) and in great good spirits. This would be too strong a statement for the postabolitionists; they needed a use for their energy and found it in a variety of worthy social causes. The exuberance I speak of showed itself in a remarkable—and remarkably articulate—collection of preachers and speakers devoted to the most public and doctrinaire kinds of open marriage and free love. Their motivation was strong enough to see them through a good deal of harassment, ostracism, and even prison. Important for us is the fact that they were so free to speak (to large audiences) and to write at great length about their convictions.

Like some of their successors in the 1960s they had a measure of important truth on their side. The questions which they raised about loveless, routine, and male-dominated marriages were—and are—vital ones. Eccentric critics, they compelled attention through their separateness. Being so visible, they forced their listeners to consider and even recognize the truth of their passionate statements and actions. They were signposts in the mind, pointing to roads not taken, to issues not being honestly addressed.

These embodiments of extreme positions did not stand alone; those who gave them life found one another in associations that seem bizarre at this distance but that derived part of their energy and success from one another. The aggressive wing of the women's movement found that it had a good deal in common with the nascent labor organizations. Both were searching for the dignity of recognition and they found it together. A similar resonance emerged between the liberalism of the free love movement and the highly personal and individualistic populism of the frontier. For those few years a surprising number and range of kinships were established. They did not endure, but they gave the period its crazy-quilt color, variety, and drive.

The period was, in this way above all, an analogue and precursor to the 1960s. No more than any of the others I have alluded to were they *inevitable* forerunners of our own singular decade. There is no fated recurrence of patterns, but the similarities help us to look harder—and perhaps with more sympathy—at a period so much a part of our own lives and hearts.

In this opening section I have been concerned with sharpening in a variety of ways our perception of the 1960s. I have steadily widened the circle of our comparisons, from the years immediately before that remarkable time to years far distant and styles of life quite at variance with much that the sixties will show. But the rhythms are there, and some of the major themes are developed for us in considerable detail. It is my hope that they will give us a sense both of some distance and of some familiarity as we step inside the sixties and look for the springs of action there.

Decade of the Dream

In the Beginning

When John Kennedy asked Robert Frost to speak at his inaugural and invited Camelot as a metaphor for his presidency, he must have been building better than he could have known. Poets, as Plato pointed out, are dangerous people to turn loose in a well-governed country; and Camelot stands as one of our most enduring symbols of a failed dream. "Go away, save yourself," King Arthur says to the eager young boy at the end of the play, "and live so that you can tell others there was once such a place." The history of this decade is a chronicle of those who (starting with JFK) articulated a dream more or less coherently and then discovered at great cost what happens when we dare to bring our dreams into the light of day.

The stirrings and portents to which I alluded in the opening chapter were not much in evidence for official Washington at the decade's start. They would show themselves soon enough, but at first there was movement of another sort. The Kennedy emphasis on the young, the bright, the chic, and the tough was enormously appealing; it dampened criticism by its very style, and so begged for a while the questions of substance which must inevitably come. A program like the Peace Corps seemed to say that one could change the world a little for the better and have an exciting time doing it. It could also shake up establishment liberalism, which had become shopworn. The Kennedys brought individuals back into government at the levels of publicity, public culture, decoration (as in the restyled

White House), and an assertiveness in rhetoric which was often unmatched by equal success in policy and action. Even its tragic ending was a spectacle, the most visible and carefully staged funeral in the country's history.

There was a tone of assurance about these years, perhaps their most remarkable and—in view of what was to come—their most haunting quality. It was often at variance with the anguish that went into the missile crisis, for example, or civil rights issues in Mississippi and Alabama. Again, this tone of assurance went with a sense of style, with that optimism which makes many good causes seem easy and available and gives liberal politics its warmth. Since we were never to see the unfolding of events under a two-term Kennedy tenure, very little of the conservative common sense, the tentative excursion into the dark politics of Vietnam, or the inevitable tangles with Congress showed beyond their embryo states.

Kennedy's death contributed in several ways to the complexity of the 1960s, to the human and very personal way in which larger issues were summoned up. All the hopes and partially realized plans suddenly became might-have-beens; the shock of so sudden a change was traumatic in itself and was made even more so by the destructive deaths to follow. Seen as stimulus and response, those three years were not only connected to a terrible loss but also to something permanent and persistent, something which had been and suddenly was not. They were fixed; they could be looked at, held up as a benchmark, even dreamed about. This was not universally felt, of course. We are all aware of the many Americans who shed no tears, then or later. But the young felt both sides of the death; they perceived what was lost and equally what was made permanent by the loss— a complex view of Kennedy's death which was to be used again and again as an attitude, a stance with which to meet major issues as they emerged.

And one of those issues, of course, would be the attitude which the activist groups in particular would adopt toward LBJ. I shall have more to say about that dazzling politician and complex human being. Here, it is important to recognize that Kennedy's death would contribute to LBJ's special pain when his years of purgatory came to their own terrible life. He would be judged in many ways; among them would be by sinister contrast with the vivid, young, last president.

This sense of the sinister, of the unexplained darkness of people and events, was a legacy from which many of us in positions of authority would suffer. The Kennedy murder was only one strand in that fabric of the hidden, the alien, which provided the basis for a good deal of the fear and anger of the time. Not seen fully in 1963, it was one of the conditions of mind and heart which made the later causes and conflicts so overt, so strident, so emotionally overwhelming.

As we shall see, there were several nodal points during the decade, times when the major movements took a long step—not always forward, but at least a step. The last eighteen months of John Kennedy's life embodied a half-dozen of these events which were to be instrumental in shaping the immediate future. I describe them serially, but we need to picture them together, creating a particular texture for national life and a dynamism which would become steadily more frenetic in the days to come.

The concerns of women had (as we have noted) seemed muted, in the shadows, during the 1950s. This was partly an illusion, of course, and partly preparation time for a generation of women who were not yet ready to assert themselves with clarity and creative energy. We often take that word *assert* in its negative sense; certainly there is a negative side to any assertion, a prior position pushed against as the necessary precondition if a new action or stance is to be espoused. In the two examples which concern me here, however, the positive action is at the center, the negative merely a place to start. The first is the formation of *Catalyst* in 1960, and the second—of course—the publication of *The Feminine Mystique* in 1963.

Catalyst is a remarkable example of an idea brought into existence by a small group, initiated largely in fact by the energy and insight of one woman, and moving through the sixties into the seventies as a steadily growing force to establish women in the working life of the country. I was fortunate to see it as a board member for the first twelve years or so. It was effective from the start because it was dedicated to active programs, not to political manifestoes. Our question was always, "What is needed to help women use their competence in jobs and careers? What are the barriers, and how can we present effective solutions both for women and for those who should be employing them?" We were not doctrinaire, and Felice Schwartz set a tone of quiet and businesslike effort that kept us, I believe, from being self-important. As a result, we were never in the noisy news of the time, but by the end of the decade we had a small, strong organization devoted—as one example among many—to matching part-time employment to the needs of business and the professions.

Betty Friedan's pivotal book was quite another matter. Its public and controversial impact came through the articulation of a complex group of women's concerns, balanced by an equally complex pattern of imminent change—change both in attitudes and in the new modes of life which might be established. That is an abstract and highly generalized statement. What in fact did she see, and what made the book influential far beyond her expectation or that of her publishers?

Evidently she saw and heard the exact opposite of what the advertisers, the slick magazines, and conventional trend-setters chose to see and hear. (With hindsight we can question, of course, whether they claimed to be hearing what they merely felt they *should* be hearing.) She had done a great deal of private interviewing of her Smith College peers and others and had come to some intense convictions about their discomforts with their place in society, about the ambiguity which they felt as they tried to combine careers and marriage, about their desire to get beyond these either-or choices which were all too likely to leave them dissatisfied no matter which way they tried to move. These women felt that the tensions they described came both from within and without, and they were candid and searching in ways which surprised them as well as her. We might say, indeed, that their very perception was "revolutionary"; nothing of this sort had been articulated before with such passion and coherence. The actions of the 1960s were remarkable in many ways, but they owe a good deal of their power and effectiveness to these perceptions. Once articulated, they quickly became a firm basis for action.

The high emphasis which the 1950s put on domestic achievement and the public emphasis (from many quarters) on family, femininity, and volunteer work as adequate answers to women's aspirations were cut across by the steadily increasing numbers of women in the work force, as well as by the inner desires of these women themselves. In many ways this group was in an ideal position (though they would hardly have used the word *ideal* in describing it) to experience the crosscurrents of emotion and action which characterized the college class of 1942 and those nearest it. These women stepped out of college into the unusual demands of the wartime years—either early or delayed marriages and then demanding work during the war which in turn was succeeded by an abnormal public desire for a simplified version of the "normal" life. As we have seen, the serenity of the 1950s was in many ways an illusion, a fond hope. As with so many other aspects of the time, the emerging reality was at odds with the official views. Betty Friedan articulated the self-doubts, the frustrations, the unphrased and still inchoate aspirations of millions of American women. Simone de Beauvoir had, of course, been a pioneer in articulating their hopes and needs, but *The Second Sex*, first published in 1949, was still the property of an intellectual elite. In 1963 Betty Friedan made many of those earlier insights and a whole range of her own widely available to American women.

Here, as so often in the decade, we see the beginning of an assertion which by itself would not have moved so far or said so much. But as their public docility was being shaken off, and while they were beginning to move ahead with programs of both thought and action, women found themselves in surprisingly active company. There was nascent political ferment of an intensity and range not seen for decades; there were university students who were beginning to feel alienated without yet using the word or playing games with the concept; and there were enough black movements in embryo to inflame that community and bewilder the rest of the country. (And that bewilderment had an important part to play in the tensions of the latter years of the decade.)

When I mention political ferment, I am for the moment concerned only with that one band in the spectrum which was Southeast Asia—not even seriously discussed by area in the Rockefeller Report. After the French left in 1954 and the new South Vietnamese government asserted control, it seemed more and more to be that subversive political/military movement which we had been taught to fear. We began to react much as we were reacting to the new regime in Cuba. But while Cuba was so close that we felt secure (at least in our power to maintain constant surveillance), Vietnam was out of our normal orbit and therefore all the more threatening. We underestimated the difficulty of taking action in Cuba, and we exaggerated the need to take definitive action in Vietnam. The overt moves were slow and only gradually became visible to most of us. But the country had an agency for covert maneuver thoroughly established; and it certainly did not use up its energies with the Bay of Pigs disaster. What was needed was a countervailing force, a dictator who was our dictator, to paraphrase FDR's comment about Batista. And so we were set to embark on the long path which led from covert action (including the first of many political assassinations) through the establishment of an advisor group, and on to the supply of air and ground support, which seemed to lead inevitably to a major war. I mention the whole sequence at this point for two reasons: its impact on the chief domestic movements of the decade, and its own special inner dynamism.

Little as we knew of the policy being evolved, we were being stirred by the presence of issues dimly seen but constantly felt through the press and television. The unrest we began to sense in many corners of society between 1960 and 1963 had international conflict as one of its growing preoccupations. We felt it in Cuba, as we had in Korea; and some of the concern about Southeast Asia followed logically enough from these past events and associations. We were already positioned on knife's edge some time before we began the series of irreversible commitments to Vietnam.

The inner structure of our political/military stance was, oddly enough, dominolike in nature. There is a bitter paradox here, of course. Concern about Southeast Asia was often expressed by the State Department in the image of falling dominoes; we see now that it was hopelessly simplistic and did little to describe the separate nationalist aspirations of each country in Southeast Asia. Very largely a myth as far as international politics went—and the whole history of postcolonial Africa is a further proof of this fact—the domino theory provides an ideal metaphor for the steadily deeper and sequentially related involvements which we endured between 1960 and 1972.

College and university students formed a special group throughout the decade. They were not all of one mind, naturally, but they were seismographic in registering the international issues. And they had their own separate culture—their space—in which to debate and ponder the major questions. They also had the time and interest to respond to cultural or political events, first by excitement, then possession, and often finally by action. They were moving in a tradition of student activism as old as the universities themselves. It is important as the decade begins to remind ourselves that students —and universities—have repeatedly mirrored the major events of their time, though often in symbolic and exaggerated form. Student activism in the 1960s was remarkable, not because it existed, but because it mirrored, focused, and projected simultaneously so many of the major movements.

American students have not been as politicized as their continental European counterparts. The residential nature of American colleges and the great British universities has had a good deal to do with this fact, and the British universities had the added discipline of a political establishment to which, until the 1930s, most students already belonged by the time they were admitted to the universities. The students who lived in the great continental cities were much more accustomed to taking to the streets and the barricades whenever there was an issue available for them to seize on and enjoy.

This does not mean, however, that American students were historically immune to sudden and direct action. Yale in the 1850s was a center of southern sentiment, with a substantial group of students accustomed to firearms in their homes. They were ready and able to express their regional opinions with more than words. When tension with the New Haven citizens broke into the open, the resulting deaths turned the campus into a fortress for two weeks, with gates barred and chained to keep the students in and the enraged citizens out. At a different level in 1939 at Yale (and many other campuses) a seemingly spontaneous peace movement broke into the open. I took part in it, as did nearly half of the Yale undergraduates. Our principles were of the highest and most simpleminded sort; we responded in part to a group of charismatic pacifists but also—though we did not know it—to a well-orchestrated leftist campaign to neutralize American support for the war in Europe. This movement vanished overnight when Hitler invaded the Soviet Union, but it has stood as a constant reminder to me of the speed with which a movement could take hold of large numbers of students if the external climate was right.

And so in the early 1960s there was once again a readiness to respond to new issues, new styles, a new beat in the music. As the decade heated up, it seemed as though that music, the violent verse, the metaphysics of alienation and anarchism were all new and immediate responses to the time. Their sudden public emergence, their cresting popularity, certainly were in good part responsive to the moment, but many of the actors, like the themes, were already in place. Some, like Paul Goodman and Herbert Marcuse, had been in place for years; but suddenly they and the times found one another. So with undergraduates; they were, like many women, already in vigorous motion away from the outer facility and acceptance of the 1950s. Those of us busy with university administration got the sequence backward; students in the 1960s were already on their way to a new, assertive, experimental culture *before* the great disruptive issues emerged.

Similarly with the variety of black movements. As we have seen, there was enough ferment in the 1950s, geographical mobility with all its unsettling results and lingering bitterness from the war, so that only a group of brilliant young leaders was needed in order to bring a whole spectrum of activity into passionate being. By the early 1960s those men were in place and building their followings. The lines were not yet sharply defined, of course, the bridges between movements not yet built; and white liberals still seemed to have a part to play in helping unfold the implications of the major legal actions taken in the 1950s. More than any of the other major groups, however, blacks were poised for independent motion at the start of the decade. They sensed clearly both what they wanted and what they were pushing against. The issues which they faced were tactical issues; and these would be the substance of argument—often violent —in the years to come. But Martin Luther King and Malcolm X did not have to debate what black people needed and deserved. Instead, they were involved at the start of the 1960s—and some years before it became significant for the women's movement—in major efforts at consciousness-raising. This was a necessary first step if blacks in any considerable number were to establish enough self-confidence so that they could hope to act effectively.

Moving through and often beneath the overt actions of all these groups were the young radicals—some of them Don Quixotes, some guns for hire, and some dedicated crusaders. Suddenness, change, drama are qualities which run through the 1960s; the radicals of the new left were always ready to supply them if one of the other movements seemed to flag. In a time when "co-optation" was one of the shibboleth words, they showed unusual skill at practicing the technique while they scorned and rejected it in the establishment. They were certainly catalysts in the whole surge of movements; but next to the drug and flower cults, they were the most ephemeral. They left no figure in the carpet, while the black and women's movements draw major elements of their strength today from the patterns which were explored and developed in the 1960s.

I have moved rapidly over the various groups which would be involved in the actions of the decade. I shall return to each in some detail, but as I do I must inevitably lose that kaleodoscopic quality which was so remarkable in their common activity. That kaleidoscopic effect was one of the most important and somber aspects of the decade. Many loyal Americans were caught up in these issues with no preparation and little time to understand them. As we shall see again and again, the tempo was extreme. I have described movements just as they began to accelerate, but all of them—including the war itself—would change at a pace which made it extremely difficult to grasp the true meaning of events. And this difficulty showed itself right across society; the generals knew as little of the forces they were in fact dealing with as the most ingenuous college sophomore, who discovered suddenly that you could trust no one over thirty. We were all caught in a net of hopes, fears, and desperate missions, and this fact provided a special quality to the decade which should be understood before we look at the individual movements.

The Curve of Action and the Common Bond

The "curve of action" during the decade is my metaphor for a pattern remarkable in many ways but most of all for the fact that it was —unknowingly—shared by all of the major groups and by the individuals who dominated them. General Westmoreland, Malcolm X, and Timothy Leary do not have much in common, except that they walked the earth together, but they do have one shared human quality. Each of them had an articulated dream, a conviction about certain goals and how they should be reached. (And the *how* is as important as the *what* to men and women in this special position.) Some of the dreams held were so bizarre, so spectacular in their statement, that they have distracted us at times from their ubiquity. Each dream was carried forward through conviction and into action, and it produced some singular correspondences. Indeed, bitterly opposed groups influenced one another to shape some of these "agreements in disagreement." Taken together, they represent a curve of action in the sense that they carry us through the decade as initial decisions are played out and modified by events, which in their turn modify the very decisions which underlay them—and by those changes modify the action of others who themselves are building patterns of judgment and behavior.

Vietnam was a prime example of this complex field of force. The official conduct of the war was remarkable in many ways: its heavy use of equipment and supplies, its dependence on techniques of saturation—including a good deal of chemical oppression as well as bombing and low-level air power. But it was most remarkable for the unfounded conviction that a little more force of various kinds would surely produce a military victory. We can still hear that conviction today in the voices of the revisionists and the reminiscers who quiet their own doubts—and try to still the doubts of others— by the poignant assertion that "we were not allowed to win the war." Our military history shows few claims with less foundation.

Important for us here is the fact that the very weight of the war's prosecution brought forth a corresponding weight in the reaction of many groups and most of all among students of military age. The constantly increasing demand for more men, more sophisticated and destructive equipment, brought into being not only disagreement at the most basic emotional level but a great deal of reasoned analysis of the uses and limits of military force. This intensity of criticism was very largely the result of the heavy demand laid on society by the military. In their reciprocal relationship the two groups shared one common attribute—the active and aggressive pursuit of a position, which became more entrenched and rigid on both sides as events in Vietnam grew steadily more somber. And this criticism was no mere verbal matter; young men went to Canada, went underground, went to jail. Action was matched by action, and the self-awareness of millions of young Americans (as distinct from those who gave the orders and enforced the laws) moved in markedly new directions.

This was the greatest single conflict of opinion and action, but it was ultimately primus inter pares, and it might not have had its full impact without the support of a dozen other paired conflicts which mark the decade. Before we look at them in detail it may help us keep our footing if we identify the most significant quality they shared. Different as they are, they draw much of their life from the fact that they are conflict positions; their own nature is established by pushing against another standard of value. There are times of course when the positive assertion of a new attitude seems almost to stand by itself; it builds on another style without being locked in mortal struggle. Even the French Impressionists did not face an equal and opposing energy (though scorn and derision were bad enough). The pairs we are now considering draw a significant part of their energy quite precisely from their conflicts.

The black movements which proliferated so dramatically in the 1960s present a multitude of surfaces and attitudes, but one issue gave strength to them all. Should the assertion of black rights and black equity be nonviolent, or should it use every means possible? *Bullets or ballots*, as Malcolm X put it in a virulent Newark speech during the summer of 1964. (He recommended them, in sequence, if necessary.) The tension and discipline of the nonviolent movement was lent a good deal of its power not only by the white extremism which opposed it but by the explosive and enraged black movements which paralleled it. Similarly, many of them—and many of their leaders—were not only skeptical of Martin Luther King, but drew strength from their steadily increasing opposition to his methods and his metaphysics. As their impatience and frustration mounted, so did their open doubt that his approach could create what blacks needed and demanded within a reasonable time. In ways both subtle and obvious the major black groups were foils for one another. Their antagonisms defined the basic problem and set many of the limits and conditions for its solution.

Political activism is for many their most vital memory of the 1960s. It was manifest in many forms for most of the period. As a result, it was paired in its opposition, not just to one major movement of the time but to several. These deserve our special attention; they are important for the true action of the decade, which goes far beyond its activism. Most simply they are the drug culture, the quietists or Aquarians, and the liberal establishment. In all three cases young voices were loud, and in each case there were older gurus who set much of the style and many items of the agenda.

If we had to pick one conviction which drove—and always drives —the political activists, it would be that the course of events could be changed suddenly, radically, and for the better. Many methods were tried in the attempt to build a mass political movement. Ironically enough, one major opposition which they faced came from a political movement far more radical than any devised by any of the "official" activist groups. This was the drug culture, political in the most basic sense since it had a sweeping program for the reform of society. Swarming with cult figures, so that at its height everyone involved seemed to be both follower and leader, it created a political theater of the absurd in which the major action was to step out of action altogether into a shared but private world, where the nonexistent was made real—sometimes in joy, sometimes in terror, but always in opposition to public causes, manifestoes, and pressure politics.

The edge of new left activism was sharpened by this opposition, which was officially directed against the straight world but in practice appealed to some of the same groups on which the young activists depended. In the opinion of older America, furthermore, the absurdities of one group mingled with the extremism of the other.

They tended to flow together in the common mind and to create one reaction of distaste and rejection. And they supported one another, grotesquely enough, in a progression of events which led over and over again—for soldiers, women, students, blacks—from initial conviction to final disillusion or defeat. This seemed to be a basic pattern of action which was repeated by the most disparate people. It is not too farfetched to speak in the metaphor of a lifecycle. Each of the major movements or events started with a germ of conviction; each grew through discussion with the like-minded and the addition of converts; each found a plan of action which was followed by a good deal of passionate commitment; then, and most singular of all, each movement through its organized activity built toward its own defeat —or at the very least its radical modification.

There was a bondage of loathing. The groups came to detest one another while they repelled large segments of the society around them. As a result, activists of various sorts failed to establish a hearing for many sound ideas. They did get some visibility, however, from two further contrasts beyond the drug culture. The first of these was provided by the gentle people, the Aquarians. Their quietism was not sick, not self-destructive like that of the drug people. Instead, they took the world, and one's experience with it, to be at heart good, peaceful, and Edenlike. To create that state one had to will it and then celebrate it. Where the activists were fighting with their world in order to improve it, the Aquarians were proclaiming it. They were born-again, but without the self-righteous edge that often goes with the term today. Their own dream might not hold up, but its rebuke of the contentious bustle of the activists held up very well. They were prophets of the word, the song, the existential Now, and the only sharpness about them was the light they shed on others.

These were modest opposites, indeed, compared to that which developed through the decade and with increasing fury between the liberal establishment and the new left—and its half-formed counterculture. "Liberal establishment" is a trite but compact way of indicating that complex group of organizations, government agencies, and individuals which had long provided an official approach to social and individual needs. It had started with a rush in the 1930s, had matured so that much which once seemed radical was now normal and accepted. In fact, one could argue that these programs and attitudes had become too routine, that they were losing their effectiveness. (In one of the great ironies of the 1960s, Lyndon Johnson, the most valiant political champion of these national concerns, would try to breathe life into them while sinking into a Vietnam morass which negated all his hopes and plans.)

The frustrations and the final disillusionment of Lyndon Johnson will occupy us shortly. Here we should recognize the intricate conflict and dynamic interaction between the explicitly liberal political stance of an Allard Lowenstein, or (in more substantial form) a Hubert Humphrey, and the brightest of the young radicals. The tension between them is similar in many ways to that between the two major wings of the black movement. A good many of the purposes and hoped-for ends were shared, but the means caused the profoundest kinds of mutual suspicion and conflict.

It is not easy to explain why their overt conflict emerged so suddenly, but an analogy to the genesis of hurricanes may be an apt metaphor for the dynamics of the decade's early years. It is only by some such image that we can understand the suddenness with which both national priorities and the means of attaining them changed radically in so brief a period. The heart of the analogy is the fact that political or cultural atmosphere can act like the physical atmosphere in this one respect. Once a change begins, it can build dramatically and swiftly from a modest base, and there is a quality of self-generation in both cases. The initial depression becomes a minimal tropical storm, increases in intensity as it draws more and more energy into its own center, and finally emerges as a full-blown hurricane. So a few sources of unusual agitation in the early 1960s provided a self-generating and steadily increasing energy, and that energy increase is particularly important for our understanding of the political turbulence of the 1960s.

This is so because the liberal movement itself had already articulated a broad range of principles and political objectives. The trigger mechanism for the radicals was the sluggishness of the liberal program to achieve anything beyond its formal expression through the government bureaucracy. Suddenly, a group of young, articulate, and often thoughtful people were looking for immediate action to deal with all the issues which liberalism had espoused for so long. They did not want to be co-opted (that favorite sixties' word again) by the liberals, whose effectiveness they questioned more and more deeply; and out of these initial disagreements there grew with fateful speed a fully articulated opposition which set out to provide a viable alternate to liberalism at the left end of the political spectrum.

The liberal position during the 1960s was itself a bundle of conflicting attitudes and approaches. LBJ's Great Society was, despite its young critics, an honorable and ultimately tragic attempt to push forward the best of official liberalism with new legislation and new organizations to carry out the law. At the other end of the liberal spectrum, we see Allard Lowenstein attempting to surf with the young activists and still keep his more orthodox liberal credentials. He is almost in his own person a demonstration of the bonding of opposites in the political arena—which he tried to accomplish by eliminating them through his sheer versatility and energy. This reconciliation was intermittent and superficial, however, compared to the much more profound tension which held political antagonists together through their zeal for combat and their constant fear of co-optation. This fear was an important aspect of the paranoia of the young (which made honest discussion with them so difficult during these years). With suspicion rampant, we can begin to understand why the old-line liberals were often the sworn enemies of the new activists. They were too close, they *seemed* to be discussing the same issues—indeed, trying to keep possession of them—while in the eyes of the new left they were out to protect their own positions rather than to change society in any significant or timely way.

And *time* was a major issue, both in the adversary relationship between establishment liberals and the new left and the wary, finally contemptuous relationship between those same liberal groups and the major black organizations. The more radical, the more contemptuous, of course. One of the chief grounds for black resentment toward Martin Luther King or the NAACP was their influence with whites. This conflict within the groups moving for major change in society would have a heavy and largely negative impact on the results they hoped to achieve. At this point, however, I want to stress only the weight of the disagreement. Initially, it heightened the tension among all of these groups, and between them and the far larger number of Americans who did not consider that there were in fact issues to face.

Animosity of quite another sort developed between those committed to an unquestioned acceptance of all that technology could do and those who were beginning to feel that the significant questions were not being asked of it. These questions came more and more to emphasize our relationship to the natural world. Ethical issues about the environment were raised with an intensity which forced issues of pollution, use of resources, and dependence on nuclear power (whether for peace or war) into positions of prominence. And, as we have seen with the other antagonistic pairs, those with the newer point of view—the challengers—were not satisfied to spend their energy in talk. A major characteristic of the 1960s, indeed, is this counter-activity among those who most feared or resented the official actions of the time. Even Timothy Leary's drug communes were active in their rejections; the far more coherent antitechnical groups took action by forming alternate communities which would place them directly in the natural world—caring for it, enhancing it, and resisting further depredations against it. These were groups with spiritual roots leading back to some of the nineteenth-century Utopian communities, but they were very much of our own time in their antagonisms.

These alternate life-style groups of the 1960s were—at least in their judgment about the heavy technology of post-war America and Europe—even more prophetic than they knew. In chapter 4 we shall return to the problems of chemical pollution and ecological damage which they addressed so directly. Here, it is important to note that the exaggerated and uncritical claims of the 1950s about the dawning world of infinite energy and automatic abundance were already forcing thoughtful people to consider alternates to "What's good for General Motors is good for the country" or "There are no problems with nuclear power that a billion dollars won't fix." It would be wrong, of course, to assume that these voices, these alternate life-styles, were always the result of careful critical thought. They were often the intuitive conclusions of men and women already out of tune with their society's dominant styles and dogmas. Those who were disaffected for a variety of reasons found the alternate and nature-related life-style a sharply focused way to express their disaffection. As a result, the reason was often reason in madness. The texture of the sixties owes its singular quality not only to the constant bondings of opposites, but to the crazy sanity which shows up again and again in the programs of many of the movements.

The bond of conflict between traditional sexual morality and the freedom made feasible by the development of the contraceptive pill is perhaps our best example of cross-bonding. Sexual freedom was obviously and directly related to the assertiveness of the young, particularly in the universities. However, it equally allowed young women to "prove" their allegiance to a cause by bedding down with its proponents (and it allowed the proponents to exploit the young women much more comfortably). It was a component of many of the communes, and particularly evident in the drug-oriented ones. The new freedom in sexual relationships thus became not only a cause in itself but an important supporting element in a dozen other causes. The antagonism between generations, for example, was often expressed in sexual terms—too available as a way of outraging the elders or castigating the young to be ignored by anyone on either side of that magical thirty-year line.

The most dramatic and complex example of cross-bonding in the sexual area showed itself in the constant tension between straight and gay exponents of sexual freedom. This produced a double-barreled charge of antitraditional morality, of course, and a great deal of group tension, particularly in the women's movement. Here we see how convoluted the substructure could be. Straight and gay could unite in an attack on their common enemies in traditional society. At the same time there was deep cleavage between the committed gay groups and those who believed that the gay issue was merely one element (often disruptive) in the larger issue of equity for women, blacks, and other minorities. The sexual element was inescapable, however, no matter which group was considered. It created issues of bonding so close that they were familial.

To state the matter so is to bring up again the archetypal bond of the sixties, that between the bewildered elders and the embattled young. The generational conflict of the decade is a curious particular case of that genetic tension in parent-child relationships. Like the issue of sexual mores, it was a ready-made cause for many of the sixties' movements to use and abuse at will. One would have predicted it in the various movements and groups of the young radicals; actually, however, it came to prominence most of all in the work of Paul Goodman and other far from young exponents of the "Don't trust anyone over thirty" schools of thought. (There were obviously some quiet personal disclaimers being spoken while the use of that phrase was at its height.)

The significance of finding it in the verbal tool kit of analysts like Goodman does not, of course, exist merely at this surface level. The phrase is used to embody a sense that the elders had lost their innocence, their power to see issues clearly—and, most of all, to act on them in an honest way once the issues were described. The weapon of age becomes powerful indeed in the hands of eloquent speakers and writers; in the hands of brilliant filmmakers, it can be devastating. *The Graduate* gives classic expression to this attitude, and I shall return to it. Here it is most important to understand how the particular emotional charge of the 1960s was strengthened by this special use of an age-old issue of generation conflict. The result when one takes this together with the other patterns I have discussed is a remarkable richness of texture: emotional color and sound blended with substantial (though often confused) intellectual content. As they reinforce one another, we can begin to understand why the atmosphere is often too heavy to bear, often out of control.

A Special Strength

The relationship of the women's movement to the other major events of the sixties is unique. Not only were there bonds of conflict like those in the other major movements, but there was a coherence and a sympathy with certain other groups which was not commonly evident or fully reciprocated. There are many reasons for this unique position: the sheer size of the women's movement, the fact that it had existed in one organized form or another for so long and had already won so many hard-fought victories; the nature of its potential members and their high responsiveness to the aims of many of the other active groups through a long-standing formal tradition of support for blacks, for the abused families of the inner cities, and for men and women working under inhuman conditions.

The size and variety of its potential constituency ensured that bonds of conflict would exist within the movement, as well as between it and certain of the conservative groups resisting equity in the professional, career, and personal treatments of women. Given this texture within the women's movement and in its relationship to other major activists, the interaction between conflict and cooperation becomes dramatic indeed. Like the bond of conflict between parents and children, which ran deeper than any of the more spectacular young rebellions of the 1960s, underlying all the richness of relationship between the women's movement and others is the basic conflict between men and women. This statement would be a mere truism were it not that so much of the energy in the women's movement has been supplied by that tension. When it is combined with the other relationships which we see in the 1960s, it is a movement set apart.

The conflict-bonding with a variety of groups is clear enough. The relationship between the women's movement and certain broad aspects of the black movement is so striking, however, that in itself it makes a distinct and separate pattern in the sixties. This support went back at least as far as the 1840s when the women's groups of many churches began to find their mission through reaching out toward blacks. To a surprising degree, those women before the Civil War pictured their bond to slaves as their descendants did in the 1960s. That bond was the bond of oppression, and the sense that women were members of a minority in this particular meaning of the word. Majority meant power, not mere numbers, and they were denied it.

I have suggested that the women's movement, like others, came to a time of conflict, self-doubt, and disillusion. It would be inaccurate to say this, however, without one major qualification. Despite the obstacles and frustrations, the women's movement—or movements—reached many major goals. Some were to be denied or heavily modified in the decades to come, but women did what (as we have seen) they had done many times before in American culture. They persisted in the face of scorn and contempt; they established their claims to parity of opportunity, and—ERA or not—those claims would not be swept away. Most important (and far too little acknowledged), they managed, in the course of strenuous efforts to heighten their own awareness, to bring a new awareness and perception to millions of American men.

When I say this I am not trying that trick of co-optation which the radical groups of the sixties feared so much. It was obvious that the women's movement must make several of its major affirmations apart from men; that had been the case over and over since the eighteenth century. What made the movement of the sixties so remarkable and so different from earlier times of great effort, however, was the fact that in order to succeed it had to place women in a different position in the professions, in business, and—as a direct result —in the structure of the family. The assertion was made by women, but it was made about aspects of the world dominated by men until that time. It was a women's movement that had to become a social movement in order to succeed. In the great earlier causes with which women had identified themselves they were at the service of a major social movement—universal suffrage—or an intense moral as well as social crisis—abolition in the 1840s and 1850s. The battle for education at the college and university level was a truly remarkable enterprise; and like the other major causes it greatly modified the position and influence of women in our society. All three were contributors to the movements of the 1960s, but they did not prepare us for the mass and richness of the events which took place. The questions and the causes were many, but they became one: What does it mean to be a woman? And there was the inevitable working corollary: if we can establish our identities as women, what steps must we take in society to guarantee that this complex feminine identity will flourish?

Put in this way, the issue becomes singularly at home in the 1960s. Simone de Beauvoir had raised many of the major questions in the late 1940s, but (as we have seen) the current of the 1950s flowed strongly against any major concern with feminine identity if it implied independence, separateness, strength. But suddenly there were voices of many sorts—not just women's voices—discussing the issue of identity and pressing for a particular place in the sun.

And there was Betty Friedan. As she herself said, she did not expect her inquiries to unfold as they did; she met in her peers the issues of significance and direction which she had felt but not yet fully worked through for herself. She discovered as she wrote, and with the appearance of the book moved her discoveries to a whole new level of national importance. The feminine mystique and the feminine reality turned out to be a serious concern for millions of women.

We see here an unusual form of the "suddenness" which was so important a part of each major movement in the decade. The women's movement stood apart, however, because its base was so broad and so multiple, and equally because it had (as we have seen) so solid a basis in the history of American culture. These varied strengths helped the movement greatly when it had to cope with the excesses of certain subgroups—and I would say in particular some members of the lesbian sisterhood. There was no parallel to this particular tension anywhere else in the psychic history of the time. Gay men often joined with women in public assertiveness, but the men had no single larger group to which they might belong. This denied them the power and the visibility which were available to lesbians through the women's movement.

This setting, the women's movement as a whole, was often shaken by the stridency of the lesbians. Though some of them disclaimed it, there was a well-articulated and clearly argued position which maintained that lesbians, being purely concerned with feminine matters, were the real vanguard of the movement, its essential and unadulterated core. Women who had to—or chose to—maintain complex relationships with men were to that extent compromising the single vision which was necessary if the messianic sense of mission was to be maintained.

Despite our best effort, this still seems like strange doctrine to many of us who are involved from a masculine point of view in these relationships. We are forced to ask whose femininity we are discussing, just as the gay movement—or the gay reality—forces us to look into ourselves as we try to understand whose maleness is under definition. One of the most remarkable aspects of the sixties, indeed, was the fact that the questions could be felt, articulated, and endured even if we had no easy answers. One of the great triumphs of the women's movement was its recognition that all of these questions had somehow to be maintained and understanding of them enhanced. The very complexity of this understanding marked both the movement and the decade. Nothing like it had ever happened.

And it was of course also a complexity which invited scorn and cheap humor. The bra-waving was a parody of freedom, and some of the aggressive anti-male positions seemed overstated. These statements, however, are made from the higher ground of privileged masculinity. Left unqualified, they ignore realities of prejudice and injustice which the movement of the sixties confronted. Here, it is most important to realize how well the movement kept its balance and its vision of the goals to be pursued. Some of the resistance which occurred in the 1970s and 1980s—to the ERA, for instance— was predictable. Far more important is the fact that the issues of work, of varied styles of marriage and family, of independence and yet social acceptance, of sexual initiative, were clearly established by the end of the sixties, and they did not disappear. Instead, they became central, even determining, aspects of our social life in the 1980s.

The clearest demonstration of this vitality is the fact that I have such difficulty keeping the 1980s in their proper place. When I write about the women's movement I cannot escape the continuity, the persistence, as well as the change of emphasis within it. It is easy to separate the black or student movements from their past in the 1960s; the *discontinuities* are apparent and—as we shall see—they often suggest the loss of positions and understandings which were clear for a brief time in the sixties. There is certainly change in some emphases of the women's movement, but it is change within the boundaries of clear consistency. That is a major achievement, and one that sets the movement apart.

The women's movement was obviously more complex as well as more broadly based than any of the others, and its conflict-bonding went on intensely among its subgroups—not unlike the subgroups of

the black movement. Whatever the differences or similarities, however, we have a large pattern of relationships among groups, movements, and ideas which is striking for its intensity, for its complexity,
and by and large for its positive consequences. It is nontemporal; the
bonds result from common concerns, not from the fact that event A
took place before or after event B. But these bondings are only one
part of the decade's dynamism.

As a result, we find that we are dealing with a grid of aspirations,
actions, and relationships. The movements come to their passionate
life in these three dimensions: first, through their explicit contact
as black, student, political, military, women's movements; second,
in their relationships, bonds of antagonism as well as cooperation;
and third, in the dimension of time by which they come to some
resolution through action. And it is these resolutions which create
the unpredicted, unexpected patterns of the decade.

The student left, to take perhaps the most familiar of the sustained
movements, was born from the fertile interaction not of two but
several events: assassination, the looming of war, the failure both
of the old radical left and the old official liberalism, a fair amount
of Utopian talk, music, and instability in life-style. As those came
together in the earlier 1960s, they guaranteed not only a good deal
of heat but a good deal of hope; and both in its genesis and its
sudden flaming into full life this movement embodied the others.
Each owed its vigorous beginning to a coalescence of causes and
opportunities; as a result, each started in hope and was emotionally
poised to move at high speed to its unforeseen destiny.

Speed and suddenness, indeed, would be hallmarks of each movement throughout the decade. It was particularly striking in the shaping of all the student ventures, of course, but it was a constant pressure on those of us who were seen as the establishment. The tempo
of the battles which developed later in the 1960s was never siege
warfare; it was the panzer attack. Important for us here is the fact
that this urgency moved the student left rapidly into the issues which
were to be bywords of the middle sixties: "free speech," participation
in the governance of universities, the redesign of the curriculum to
meet student definitions of relevance, rising and increasingly organized opposition to the growing war.

The inevitable results of this rush into action were two: first in time, a heady conflict with the authorities at many levels and ranges of importance; second and later, an internal conflict among the major groups of the movement. The techniques of conflict were many: mass meetings often leading to mass hysteria; the boycott and the strike whenever an issue presented itself; the non-negotiable demand for changes in the rules, the personnel, the structure itself. This was familiar from 1964 on, and reached a grim climax with the Columbia adventure in 1968. It is not clear how long this pattern could have continued; given the unresolved state of the war, it might have persisted in an equally intense way for two or three years. Internal conflict, however, turned the student movement against itself, as it did with several of the others.

For the student left in particular, the dominant push was toward steadily more violent confrontations. Though many confrontations were contrived, the violence of their expression was real, and it came to dominate other and more sober expressions of dissent. These in their turn had not changed society in any consistent or dramatic way; and the Weathermen faction of Students for a Democratic Society came to feel that only the most direct action stood a chance of success. From this conviction came the bombings of university facilities, with loss of life at the University of Wisconsin and heavy property losses elsewhere. This violence, which was designed to introduce a whole new chapter in the effective life of the young radicals, turned out instead to be nearly the end of their book. They lost the great mass of the American student population at that point (and indeed the radical wing of the movement had called forth heavy commitments in only a small minority of students at any given time).

The result could probably not have been rightly predicted; but the radical wing of sds predicted it in exactly the wrong way. The members were sure that there was a logical sequence, which they worked hard to arrange, from peaceful protests to disruptive, then violent, direct action; this was the revolutionary sequence, and there was good historical precedent for it in Russia, in China, in Cuba. There was a dialectical sequence, if you will, and its logic had to lead sooner or later to the use of force. Too late its leaders discovered that the spirit of a centrist society was not open to this reshaping.

Naturally concerned with their own positions, they had moved well beyond the realities of their society. Their society in turn rejected them for the most basic reason: it did not see and could not accept their version of the real.

The final stage of this movement, like several of the others, was a move into dreams which were taken to be reality. Exactly as with the proponents of victory in Vietnam, dogmatic assertion of what ought to be turned into the fanatical assertion that it must be so in fact. There was a society ready to be overturned, there was a war ready to be won. This was the terrible delusion, and the worst dreams came at the end in each case, when the proponents of a particular position stepped off the edge of the world—east of the sun and west of the moon with a vengeance.

The Corridors of Power

The decade was one in which issues of power, control, authority, and order were constantly alive, often in their most extreme form. We have looked at the inner dynamics of the various movements and at the "bonding by conflict" which went on there. Naturally, those bondings were constantly posing issues of power. The purpose in each case was the firm establishment of the cause; but the means to be used forced issues of power constantly into the open.

This fact by itself would hardly set the decade apart. What distinguished issues in the 1960s from their more normal form (bickering between presidents and Congress or central government and the states) was the high degree of philosophic debate which embodied them. (Equally, of course, the significance of the issues went far beyond that which a normal period would provide.) The very depth of these debates in turn enhanced the issues of power; from General Westmoreland to Eldridge Cleaver a position under fire would be held and developed with the greatest tenacity.

These human extremes showed a common approach; each walked the corridor of power right to the end and asserted a position until it met absolute resistance—resistance which nullified force with equal force. They are prime examples, among many, of the lengths to which these disturbed years encouraged able men to go. In the bafflements of war—whether for control of a country or a cause—the very obscurity and difficulty of events urges us on to find more and more extreme solutions. It may be hard to picture Westmoreland of the Citadel as an extremist, but in the prosecution of the war he certainly was. After all, as Barry Goldwater remarked, "Extremism in the defense of liberty is no vice. And . . . moderation in the pursuit of justice is no virtue." Both Cleaver and Westmoreland would agree, though each reserved the right to define his terms.

There are many kinds of power, obviously; what makes the sixties almost a laboratory in its uses is not only the range of ends but the range of means—from Martin Luther King's dazzling assertion of nonviolence to the Weathermen's ultimate social disorder. We are confronted with a grid of forces which are highly dynamic—constantly in motion, constantly changing their emphasis as opportunity and the emphasis of a particular struggle demand. We saw that the various movements showed comparable patterns of growth and change during the decade; when we look at the individuals who shaped or headed those movements we see an equal dynamism. The shock of contrast between them is as great as the unexpected shock of certain major similarities—which Cleaver and Westmoreland would certainly not have recognized or accepted.

The decade embodies major elements of a conflict as old as society —that between those whose urge to power constantly moves them toward force at one level or another, and those for whom the realities of power are constantly shaped by the demands of interpretation and understanding. This second group is as a result nudged away from the varieties of force and toward the equally strenuous and far more ambiguous demands of persuasion, manipulation, and the uses of principle as a means to exercise power over events. The 1960s stand apart because so many variations and combinations of power were being publicly tried at the same time. And only twice before in our history had the extremes of force and philosophy—war and the interpretation of society at its heart—been so urgently and intimately alive and so intertwined. The two world wars had put enormous demands on us, but they had not insisted that at the same time we confront basic social and political issues as equally important and moving in tandem with the prosecution of a war. The American

Revolution and the Civil War had this character in common with the sixties as the two world wars did not; they posed the great questions far beyond the ability of war to resolve them.

The oddity is that these major questions were so often raised in eccentric, partial, or extremist ways during the sixties, and by individuals and groups who had to speak against the established power structures if they were to speak at all. These were not the country's founders or shapers; they were often bizarre or ragged, and they belonged to none of the available power structures. (By contrast, Samuel Adams and the other Massachusetts extremists had their position well-developed when the chance for action came.) Yet these offbeat folk drew their power precisely from their ability to put the questions which had been equally familiar and vital for Washington, Jefferson, and Lincoln. What is a just war? How do we deal with minority rights? Who is to define the good society, and how do we implement it? How do we shape education to serve the purposes of our society? These are the central questions which our antiestablishment group asked with increasing urgency as the decade moved on —an urgency heightened by the death of some of their true leaders and the bypassing of others as issues changed and styles of rhetoric lost their freshness. At the same time we should recognize that the most senior members of the administration shared both this sense of urgency and the moral complexity which underlay it.

Even those who vilified him the most recognized, for example, that Robert McNamara was a man of formidable skill both in interpreting evidence and organizing operations. Those opposed to the war naturally hated him for his talents; he made a target no mediocrity could match, so that he was a highly satisfactory villain in the play. Many things were left out of this caricature, and an understanding of one major aspect of his nature would have made the caricature impossible. Beneath the incisive brilliance, and even more important to his career, was an almost puritan dedication to defining the reality of any given situation. Then he would act on it, but he would allow no pat answers along the way.

There is a striking film clip from the most agonizing period of the Vietnam War, when men and matériel are being pushed into action in the maximum numbers and with the most effective deployment of weapons. So the official script reads, and McNamara is sitting under a canvas canopy discussing with the senior generals their conviction that the war is going well, but we need one more push to bring the enemy down. Suddenly, McNamara speaks out, "That's baloney, and I can prove it." He has seen the terrible fallacy in the judgment of his generals, and he challenges it with an integrity which leads inevitably to his resignation and his move to a radically different way of meeting the needs of society. The man who seemed dedicated to the means of violence was dedicated in fact to principles which his severest critics should have shared and often (in their own antiwar violence) failed to understand.

If the period forced paradoxes of this kind on many of its actors, it was given one paradox incarnate in the president of the United States. A man of legends, and not of the kind created by publicity agents, Lyndon Baines Johnson has been analyzed almost beyond credibility. Most important for his place in the 1960s is the fact that his phenomenal skill at manipulating political influence could do little for him when it came to the greatest issues of power and the limits on power. For LBJ a personal limit seems to have been imposed by the honesty of his push for the Great Society. There has been a good deal of cynicism about this massive program. Reductionist thinking has a way of saying "only politics" or "just for public consumption." The evidence from personal journals and private interviews suggests strongly that the commitments were real. If they had been less so, his entanglement with the Vietnam War would still have been destructive (for him as for the country), but a dimension of the decade would have been missing—the anguish of power turned powerless.

As we all know, it became impossible to pursue the social ends LBJ had in mind and at the same time prosecute the war. (Lady Bird Johnson refers to this intimate frustration at several points in her personal journal of those years.) He was as entangled in the net of events as his severest critics—and he could no more break the nets than they. The dilemma of power in the late 1960s is exactly this, that those who were at the center of it had so little control and were

in fact most vulnerable to the crush of events. They could ultimately
see, but they could not control, and so both McNamara and LBJ
stepped out.

We must take great care with our language when we say that
they could see, however. The apparatus of power is so dazzling at its
center that those who live in it are even more likely to be deceived
than those of us who move into it for brief moments and then move
out again. Small personal encounters which I had with both LBJ
and Dean Rusk during the period tell a good deal about the limits
of insight which seemed almost to grow from their positions.

These encounters came about because university presidents have
always had a particular window on the political world. By chance,
design, or desire, they are tied into national commissions and agencies of review. They lobby and they cajole; the politics of their institutions impinge on the goals of state and federal government, and
often they are heavily supported in return. In the 1960s the interaction was traumatic and often highly frustrating. The impact of
government policy was heavy, and in the universities we responded
in ways which would not have seemed wise or even relevant a few
years earlier. One of these encounters related directly to the anguish
of the late 1960s; the other was concerned with long-range issues of
library and information-handling resources (or so I thought before
the meeting). Both were revelations to me of the limits of power and
of the limits which power imposed on insight. And I do not want
to be judgmental. Both Dean Rusk and LBJ were under the most
extreme pressure, and in any case my concern goes far beyond any
easy criticism.

In the spring of 1968 the Association of American Universities
asked Howard Johnson of MIT and myself to represent to the secretary of state our collective view of the desperate campus situation. Resistance to the Vietnam War was becoming so intense that
it shadowed everything else our universities did or tried to do. The
country's official position on the conduct of the war seemed to have
no flexibility at all, and we needed to know, if possible, what hope we
might take to the embattled groups back home. Was there any room
for maneuver within the limits of that policy, and if so how could
we employ it to defuse a hundred explosive situations on our cam-

puses? This was a tall order. In other times the questions would have seemed impudent, and it was a measure of the depth of our trouble that we all assumed the asking of such questions to be essential. We had to know.

Dean Rusk was a most affable academic that afternoon. In the great quiet office, with our glasses of bourbon, there was a remarkable quality of serenity. Only one person could trouble the secretary of state, the room seemed to suggest, and he was not doing it on that sunny afternoon. The eye of the hurricane is quiet and even beautiful (at least the one I lived through had that eerie quality), and it was certainly present during that hour! Howard and I, coming in from the northeast quadrant where the winds blow hardest, did not really know how to cope with this quiet. We made our case, and the feeling grew in us as we talked that it was simply not very relevant. The secretary knew what we were talking about; he read the papers, after all. But if we realized how matters really stood, perhaps we and our students could recognize that our concern—or at least our expression of it—was rather misplaced. As the conversation unfolded, it began to seem that we should be talking to the North Vietnamese. There had been repeated attempts to discuss a settlement, and they had all been rejected. With no one willing to talk, what could honorable men do but push on? Our talk went back and forth for an hour or so, regretful, pained, cordial on both sides. Howard and I left with clear minds on one subject: nothing was to be done at that level; there was no word to take back. At this distance it is easy to see how foolish we were to expect anything else. I hope it is equally easy to see why we had to try. Not so easy is my contemplation now of the true reason for our failure. Men are still talking about how that war could have been won; they cannot bear to say that we lost because the war itself was wrong—strategically, tactically, and morally. That is an ugly statement now; it was an unthinkable one in that office on that afternoon. To look at these issues, and at what was happening to the country because of them, was not an available option. As a result, we had to leave and muddle on as well as we could with communities which were deeply critical of all authority figures—including ourselves—because we could not or would not come to grips with these questions.

Sometime later when I could reflect on the meeting, a picture from another past bonded to it in my mind. Those nights that Lincoln spent alone with the telegraph operator, huddled in his shawl against the cold as he tried to re-create the patterns of the war from the terse, fragmentary messages, were nights of a search for reality. What was out there in the dark, what were its true patterns, and how could they be shaped? This was, of course, a man who commanded his generals, often without their knowing it; and he was able to do so because he went to the evidence as McNamara finally did and built his strategies from it. Dark, brooding, living with the tragedies of the war: the contrast with our imperial blindness will not leave me when I think about the Vietnam years.

There was certainly nothing superficially dark or brooding about my one direct encounter with LBJ. In 1967 I had accepted the chairmanship of the National Commission on Libraries and Information Services. It was the worst possible time for such a commitment, but now in the fall of 1968 the report was finished and must be presented to the president—who certainly had other matters on his mind at the moment. When the call came, I had about three hours of lead time, chartered a plane, and at 4 P.M. found myself looking at the fish tank in the outer waiting room. The president and Clark Clifford were deep in discussion on Vietnam, and the minutes dragged along. Douglass Cater, assistant for educational and cultural affairs, filled in the time with sound advice. "Whatever you do, don't let him get started on the presidential library." After thirty minutes or so, Mr. Clifford left, and we were ushered in, along with two photographers who used a vast amount of film in the next twelve minutes as the president and I moved around that remarkable little room. I went through the ritual formula: "Mr. President, I have the honor to present to you the report of your commission." "Ah, libraries I see," said the president, taking my summary report and tossing it on the table. "That reminds me, I've got a little library of my own buildin' down in Texas." I saw Doug Cater wince slightly, but he had no time for more. "Say Doug, what's the name of that young feller downtown with the museum—Douglas Dillon?" "Dillon Ripley," said Doug Cater. "That's the one; now he's got a lot of material on Congress, and I mean to have it." Then back to me. "You know, people think

the action is here, but it ain't. Congress is the place where things
get done." I thought of his years of legendary success there; without
overstating his nostalgia, there was a great yearning in his voice for
a setting which he knew better than anyone and players whom he
could move to action with a clear sense of what the outcome was
likely to be. Who could blame him for the nostalgia? He developed
it eloquently for several minutes. I can't recall that I said anything,
and it would certainly have been redundant. Suddenly, books came
up again. He took my arm and pointed me like a weather vane
toward the bookshelves which were next to the fireplace. "You see
them books over there? Nobody looked at 'em in thirty years. But
you take that picture of FDR, or the one of Andy Jackson, or this one
of Ev Dirksen I've got hid down behind the posies." And with that
he plunged one huge hand down behind a credenza and came up
with a magnificent photo portrait of Dirksen behind a dozen micro-
phones, his hair streaming out behind, and his mouth well open.
"Now, people will remember those. Well, good to see you." And with
that the hand propelled me to the door. "Doug," I said when I could
breathe, "there went eighteen months of work." "Don't worry," said
Doug Cater, "we'll see that something comes of it." And indeed he
and others did just that.

The stories have a minor and a major theme. Certainly the library
report was minor, but it was an example of the kind of work that
many of us tried to carry on—often desperately—in the midst of
everything this book is about. The major theme, of course, is the
president himself, a man who knew more about the various kinds
and applications of power than anyone else alive. His brief interlude
with me was a respite, but also a revealing commentary on the large
world. He was leaving; and to talk to me about the congressional
past and the library's future was really to show me where his focus
now directed itself. I was too overwhelmed at the moment to think
of any of this, but I felt it deeply, and with great sympathy. Here
was a man whose dreams had crumbled away, and equally his power
to influence events. Presidents had seen everything collapse around
them before, but never anything quite like this—though Woodrow
Wilson would certainly disagree. I was privileged to see it, and I now
realize that it was one of my major images of the personal dynamics

of the time. Like a great sonnet it was tiny, but it carried a heavy freight of meaning.

There were even more ultimate bafflements of power than these, however. The murders of Martin Luther King, Malcolm X, and the two Kennedys mark the decade as singular even for a violent country like our own. And in each case there was a common reality. Though the motives for the killings were disparate in the extreme, and obscure at many points, the result in each case was the abrupt end of everything that power might accomplish. Each man was a major symbol of one special brand of power—perhaps *the* major symbol at his particular moment in time. And that, alas, was precisely the point. The very qualities that made Malcolm X a brilliant demagogue put him in the path of the assassin. We can say the same of each of the others. Their talent (in the biblical sense) was being fully used; and for that very reason they were prime targets of the hatreds which they themselves helped to raise.

One great casualty of the time was shared by us all. When power and authority are besieged, something terrible happens to the hearing; our hand may not be raised against our neighbor, but our tongue certainly is. Talking, explaining, defending, we found it almost impossible to listen; and as a result other views (and the people who held them) were in constant antagonism to us, and we to them. At times there were elements of grotesque humor about this. I found myself at cross-purposes with Paul Goodman in a very public way, for example, once at another major university and once at home. Away, I was free to make merry at the spectacle of a sixty-year-old guru of anarchism telling his audience to trust no one over thirty; at home he more than paid me back by demonstrating to the clear satisfaction of his audience the inadequate grasp of the day's great issues which—always by definition—I was bound to show in every word I uttered.

He was formidable, but the sad fact in retrospect is that the anarchist and the authority figure held so many ideals and hopes in common. In that time and those places we simply could not communicate, and so it was with LBJ or Dean Rusk and their critics, the black nationalists and their white liberal "friends," or the student left and Robert McNamara. This collapse of understanding was one of the great disasters of the period; and it was the clear, almost ultimate demonstration of the limits of power. There was, I suspect, a good deal of commonality in the frustration of those of us who were forced to inhabit day by day a major conflict between our traditional responsibilities and a swarm of challenges to them. Most events taken singly would have been no more than a bee sting; their mutual reinforcement was quite another matter.

But we seemed clumsy within ourselves as well, and for the most legitimate reasons. We had highly visible positions and traditions to maintain. This was equally true for those of us in the universities, and for the professional politicians, and true in an inverse way for the leaders of dissident movements who were often as bound by what they were against as some of us were by what we were officially dedicated to. The positions we "naturally" took invited conflict in a time which felt no automatic respect for our views. The result was that we often felt we were speaking in some kind of "prepared" room, where our words were either totally absorbed or distorted into something quite alien. Very Kafkaesque, and a formula for chronic frustration.

Power and authority, then, assumed some highly distorted shapes during the decade. I have looked at only a few central examples of the problems posed and the responses called forth; the individuals who embodied these could not have been more divergent, and yet we were all caught in the same web of greatly heightened expectations and deepened failures. This consonance of our disparate experiences is one of the most fascinating aspects of the time. There were virtually no winners among us, except for the somber victory in death of Martin Luther King, or the triumph of painful intensity in a McNamara. To compare small things with great, the decade did not allow the prosecution of some single great aim such as FDR and Abraham Lincoln endured. As with so much else about the period, the great questions were constantly present but in crazy, Don Quixote forms; like him, we often revealed the importance of events through our misunderstandings and defeats, not through our insights and our accomplishments.

Poets, Playwrights, Prophets

There are other kinds of power, less compromised by the decade. The art of the sixties, if we take a comprehensive view of it, is so rich and multiple that it calls for a five-foot shelf of discussion. At the same time a small number of musicians, plays, and films carry a freight of meaning which demands our attention beyond the babble of the others. And they demand it because they are more than images and reflections of the time; they are shapers of it as well. This is particularly true of the music—and more specifically of Bob Dylan, who towers above the others both as performer and poet. In addition, we must take note of three remarkable plays/films: *Hair*, *The Graduate*, and *Tommy*, that astonishing rock opera of the early seventies which embodies the hatreds, the innocence, the passion, the mud and metaphysics of the decade which preceded it.

Music always seems central when passions are turned loose; then discourse of other kinds is often meager or confused, and this most widespread form of folk art comes into its own again. There were events and attitudes which made the assertions of music doubly forceful in the sixties. It was a wandering time, and even those who stayed at home had the symbolic guitar always at hand (and often, incredibly enough, the expensive camera—but that is another part of the story). The increasing restlessness which we have noted in the writers and emerging folksingers of the late fifties fed this old myth of the wandering minstrel, and the vibrant "new music." Presley and Holly as well as Beatlemania, all provided rich and nourishing food for Dylan's emerging talent. But none of these events accounts for him; they are simply pointers along the road which leads us to this poet, performer, and prophet of the very insights which he helps to bring into being.

Hyperbole in this statement is justified, for Dylan—who exists in many traditions—is directly in the line from Blake and Keats, and with the latter he shares the pain and excitement of moving almost abruptly from adolescence to major poetic stature. This formal, academically romantic aspect of Dylan is intertwined with major elements of sixties' life, which are equally romantic in a larger and less formal sense. (The antiestablishment social criticism of the

Guthries' music, for example, is one aspect of a "legitimate," even traditionally romantic view of existence.) Even though it is called earthy and bitterly realistic, Dylan's music speaks with an individual voice and anger; this sets the personal insight apart from that of the mass—apart and above. Here, we have politically romantic music; it is anathema to the doctrinaire left and the dogmatic right, while at the same time it is a direct challenge to the comfortable center. Dylan draws equally from the great romantic metaphors and experiences—of love suddenly found and as suddenly lost, of movement, "voyaging," which may lead anywhere or nowhere and is often an end in itself, of liberation and enslavement through drugs, which embody a voyage, a change of reality, and a direct affront to the sameness and squareness "outside." The romantic makes and then modifies his world as he moves through it, and at this Dylan is unusually gifted and versatile. (Among many other idioms, this is the quality which ties him to the blues tradition.)

As we look at these aspects of his work and meaning for the decade, it is striking that his allusiveness is so wide-ranging in a specifically (but not self-consciously) literary way. It is a reminder from the start that the whole course of Dylan's development and influence will be different from that of the popularizers and faddist artists of the decade—harder, not easily predictable, complex, searching. It is these qualities which draw him not only to the great poets of the romantic tradition but to the metaphysicals—Donne at one end and Eliot at the other.*

These poets are, like the Guthrie tradition or the basic blues, anchors for Dylan's personal journeys and explorations. More than that, they are models. He has the gift of assimilation, so that what he learns from others sharpens his insight where a lesser poet/composer would be intimidated by the heritage which Dylan claims for himself. My concern is, of course, with what he makes of this great and

---

*Michael Gray, *The Art of Bob Dylan*. I am indebted to this brilliant book, not only for its confirmation of Dylan's debt to the major poets of the nineteenth century (with a strong line also to Donne and Eliot) but for his equal insight into other elements of the Dylan world where my knowledge is flawed or nonexistent.

living array of allusions, traditions, styles. It is important to remind ourselves that he makes songs; the poetry is so fascinating and intricate by itself that one can read it, be baffled at times by its seeming partialness, and forget that the full realization of his meaning comes only with the music. When he calls himself a song-and-dance man, that is part of the ironic put-down of himself, like Chaucer's inability to tell a story when the host calls on him. This ironic distancing of self from the action of the song is essential, because there is so clear a persona in the poems that Dylan could easily be celebrating himself rather than reaching into other selves. Romantic poets get into trouble at this point unless they put the persona ahead of the person. Dylan saves himself through his skill at creating a world in which both he and his audience can play a part, become involved and in some sense revealed. A personal lyricist could not make that space for his hearers.

Strangely enough, when we look at the other song-and-dance men of the long generation before Dylan, Cole Porter demands comparison, not only because he fuses the verbal and musical so completely and individually but because he too has the gift of creating a world in which we participate.

This sets both of them apart from the poet/composers (or pairs of them) who are simply writing—no matter how brilliantly—about something. *Gigi* and *Oklahoma*, for instance, are fantastic shows; Porter and Dylan create encounters with a worldview, and one that cuts into us, that comes to the core of our experience. That those worldviews differ profoundly is secondary to the fact that there is a world created in each case.

Porter sees the anguish, as well as the glitz, of the privileged, the chic; he does not celebrate these but rather uses them to get into the troubled heart. Dylan sees the abrasiveness and emptiness of the dispossessed—or at least unpossessed—and sets against an uncertain, dark, meandering world a quest for love, relationship, significance. But look back at Porter; the themes of loss, deception, transience are equally constant in him, equally used as dangers in the quest for assurance, for love. Porter often shows the heartless, the ugly, just beneath a glittering surface. "Love for Sale" is an extreme example, but the basic contrasts of false/true, surface/depth, gain/

loss, up/down, and blindness/insight are as present thematically in Porter as in Dylan. We can say that we dislike one world and like the other, but that is irrelevant; there is the same sense of complexity, ambiguity, and longing in each.

What, then, does Dylan tell us specifically about the sixties, beyond these thematic concerns? And what does he shape for the period? Here we find a great difference from Porter or the Guthries. Dylan is partially creating the culture he writes and sings about. In this sense he is prophetic, but beyond the usual prophetic voice he helps make it happen.

What are his images? The road, the river, the shelter for a night, but only a night, the railroad, the evil or at least threatening city. He evokes and explores these, and then he gives them life for others so that they become the "chosen reality" of millions of people. We all look through glasses; Dylan found ones that for much of the decade fitted a host of hearts and minds.

In particular he is a genius with the innocence/experience relationship. This is revealed constantly by his reaching into the high romantic poets for so much of his resonance. (Even the drug-related experiences have their parallels there.) And he is obsessed with the metaphors of search, which lead him to the most painful issues of the decade. Superimposed on the whole romantic-pastoral tradition, and increasingly as the decade develops, are the issues of war, violence, and instability as they grow steadily more insistent in society —especially in the society of the young. Again, Dylan is shaped by these, but equally he shapes them, gives high coherence to their inchoate existence.

Auden's "images that hurt and connect" could have been written about Dylan. Sometimes he is partial, obscure even while he illuminates; but always he seems to reach for some central insight, a point where a "subject" flashes into fire. The epiphany, the spot in time, is characteristic of Dylan's art as it is of the decade (and as it is of writers as diverse as Joyce and Wordsworth).

He *is* the decade in certain ways. One of them lies in this quality of flash, of suddenness. We have seen that it shows in many of the major shifts of the time, which keep rushing at us; Dylan evokes that sense of the fragmentary, the bright and partial moment or hour, set against the dark, the uncertain, the provisional. In counterpoint (not opposition) to that suddenness Dylan constantly evokes the tenderness in experience, the openness which allows one to be seriously hurt but which permits encounter and—crucial for his approach to reality—keeps us from depending on ready-made emotions. He draws on his whole array of traditions and styles precisely so that we cannot stereotype his idiom or his insight. "Prohibit sharply the rehearsed response," says Auden again, and that is exactly what Dylan sets out to do with us. He establishes for those who listen to him with care—and in that way establishes for the whole decade at its best—a refusal to accept conventional humbug and a commitment to search for what is substantial, indeed central in our encounters with an uncertain and often ugly world.

In this way Dylan, who could easily have become glib and trendy, turns instead to pathways of meaning which are constantly changing and often lead to new levels of insight. It is a journey of enlightenment, and the fact that his followers for the most part saw only the surfaces and fragments of it is irrelevant. They took his criticisms of our society to heart, and he led them through all the major issues of the time. Characteristically, he did this in oblique and mocking ways, since he was not ultimately a poet of issues and movements; but along the way he illuminated both the movements and the people who were caught up in them.

Through this type of encounter, however, Dylan managed something far finer and more inward. Indeed, at his best he made the outer and inner worlds comment on each other; the search for compassionate life in society was a counterpart of the search for inner harmony and integrity. Here he was at one with the poets whose faces constantly appear behind a phrase or a line; and here also he gave voice to an attitude toward self and society which would shape the lives of many of his best auditors. I have had striking, recent evidence of this influence in discussions with a group of Duke graduates who were among the most active members of the class of 1969. Their lives since graduation have been as varied as any others one might pick, but with one major difference. Each one quite independently of the others told me of the difference that the issues, the searchings, the actions of the late sixties had made in shaping

patterns and goals which turned out to be permanent. It is the articulation of issues at this bedrock level of importance which sets
Dylan apart from the other artists of the time. He poses the questions for himself in these terms, as his own evolution makes clear; it
is still remarkable that he was able to pose them so compellingly for
his diverse and shifting audience. Naturally, he did not stand alone
in evoking the myths of the time. What sets him apart is both the
fact that they were so intimately part of him, and that he made his
audience partake of them too.

Among the many bright and sensitive dramatic examples of
mythic statement during the decade, two stand out: *Hair* and *The
Graduate*. The first was a remarkably tender treatment of our eternal
dream of Paradise, including all those interpretations of the world
which made the flower children so appealing at one level, so infuri-
ating at another. The fall of man had never occurred—or at least in
the eyes of these innocents never *should* have occurred. Where the
radical left was determined to force the world to change toward their
belligerent Utopia, the innocents of *Hair* (and a thousand street cor-
ner encounters) simply said, "Look, it's easy. Just act like us. The
world of love is right here in our hands."

The climax of the play, where the actor-singers stand naked as
they evoke the age of Aquarius, caused a ripple for all the wrong
reasons. They were naked because they were reentering the Garden
of Eden. It was an indictment of the elders that so many of them
snickered as though they were at a peep show, or watching *Oh! Calcutta! Hair* was one boundary of the sixties, the boundary of hopeful
innocence; perhaps everything would change so that the ugliness,
the evil, the violence would vanish in the face of conquering love.
It turned this perpetual dream into a momentary absolute; it made
its claim on reality by taking us back to all that had been lost or
destroyed in the crush of common experience.

The Graduate also made a major claim, but by the path of satire
and indictment. *Hair* would convert the elders to the vision of the
young; *The Graduate* exploited the gap between them, and the elders
were left naked in their middle-aged banality, insensitivity, and old-
fashioned wickedness. They were for the film a special kind of lost
generation. *The Graduate* was a dual celebration, satirically of those

who were beyond redemption, and romantically of the young who defy their elders and set the value structure straight again. Over and over the parents try to seduce the young by money, by sexual advances, by manipulation—finally through the forced coupling of a miscast and therefore immoral marriage. The music was as devastating as the action; who can forget or ignore "Mrs. Robinson"? The magic of the film was like so much else in the decade; there was enough truth in that compelling brilliance so that one felt both foolish and petty in trying to refute it—thoroughly on the defensive. All of our disagreements with it simply put us firmly and uncomfortably in the ranks of the enemy. To protest at all was to protest too much.

The most astonishing indictment and celebration (here again we find the bonding of opposites, now seen through art as we saw it earlier in political and social alignments) appeared after the decade had altered its character toward the self-concerns of the 1970s. The film *Tommy* was a true rock opera, with the most formidable use of the music of the sixties and an equally brilliant array of surrealistic visions which deserve attention quite apart from *Tommy* itself. The appearance of the film in the early seventies is significant; many of the major philosophic issues of the sixties are absorbed in it as they could not have been a few years earlier. The story itself is a nightmarish *Pilgrim's Progress*, with the "hero" subjected to all that his materialistic world can do to distort and stunt his spirit. This is no simple matter of scorning the bourgeois, however. One of the most moving and horrifying sequences is a drug encounter; equally enthralling is a rock mass, a session of faith healing which is blasphemous on the surface, deeply religious at heart, and a preparation for the saintly apotheosis of Tommy after he has survived every snare that his world can generate. Put so baldly, the meaning of the film is simple and a little naive in its affirmation that after all good can triumph. The nightmare realities, however, are so overwhelming that they temper any sense of the familiar or comfortable. Tommy wins through to a new reality, and the shock of what he (and we) endure in the course of the film goes a long way to justify emotionally the curious victory at the end. We and he are not asked to contemplate our world; we are forced to endure it in the symbolic outer forms of its inner reality, and these forms constantly grow from external shapes which we know and accept. A plush bedroom scene is lifted straight out of Hollywood; its sensuousness is superbly trite, until the television set at one side of the room intrudes, first with fleshy images and then with a horrible flood of blood and excrement which judges, condemns, and obliterates the whole scene in one hideous visionary moment.

Spenser creates this same visionary nausea at several points in *The Faerie Queen*; indeed, *Tommy* is in the great tradition of morality literature which runs from the medieval folk plays through to the Nighttown episode in *Ulysses*. In this way *Tommy* is not alien or singular but, like so much of Dylan, alive in a great tradition of spiritual concern which our dominant culture of the 1940s to 1960s had certainly set aside. When we move beyond the surface extremes of the decade, indeed, we discover that some of the sounds and shapes that seemed so far-out, so insolent in their treatment of our straight ways of life, are actually an affirmation of hard traditional doctrine and tough morality. Obviously, this is not to suggest that the radical left had a grip on the ethic of love (whether Buddhist, Hindu, or Christian) or that the trendy young and not-so-young were always asking the central questions about our society. But the best artists were, and in so doing they put themselves exactly where the arts have always been. Their material takes them into their society; their style and idiom often form and guide the world around them; but their inner and insistent meaning is an illumination of that society —and surprisingly often a judgment on it. Plato knew that poets were likely to disrupt his ideal world, and they have run true to form ever since. In the sixties they were given some unusually rich social material to work with. The multiple conflicts and equally varied alliances allowed them to be eclectic in their materials, and the constant questioning of conventional wisdom gave them openings to carry those questions much further than most of their contemporaries expected or understood. Despite his enormous popularity, Dylan was never content to rest on it; he was always out in front of his audiences, exploring further ranges of meaning in their kaleidoscopic world.

Force and Insight: The Dynamics of the Decade

We have explored many of the complexities of the decade, but what
do they say to us when we step back slightly in an attempt to see
their larger patterns? Most persuasive is the complex interaction of
innocence and the loss of innocence. It is everywhere in the major
movements, in the individual dreams of the young, in the prosecution of the war, in the bafflement of university presidents and the
pathetic commitments of the drug and flower cults or the trendy
searchings of the churches, both established and newly created. A
great deal was urged by those of us with a primary allegiance to one
or another of these groups. What we did not know, of course, was the
extent to which we were going through a common experience, and
one which would lead us to perceptions of the world markedly different from anything we anticipated or—often—would have wanted
if we had been allowed a choice. In one decade many of us went
through the kind of individual and collective growth which is usually
the experience of a lifetime.

The two major movements which show this transition most clearly
are of course the black power push and the new left venture. The
bold assertions which put many of us on the defensive were ingenuous in many ways but most significantly so in their failure to
estimate the countervailing power which they were constantly evoking. It was heady indeed to challenge the various establishments;
the challenges were innocent in the root sense of the word, and the
result of a whole array of confrontations was exactly what we might
expect. The opposition became just as assertive as the movements,
and by the end of the decade a great deal had been learned about the
boundaries within which dissent and disruption would be contained
or tolerated.

As I have mentioned, Malcolm X gave one of his remarkable
speeches in Newark at the height of the trouble there. "Bullets or
Ballots" was a passionate call for change at any price. Some who
came after him would take a few of the steps he contemplated and
meet an anger as great as their own but far more firmly entrenched.
Mario Savio and Mark Rudd well understood the initial vulnera-
bility of the universities, but their innocence of the strength behind

the first fumbling reactions of a collegial organization led to the eventual negation of their dazzling performances—though not to the denial of the realities in which their extremism was based. In both cases the causes of a month or a year turned out to be seriously flawed. They did not have the strength to persist, in part because those carrying them forward kept changing their own positions, and in part because the hard realities they confronted were quite different from what they had dreamed.

Innocence can be lost in many ways. The young who participated in these movements must be seen in their proper complexity. They would have passed through some loss of innocence in the most tranquil of times, but normal gropings toward maturity were dramatically intensified by the availability of so many external opportunities for instant growth and change. These created the illusion of importance, and the emotional impact of so much assertiveness was hard on the elders and often a trap for the young. The discovery that earnest young whites were not wanted in the bold ventures of black power came as a considerable shock; it is always a "learning experience" (that wonderful euphemism for trouble) to find that one is part of the problem and has no role in the solution. Similarly, the young women who attached themselves to the new left found that they became at times almost regimented sexual objects. Their freedom turned to a new kind of bondage; they were the servants of the movement in many ways, their treatment ranging from the unsavory to the incredibly cruel. For them the loss of innocence was old-fashioned, though at the time the astonishing irony of this fact was lost in the rhetoric of social revolution. The young males were even more blinded to the contradictions of their position. The uniforms were a wondrous blend of new guerrilla and Old West, and the actions were an equally romantic fusion of Utopian dream with adolescent posturing. (That is one major reason for the constant changes of stance and program.) These rites of passage were noisy and sometimes spectacular; but like Stephen Daedelus' they did not shake the universe.

This is not to say that the issues were unimportant. The conduct—indeed, the very existence—of the Vietnam War was as serious and divisive an issue as any society could conjure up. And it struck with equal severity at the professional soldier and the eighteen-year-old draftee. The immature innocence of the draftee was often matched by the insularity of the professional soldier. The peacetime world of the military is a world of *what if*, and the prosecution of a war is by definition a violation, a radical modification, of the normal world. The war in Vietnam provided a further dislocation of normal experience for soldier and civilian alike. It was fought in unknown country, and it was justified by dogmas which did not move either the hearts or the minds of most Americans. Our step-by-step involvement had something clandestine about it; moments of dramatic decision we could understand, but not this serpentine adventure, with its shadowy cast of characters and its managed assassinations.

That very quality threw the military men back on their familiar technical procedures, an emphasis which—given the actual nature of guerrilla warfare—was innocent indeed. While many of the young at home conjured up fantastic responses to the pressure of the war, the military men were often equally fantastic in their appraisals of it. Their refinements of violence often had nothing to do with the success or failure of a mission. As reality finally broke through the make-believe, the innocent faith in military technology and overwhelming firepower came to an end so dreary that there is a considerable coterie of honest folk who are still rewriting that history. There was a pathetic refusal to accept the end of our military innocence—of the naive notion that, of course, all our wars were just, and, equally of course, that we would win them all. Now both the military and the moral issues were clouded, and the senior generals were, in a nightmarish way, getting an education like that of the adolescents who confronted for the first time the possibility that their country might not always be right.

Many college and university administrators were having the same severe education. The abrupt termination of jobs and even careers may have been familiar in industry, but it was not a significant part of the pattern for university presidents until the late 1960s. We were at least as innocent a group as any other I have discussed—both innocent and insulated, in fact. As I look back, I can see that there was a splendid sense of self-importance about those positions. Elsewhere I discuss their functional weaknesses in the face of severe challenge.

My concern here is with the personal bewilderment many of us felt
in the face of these pressures. We had been secure in our conviction
that the work we were doing was important, in the public good, respected. Suddenly—and here I generalize from my own experience
—we found that we were all thumbs. Our "certain certainties" were
anything but; we found, not only that we could not control events,
but that we could not even control our own participation in events.
The loss of innocence for us came in a very special form; we lost the
power to perform adequately in our jobs. A fair number of us had the
unusual experience of being pushed beyond normal limits and into
the uncontrolled flux of events. We were disciplined to look for patterns of order, and then to articulate them; that was our trade. Quite
suddenly we found that we were Kings of Misrule instead. Those
of us in the senior universities felt we stood high in our profession;
then one fine day we found that like Dean Rusk or LBJ we were
powerless. Nothing would come right, and we lost our innocence in
a singularly painful way even as we lost our careers.

The innocents caught up in one or several versions of the drug
culture might seem at the opposite extreme from those of us in the
senior university jobs, but we had one great thing in common. The
stakes were extremely high in both cases, and the druggies were
obviously playing with their lives. Just as their risk was great, so
was their hope—or their dream—pathetically simple. Many of them
seem to have felt that there was a direct door opening from now
into Paradise; some of the photographs of Timothy Leary's group
show the return to Eden in its simplest form—nakedness, semi-
immobility, the illusion of contemplating the great mysteries and,
indeed, having a direct experience of them. To change the metaphor,
they moved into a looking-glass land where the familiar objects of
events were there, but all changed in relationship, color, and final
meaning. Like the actors in *Hair*, they tried to turn the great escape
into reality.

The ironies of this drug venture are multiple: the ignorance of
those who made the major hallucinogens, for example, the unawareness of the users themselves that the drug world was the opposite of
holy ground (Aldous Huxley was no help at this point), and above
all the unawareness that half a world away many of their peers were

entering the same dark temple as an escape from the realities of
Vietnam. The cruelest assumption was the one promoted by Leary
—that one could in fact change his private world, drop out of an
inimical society, and turn on in another world. As we know, a good
many succeeded so well that they never came back but disappeared
altogether or became part of the drifting population. Utopias were
many during the decade, and they were all in fact pathways out of
innocence. But none of the others provided quite the same chamber
of horrors at the end. The drug scene was a naive but deeply shadowed prelude to the events we are coping with today. Now we can
see what a deadly child's game that particular vector of the large
and crazy world really was.

If the path beyond innocence was axiomatic for those who survived the drug world, it was by no means so clear a road for the
flower people and the other religious cultists. We find there the same
yearning for release and instant change which animated so much of
the drug world. But while the immediate result was undeniable for
the druggies, it was harder to come by for the cultists. They had at
least to *do* something to achieve it; it was not done to them with a
pill or a needle. Having admitted that much, I must go on to say that
many of the cults were nearly mindless, that they borrowed fragments of difficult Eastern disciplines and claimed to turn them into
mass Western salvation, and that they allowed real growth only as
one broke away from them.

For that reason they posed some curious problems for the established churches, which were trying to address the heavy ethical and
emotional issues of the time with voices that were muted indeed
when set beside the instant ethical solutions of the cults or the driving secular dogmatism of the new left. The decade was filled with
strange gospels, and most of them had the great appeal of their obvious differences in idiom and content from the "straight" religious
patterns of home and family. Here again, the time posed the questions of innocence and growth, naiveté and maturity. As we look
back at the various groups I have discussed, we can see that they
all have one mark on them; from the familiar to the bizarre they
were exploring (often without knowing it) these immemorial issues.
What sets the decade apart is the fact that the explorations were so

overt, so varied, and often so frightening in their results. The rites of passage spared few of us—young or older—who were caught in the millrace of the time.

This diversity of experience in the pain of maturity was matched during the decade by a remarkable variety of articulated positions. They range from Goldwater to Paul Goodman, from Bob Dylan to "Okie from Muskogee" from General Westmoreland to David Harris. Explicit variety of opinion and implied divergences of life-style have been, of course, characteristics of our society at many times in the past. The thoughtful defiance of established norms, however, had not been carried so far since the debates of the late 1850s— and before that the 1760s and 1770s. Further, a good many people carried that defiance into the activism which everyone thinks of when the sixties are mentioned. My concern is with the less obvious and far more remarkable fact that our society could tolerate and ultimately absorb such diversity into its fabric.

In the heat of the action this basic stability was not always apparent, particularly to those of us who were being hassled by the day's events. Intriguingly, many of those who were most critical of mainstream society were thoroughly aware of that power to absorb; they feared and hated it. The dangers of "co-optation" are a constant refrain in sds discussions. They are one element, at least, in Paul Goodman's "Don't trust anyone over thirty," and it helps to explain the passion for costuming and role-playing. If the normal patterns had not been at heart so powerful, it would not have been necessary to flout them so outrageously. On the other hand, those who held centrist views of society and its purposes were also alert to the possibilities of unwanted change. There was a tacit and uncomfortable recognition that the center might in its turn be co-opted by the very positions it tolerated or absorbed. This showed itself in the high degree of shocked interest in the expression of those extremes. How else should we explain the preoccupation with something so trivial as the length of hair or the assertiveness of beards? It was most curious that these masculine adornments could be seen on the walls of any college boardroom or in any historical museum; they were the privilege of our elders, and perhaps that is why we resented them in the young. Behind the Che Guevara whiskers there was a curious echo of Grandpa, and many suspected that there had to be some reconciliation of these styles, which might in turn imply a reconciliation—or at least mediation—of the ideas behind them. As a result, the most outrageous diversities came to have a good deal in common with those who were outraged. The alternate life-style which took young people back to the land, for example, had a powerful emotional and historical content. It was an echo of the whole frontier venture in our common past, that past which was rugged fact before it became romantic myth. Suddenly, we found a whole subculture returning to the myth and living it out; here was diversity rooted in our heritage and not to be laughed away.

The diversity was not then as alien as it seemed—or was made to seem in the stress of the moment. Utopian dreamers and social critics, for instance, had been part of the American temper from the beginning. The spiritual rebellions of the seventeenth century, which often led to banishment or worse, were far more extreme than anything produced by the sixties. Furthermore, virtually none of the movements were alien; the young radicals were overtly scornful of mainline, international Marxism; some of them may have bowed in the direction of Cuba and China, but their enthusiasm was pro forma (and ignorant for the most part), while their true passion was for their own homegrown version of a people's society.

The abrupt separatism of the black nationalist movement should not obscure for us the fact that the very "return" to Africa was an affirmation of one of the major aspects of our common historic past. Those of us who happened to be white needed that assertion as much as our black fellow-citizens; all of us, though for highly divergent reasons, had walked away from the reality of color. To be reminded again that it was a major element in our culture was, at one level, an assertion of our diversity. At another and deeper level it was a major step toward the understanding of our unity in diversity. Like the other extreme expressions of the decade, it belonged to us, it was an aspect of our community set forth in such a way that we had to consider it freshly. This consideration was new, often jarring and disruptive, but the nature of each movement grew directly from some persistent element of our national character. There is perhaps no aspect of the 1960s' spirit so important as this—or so unregarded and misunderstood in the passion of the time.

To say so much is to indicate how deeply I disagree with much that has been written and spoken about the 1960s during the last fifteen to twenty years. Since my own life and career were changed drastically by the period, I am not likely to romanticize it, to make it a cozy time. It was wild, difficult, and often out of control. But it was a great deal more, and a great deal more serious than we have commonly said. We can see it even in the seeming failures of the time. Three stand out: the student movements (apart from their final violent phase); the established churches' struggle with ethical and inward issues; and the professional educators' attempts to interpret the implications of college and university turmoil. In each case something major went wrong or was misunderstood. Yet in each case something of positive importance took place. It was simply not what we foresaw.

The formal student movements obviously had a good deal of impact, though they were inevitably flawed by the rapid change of student generations and by constant shifts of agenda in response to dramatic changes in events—and even more in the perceived nature of events. Even at their best and most influential, they did not catch the movement inside students, which had no capital letters and took place within a very large number of individual lives. Those lives were governed by far deeper agitations which then demanded individual commitments. The mass events were often provocative of individual thought and decision, and it would be an injustice to the depth of the latter to listen too seriously to the shrill public voices, as we certainly did at that time.

These inner issues were also central for two other groups which "failed" in their attempt to grapple with them and yet gave testimony to the significance of the questions they could not fully understand. I am speaking of the established churches and the professional theorists of education (a group often quite distinct from line administrators or faculty in the major departments). As with the groups and organizations I have been discussing, these two show excesses of attitude and judgment, while in each case they are reaching for a significant position. The perception may be flawed, but it is honest; it represents a strenuous effort of the mind and spirit.

In the churches we see a split of direction. One group chooses business as usual, which means that the legitimate ferment of the sixties will pass it by. The other wing of the established churches is responsive—even pathetically eager at times—as it considers the questions of morality and ethical conduct raised by the black, new left, and women's movements. It should be noted, by the way, that when I speak of these groups they cut across denominations. One of the most fascinating aspects of the attitude of the churches to the sixties is precisely this: there was in every major denomination both responsiveness and resistance. The vitality of these denominations was clear, but also the fact that they were not the arbiters—let alone the leaders—of the major challenges forced on society by its own critic-citizens. As a result, the established churches were in much the same position as the universities. They had a tradition to maintain, while at the same time one element of that tradition was a commitment to moral searching, to the constant raising of the great issues and questions. Suddenly these were being put in the most strenuous way by groups outside the established order. The churches and the universities found themselves on the defensive; they were being asked to respond rather than asking the questions of others. This was deeply unsettling, and it led to a range of response from William Sloane Coffin's stand on black rights to *Are You Running with Me, Jesus?*, on to the push for ordained women and equally to the beginning of a new evangelical movement whose full response to the issues of the sixties—and often its reaction against them—were not evident for another five to ten years. The Roman Catholic church showed its preoccupation with questions of heightened moral sensitivity in Vatican II, where we saw a step of liberalization in procedure and doctrine which seemed to speak to the anguished moral issues of the time but were not sustained. And of course these responses, these steps both positive and negative, were placed in a strange and livid light by the many sects and cults which embodied the moral confusion of the time in the very suddenness and extravagance of their appearance and their claims.

The established churches seemed pallid and ineffectual by comparison; the honesty of their effort made them victims of those who offered the easy spiritual fix. Their "failure" to meet this part of their challenge was in fact a clear victory. Their confusion over the specific moral stands called for by the decade was understandable, but their refusal at times to recognize these issues and demands was a serious weakness. And in the muddled process many of their constituents began to think and act independently on social and individual ethical issues.

The professional theorists of education also faced a bewildering array of demands. These were far narrower than those thrust on the churches, but they were concentrated and heightened by the focus on higher education which the major movements did so much to intensify. Above all, the professionals were faced with an issue which was both operative and philosophical. What good might be derived from the ferment over modes of governance, control of curriculum, patterns of individual responsibility? From a philosophic perspective, were the criticisms of past practice valid, and if so how did one move to something more effective, more representative of the common will? From an operational perspective (and granting the philosophic point) how did one weave the young into the fabric of the college and university system?

The young had their own answers, of course. They ranged from reasoned requests for stronger representation in decision-making to the alternate universities and the rejection of all requirements. There were heady possibilities for the theorists in some of these developments. What if the young were right? Certainly, there was a great deal that was ineffective in the patterns of higher education, much that was outworn. These limitations had long been the subject of extensive discussion. Why not look to the students as those most directly involved for the vigor and new direction which higher education so badly needed? They might not be the only answer to its defects, but certainly they could be one part of the answer.

And so they could. As long as one does not give them the sole responsibility, one has the right to expect a good deal from mature undergraduates. The problems which they posed, however, were not remotely foreseen in the educational writing of the late 1960s. There we had the explicit hope that these lively and aggressive young minds would provide the bridge to greatly strengthened educational programs. There were only two problems with such a hope. First, college generations have a specious continuity; we think of them as sustaining ideas or enthusiasms, but this is by no means assured. A given generation of undergraduates may be clear and vigorous in taking certain points of view, but no guarantee follows. Instead, the second difficulty is very likely to emerge; successive generations may in short order expect something radically different from their predecessors. And this was in fact exactly what happened with the self-centered, vocationally oriented generations of the 1970s.

One can see at this point why the educators and the churchmen have so much in common. Both make certain assumptions about their constituents, the objects of their concern. Both try to relate these concerns not only to the moment's hypertension but to the continuities, the traditions, of education and religion. And both fail, often in a highly honorable way, because the constituent groups are themselves in constant change. You cannot relate these groups to institutions or systems when they have little or no sense of continuity in themselves. The abruptness of change, the unpredictability, spell certain short-term defeat for any of society's structures which depend on a continuity of styles, ideas, or beliefs. They were among the many casualties which lent such a tone of bewilderment and weariness to the end of the decade. There was great integrity in many aspects of the decade, in many of the conflicts and struggles to make something positive, something new out of it all. The individual growth, the genuine discoveries, however, took place almost always in a context of disarray and social or institutional defeat.

As we stand back and look at the decade as a whole, indeed, we see that virtually all of its special qualities were dependent on some form of paradox, some distorted, fractured, or even surrealist relationship. There were resemblances to what we have known and will know again, but there were three aspects of the sixties which set the time apart: a very special interaction of force in its many forms and an equally varied set of insights about our society; a surrealist quality both in the unfolding of events and in our commentary on them; and a superficial disappearance of many of the most energetic movements and attitudes—indeed, of a whole social texture—in an astonishingly brief time at the end of the period.

When I refer to an unusual interaction of force on the one hand, insight on the other, I might return to the Rockefeller Report as my baseline. There, the traditional view is well displayed. National policy is to be built from decisions about the national interest in every major aspect of our society, and then we propose the kinds of supporting force or power we need to use if we are to bring about our policy ends. This is a reasonable approach, a familiar one, and it implies some effective harmony between ends and means. The issue may be social, educational, military; the method is the same in each case, and it gives us a clear way of avoiding conflicts—or at least of resolving them.

The odd fact is that in the sixties this conventional wisdom did not work. The policies which belonged to the "straight" majority ran into opposition from unsanctioned but highly compelling causes. As the normal fabric of things was loosened—by the assassinations, the Vietnam tangle, the whole vortex of forces we know so well— we were faced by countercultures which were powerful precisely because they did not have the baggage of the accepted positions. The continuum between the decades was fractured by unpredicted attitudes as much as by unforeseen events. And it was fractured further by the fact that the application of power did not produce the normal results—a fact which was true across the whole field of social action.

At the right-hand edge of that field—the traditional edge of society's structure—we saw for the first time in our history a war which failed of its objectives almost in proportion to the steadily increasing force which we applied to its prosecution. We were Antaeus, an earth giant suspended in the air; the more force we used, the weaker we got in the attainment of our objectives. The anguish over the war, which drove presidents into retirement and generals into total frustration, ultimately became the most important fact about it. It is fascinating and quite horrible to note how our traditional patriotism underwent so radical a shift that we scorned the innocent men who fought the battles. Those of us opposed to the war had more sympathy for them than their flag-waving fellow countrymen. This was the most dramatic emotional symbol of a world turned upside down. As a country, we tried to block from ourselves the fact of a lost war, even while we were acknowledging it by the very crookedness of our rejection. We gave Vietnam a bitter celebration, indeed; we expressed our bafflement by turning its veterans into victims. This was not only grossly unjust; it was a fearful expiation—truly Greek tragedy—for the innocent victims of the war.

Meanwhile, we had a second and equally lurid domestic example of force destroying itself. I say example, but it was really a group of examples leading to one singular result. Several of the major movements had by the late sixties become extreme in their acceptance of force as a means of accomplishing their ends. Political and social disruption became norms for many of the group leaders, and their thwarted performances made the Black Panthers and the Weathermen a logical development. At that point came the most dramatic event of all; their constituents turned away from them. All of us marveled at the sudden shift which changed the activism of the late sixties into the self-preoccupation of the seventies. One part of the answer lies here; when the issue was posed, the mainstream movements would not accept violence, so that the use of force destroyed the very power and initiative which had seemed so compelling. At that point the failure of the military and of the major movements became one; as a society we were sick of it all. A passion for normality —even of the most venal sort—was about to assert itself.

That zeal to return to the normal and familiar was encouraged by a particular atmosphere and tone in the sixties, a tone which disturbed millions of solid citizens, even though they had no name to put to it. It was surrealistic in its happenings, always uncomfortable in its fusion of the familiar and the odd. We commonly speak of surrealism in painting or the cinema, of course; but it is also a major idiom for a novelist like Joyce, whose Nighttown episode in *Ulysses* is a major excursion into the surreal interpretation of events. The norms of reality are extended there so that the outer and inner worlds of the two major protagonists can exist simultaneously, both for them and for one another. Barriers vanish or are realigned; Bloom and Stephen are pushed beyond the constraints that usually allow us to deny painful reality. The surreal world leaves them no place to hide; its nature is that of double vision. We are in our own world; it is familiar and yet it is not, for the patterns keep shifting, the music changes key without notice, cause and effect behave in strange ways.

I have just indicated one result of this deep discomfort with a surrealist world: the rejection of force and naked power by almost all of us. The events which we confronted for nearly a decade are right out of the surrealist casebook. The assassinations slash across the face of civilized reality and force their savagery on us. The war becomes more and more a work of terrible fiction, which imposes on us realities which our sane selves deny. How can we assimilate that exotic land, the Sin City which is our base and those jungle villages our targets? We know that the war was a nightmare for the men who fought it, but it became equally so for the rest of us—Agent Orange, demolished villages, children running naked from the combat, massive bombing which accomplished nothing. The war of high purpose we had been told we were fighting turned to something else before our eyes; the cause vanished and the horror remained.

Our preoccupations at home, meanwhile, were also an extension of the normal, a warping of the realities we commonly accepted. Their quality of hallucination, of energies and attitudes askew, frenetic or compulsively manifest, was in fact a major hallmark of the decade. Those of us who were more or less straight had a constant sense of confusion; we were the ones who saw double and found ourselves saying, "It can't be happening, but it is." This same quality had its part to play in the ending of the period, itself a piece of theater—a sudden resolution in which the characters have said what they have to say; they scatter and the curtain comes down. So ended a multitude of events and "creations" within the decade—Soul City, for example, founded in the faith that one could turn ideology into a piece of real estate, could symbolize a state of mind and help turn it into physical reality.

This intertwining of theater and reality, or symbol and action, gave much of its intoxicating drive to events. It was constantly supported by the rhetoric which embodied the movements, moved through and around them. This was a rhetoric not only of language

but of music, costumes, even lighting, even the omnipresent Leicas
at every gathering. Rhetoric is gesture and style, after all, and the
sixties were remarkably rich in their evocations, their emotional
content. As I go back into that time through its pictures, I wonder where the costumes came from, but I can see where they were
headed. Like the names of the rock groups, the clothes meant much
more than rebellion or revolution (the Che Guevara or Chinese costumes). They spoke privilege—the freedom to play, to invent, to create a new and outrageous world which constantly used the straight
world as its necessary foil. This too was theater, and it certainly
partook of the surreal. These were not alien beings; the conflicts
which they created were a clear result of the fact that they were
bound to the rest of us even in their most outrageous styling. It was
allusive and built itself from a dozen straight traditions—the western, the military, the hobo, the streetwalker and the street worker.
It was a fanciful style which provided a curious counterpoint to the
high seriousness of the causes; and that interaction was perhaps the
greatest single example of distorted reality. Many of us could understand the importance of the issues, but the languages in which they
were expressed caused us not only confusion but outrage. They were
designed to do just that, and they succeeded.

The four-letter word became a part of our common idiom for the
first time since the eighteenth century. This may have been child-
ish at one level, but it took hold, as our freedom of speech today
constantly reminds us. Equally, it was a time when black street talk
was added to our shared language; it appeared in tandem with the
vocabulary of rock. The combined impact of these and a dozen other
cult languages was to add to the sense of astonishing variety and
strangeness in the decade. Like the costumes, they brought reality
and singularity together. But our experience with the new languages
did not stop there; more insinuating, more inward than the weird
and jarring experiences of the time, they became familiar and less
surreal through use. The true end of the decade came when major
aspects of the style of the sixties, like aspects of its thought and
action, became weary, destructive, or simply outmoded by the very
speed of change which they themselves had encouraged and brought
about. But the cult languages "disappeared" in quite another way.

They were assimilated, as vibrant and imaginative forms of speech so often are.

We shall see in chapter 4 that many other aspects of the culture of the decade did not disappear but were submerged and transmuted. They served purposes beyond their own time, but they were surrealist no longer because we did not need to use our double vision in dealing with them. This happened more overtly and more pervasively with language, simply because it is our inescapable and shared expression of reality. We do not have to share beards or blue jeans or campaign hats. Private language, on the other hand, becomes public; we use it with others, and the sharp edges of its separateness are worn off. In the sixties, however, it was designed to force a new approach to experience; it was a major element in our disturbing and disturbed encounters. It was an embodiment of the dreams as well as the calls to battle, of the new life sought and the Aquarian hope for the world. Like so much else in the decade, it failed to accomplish what it hoped, but it helped bring about a diversity in society which was not its primary aim.

We were coping in the sixties with a society which seems to echo the French Revolution. "It was the best of times, it was the worst of times. . . ." I have anatomized it; when we step back and look at the whole, we see great energy, moving in directions often opposed to one another. We see a great deal of personal searching, much of it anguished and some of it tragic. We see extremes of social and antisocial behavior which are often trivial but sometimes embody a profound critique of our norms. Everything takes place in vivid color and at a high decibel level. As a result, contrast and shock are forced on events.

I have suggested several reasons for the seeming suddenness of the decade's end—the change of style as the seventies begin—but a major one may simply be exhaustion. It was tiring to take part in (and even tiring to be aware of) the oppositions which made the decade move. It was an abandoned time, and yet many of its cults were ascetic. It was stylish at the start, but after Camelot it was often grubby and deliberately ugly. It talked high purpose, and sometimes lived up to the talk. At the same time it was self-indulgent and many of its high-sounding demonstrations were ego trips for leaders and followers alike. The penetrating question and the knee-jerk response might occur almost in the same sentence. The sensual broke free and often assumed forms both bizarre and brutal. Simultaneously, the pseudo-Eastern cults claimed to offer us a path out of the magic of the senses. And at times one movement tried to do both, to liberate the flesh and lift us above the limits of the senses.

In the light of all this, it is clear that the ferment of the decade could not be sustained. In order to do full justice to it, however, we must ask what happened to its major concerns. The society of the last fifteen to twenty years has assimilated, obliterated, or co-opted so many elements of that time that it seems almost as though nothing is left. We must now look beneath that surface impression and see not only what the complex meaning was but what it is today. In order to do so, however, we should have a detailed encounter with the one institution whose experience during the decade was intimately involved with every movement and countermovement—the American university.

Looking-Glass Land

Lewis Carroll has given us a basic image for relating the "external" analyses of the movements of the 1960s to the inner and daily experience of the time, and above all the experience of the universities. Once you step through the mirror, everything has elements of familiarity but is likely at any moment to behave in an unpredictable way. Students come to the house, but it is an occupation; you invite students to dinner, and it becomes an insult. The problem for the university president, as for Alice, is that he cannot help working by his norms; it is hard for him to learn to walk in one direction if he wants to go in another.

But the metaphor governed a good deal of everyone's behavior. Both our procedures and our results were upside down and inside out. A yearning for justice would lead to violence, peace movements looked like battlefields, a cry for relevance made it impossible to relate. The universities were particularly subject to this mirror experience because their normal patterns and traditions were so open to discussion, to change, to another view. As a result, the strangeness of the sixties would be accepted within the university fabric until at last it became, not just eccentric, but alien and confused. One kept trying to pull the extremes inside, like getting all the animals into the tent; and this effort heightened the looking-glass effect, particularly when one's efforts of goodwill seemed like antagonism. The fear of co-optation is then a looking-glass event; you want to participate, but cannot accept the offer of participation. (As a result, many of the university committee efforts during these years were nothing but words.)

In the normal university world, again, fund-raising is an activity of absorbing interest; in looking-glass land it is buried by more "important" happenings. One could say that events are ranked in the inverse of their customary importance of meaning. That fact, indeed, gives the mirror world its consistency, its own strange coherence. There is, of course, a psychiatric parallel to this perverse consistency of the looking glass. It lies in the patterns of the paranoid mind as the rest of us see and endure them. Anyone who has had to work with a seriously ill person of this kind knows how wearisome the endless logical proofs of an irrational major premise can be. And it is impossible to get behind that assumption. To say that the sixties were in this sense often paranoid is naturally not to say that the individuals involved were so, but that their philosophic method moved from the unchallengeable, often nonrational premise through to its clear, consistent, cockeyed embodiment.

To confirm my parallel, look again at the many creatures Alice meets. They are touchy, combative, often suspicious, and quite consistently resentful of other opinions, even of other shapes and human forms. They are paranoid in a specifically chauvinist way; they are overly sure of themselves, and at the same time they are constantly in a state of war with those around them. Alice's world has these many meanings for us as we step into the universities of the sixties. Zany, relentlessly logical, combative, suspicious, deeply familiar, and yet at times totally unpredictable or alien. Those are some of the words which will embody our experience as we make our way through a diversity of universities—and in particular as we give our attention to Duke.

Duke in the 1960s: A Web of Purposes

At the start of the 1960s Duke was a university under stress and also in inevitable transition. The stress related above all to tension between the Duke Endowment board of trustees and some senior administrators on the one hand, and certain members of the university administration and board on the other. The question of final responsibility for the university's welfare was left unresolved after the resignation of Hollis Edens and Paul Gross and would remain so for another decade. At the same time the university felt within itself and in the whole region a stirring of vigor and change. This created a counterpoint to many traditional patterns of life, of which one—the relation between blacks and whites—would loom large in the years to come. It was one issue among many, however. The whole necessity of national stature and responsibility would be faced, as would the changing place of Duke in its regional community. The largest community employer by a factor of two and a half, the university was both dominant and isolated, an object of envy, admiration, and —to some slight degree—of suspicion as well.

The measure of this complexity and change came in the early sixties when certain crucial decisions were made. In 1962, after long and intense consideration, the board of trustees voted to admit black undergraduates. This was not a unanimous decision; there were abstentions from the vote, and a good deal of silent unhappiness among alumni and others in the region. Duke was a place of great privilege, as it is today, and inevitably it seemed inappropriate to some that such privilege should be shared. Someday, perhaps, but why here and why now?

That sentiment was hardly unique. In 1954 I met it in Wisconsin, phrased by Lawrence College trustees during some intense discussions of black membership in fraternities—and indeed in the college community itself. I had lived with it long before I had the slightest thought of moving to North Carolina. Even though my grandfather had been the first professor of agriculture at the Women's College in Greensboro (I would go to see the great trees he had planted as saplings), I was, as the Durham newspapers put it, "Yankee-born and Yale-educated." When the Duke trustees decided to look outside their own region for a president, then, they were taking a step as new and controversial as the admission of black students had been. It called forth some of the same reservations, and it would have some of the same disruptive consequences in the turbulent years to come. None of this was anticipated by any of us, of course. The adjustments which may have been foreseen were to be set against a familiar background of prosperous tranquility.

To say so much is to lock Duke firmly to its southern setting and heritage. At the same time it is clear that both Duke and its region were embarked on a path of change, of choice and opportunity which has been realized to a surprising degree both in the cutting edge of southern life in the 1980s and in many aspects of Duke as it is today. The transient flamboyance of the 1960s obscured the deeper and far more significant urgencies of that change—which might be blocked or even distorted for a time, but would not be defeated or even neutralized. To understand Duke as a revealing example of the shaping quality of the sixties, we must see it as a university whose own emerging character moved in a counterpoint with national issues and dramatic local events. It was, in fact, open to these events precisely because it was so deeply concerned to find itself, to define its own new areas of competence and new levels of effectiveness.

The creative irony of this position was not, of course, apparent at the time. It makes appropriate, however, a reasonably detailed account of what we were trying to do at Duke. And this attention to Duke's inner life as inseparable from the ferment of the time is still further reinforced by the fact that we were a target university for several of the major movements. The "right" visitors came, the press was interested, the very history of the founding of the university made it a magnetic place for those with a pitch to make and a cause to publicize.

As a result, these very characteristics and attitudes which made Duke a fascinating university during the decade laid it open to all of the major external pressures, to a variety of conflicting inner priorities, and to a degree of criticism and righteous partisan indignation which was not found in highly stable universities such as MIT or Princeton. It did not have available a strong fortification of unified purposes. The remarkable fact, perhaps, is that we accomplished together what we did. And I might take that suggestion one step further; some of the demands made on us, some of the difficulties we faced, helped greatly to increase the vigor of the following decade. For all these reasons a selective but detailed treatment of Duke in the sixties will serve our larger purposes. If nothing else, it will serve as a baseline for an analysis of sister universities which faced similar pressures but responded in divergent ways.

The preceding paragraph would have made little sense to any board of trustees in 1960. The concept of growth through stress might have seemed particularly odd, but then the whole range of issues to come to the fore would have seemed like the invention of a disordered mind. No board of trustees was equipped to deal with the quicksand events of the 1960s. Each had its own singular mixture of personalities and attitudes, and it would be tempting—and cheap —to satirize those idiosyncracies in the Duke board. Seen from this distance, the members of the board at that time are fascinating for their diversity within rather strict limits, and equally so for a substantial lack of sympathy toward all that was about to happen. As I look at the list of board members, I see flexibility in eight or nine and varying degrees—and forms—of rigidity in the rest. I do not mean by this to scorn the traditional concerns which were vital for many of them. When the water of change was flowing so fast, however, those traditions were at times like rocks in the river.

The results could be humorous at times, as well as destructive. There was a short-lived theological aberration in the early 1960s, the "God is Dead" gospel propounded by a scholar named Thomas J. J. Altizer (among others, of course). Since Duke's Divinity School is one of the most distinguished in the country, it was only natural that the gentleman should speak there. It was slightly more surprising to discover that he had been sent to us and paid for by one of the central offices in the Methodist bureaucracy. I was grateful that someone else had paid the bill and thought no more about it until I received an outraged—and outrageous—letter from a senior trustee who was himself an absolute mogul of Methodism. My letter of explanation about the heretical speaker was rejected out of hand, and in my own stubbornness I prolonged the correspondence. Finally, another distinguished Methodist trustee told me to save my powder; not even the receipted bill could persuade my disgruntled friend that his own church was responsible. There were to be many trials of this kind. Late in the decade the senior women chose a distinguished black classmate to be their queen, and I found to my considerable surprise that I was held responsible. She became known among the board members as "Doug's dusky beauty queen," and there was no way to free myself. If I had not chosen her myself, I had created a climate in which she could be chosen.

These were trivial incidents, but they must be seen as thorns in the flesh; they suggest a temper and a tone which could easily be directed toward the substantial issues which confronted us. They seem on reflection to be themselves the trivial forms of major issues; they show the edge of conflict along which we constantly moved. We did not, of course, usually discuss matters at this level in meetings of the board. Those meetings were conducted in a way which combined a high degree of gentility with a good deal of subcutaneous backbiting. This last characteristic showed itself far more in the meetings of the executive committee, which at that time dominated the activity of the full board. At its full size of thirty-six the board was unwieldy, and while there were active committees none of them showed a fraction of the executive committee's continuity and authority.

That high gentility which I mentioned was of a very special sort. It was southern and it was courtly. Some of the long-time senior members set this tone, and at its best it could be a great asset in conducting our affairs. This courtliness, however, could be used as an excuse for failing to confront urgent issues, and it was closely allied to a special quality which it took me some time even to begin to understand. This was the maintenance of silence about major issues, not because they were deemed to be unimportant, but precisely for the opposite reason. Silence definitely did not mean consent. It was more likely to mean that discussion would take place privately and informally, and that the president might well be denied the benefit of that discussion. (Though a voting member of the executive committee, the president was not a member of the board.)

The executive committee of eleven had eight lawyers and several members of the Duke Endowment board were also on it. Issues of property and finance quite properly received a good deal of attention; educational and large strategic issues did not. This was not only a matter of personal regret for me; it weakened the ability of the board to deal with the issues generated in the sixties. As a prime example of this limit, I might mention a major fear of the board during the student Vigil for higher staff wages that it might lead to a kind of union ascendancy which could have repercussions on other labor situations in the region. (This was a large strategic issue, certainly, but it was regarded as one to be suppressed if at all possible.)

The two great weaknesses of the board were these: first, it had many members who were pleased with the honor but not particularly interested in the responsibility. Second, it had a long tradition of subordination to the Endowment board, and this fact weakened its ability to move independently when issues became critical. When one couples this situation with the fact that the Endowment's interests were largely bounded by its own multiple and interlocking financial structures, it is obvious that as far as university matters were concerned the board had what I might call a fair weather view of trusteeship. When the winds of the sixties really began to blow, there were individual trustees who made serious efforts to help, but there was not a coherent attitude, a common front in the face of adversity.

I put the matter so, not because I enjoy describing this state of affairs, but because one cannot understand Duke's particular anguish without this frank appraisal. A board dominated by these attitudes was, almost by definition, in a poor position to cope with overt issues of black employee status and black student rights. The code of silence had worked for many years to keep these issues in control. There was no way in which it could be changed overnight into a task force adequate—let alone comfortable—in dealing with them. It is equally clear that those issues would play a substantial role in the creation of a far stronger board, which could deal with all the concerns of a major university and without the dominance of the Endowment.

I also feel that my own struggles for independence from that domination played a part in the restructuring which would come. At the time, however, such an effort merely compounded our difficulties. Unlike MIT, Princeton, or Yale, the senior administration at Duke could not count on the support of its board when emotions began to run high. Too many members were also emotionally involved, and on the opposite side—if by the opposite side we mean the status quo ante.

One result of these majority attitudes, when they were coupled with the president's lack of membership on the board, was that at crucial moments he was not his own man. I remember with particular vividness being kept at home by a senior trustee (and close friend) while an important meeting with undergraduates was taking place late in the decade. Issues involving the black students were to be discussed; a strong desire to protect me from any possible mischance lay behind this insistence that I *not* be present, but there was an equally strong feeling that anything to be said would come from the chairman of the board. It is still painful for me to remember that afternoon. I could not get out, and that is the wrong relationship for the president and his board to have. He should serve at their pleasure, but while he does he should be a free man.

Duke: Money and the Governance of the University

One major aspect of Duke's texture stemmed from the original concept of the Duke Endowment. Nothing could be more straightforward or laudable than J. B. Duke's desire to strengthen education, religion, and medical care in his own heartland. The indenture which created the Endowment was very specific about these matters and farsighted about the recipients apart from the embryo university which was to transform strong but modest Trinity College into a major center of learning. J.B.D. never dreamed small dreams. The photographs which chronicle the university's rise from the Carolina clay have an astonishing quality of unreality; so much was there all at once, which immediately set the university apart from all those which had grown, step by step, from simple beginnings.

And the financial underpinnings were also to be there. Duke had no group of wealthy alumni; one could not create *them* ab ovo. The generous provisions of the indenture would get the university started in handsome style. But over the next thirty-five years a number of patterns developed which were not basic to the original concept. The interlocking directorate which ran the Endowment and the Duke

Power Company also came to look upon the university as its special province—definitely a Gaul divided into its three parts. There was no malice in this, but the major result was the creation of a shadow board which could carry on its own deliberations quite apart from the university administration and trustees; and it could then enforce its opinions with the power of the purse. This development created serious problems for two presidents, and more generally it weakened the independence of the university trustees—except as they were also members of the Endowment board. These negative influences in turn made it extremely difficult to pursue the development of other sources of support. During Duke's early years this outside support did not seem to be necessary. But as the years made it so, issues of control and power loomed large and created real barriers to pursuing anything new in the way of funding.

In discussing this issue it is important to remember that much more than money is involved. New projects are, after all, new ventures in the world of ideas. They are essential to the continued vibrancy of any university. And except in the medical area they were not emerging at Duke as they should have after the Second World War. There was a sense of self-sufficiency and paternalism. D.E. would provide, and new ideas were not encouraged, in part because they would take resources from the standard programs—fair enough, so far as it went, but no stimulus to growth.

There were some significant consequences of this limitation on funding. When new buildings were built after the war, they tended toward the brick box style of architecture—like Kannapolis, North Carolina. This was hardly surprising, since Charles Cannon was chairman of the buildings and grounds committee. His own sense of economy and the funding pattern of the university were in complete agreement; there was no perceived need for style or imagination.

This attitude set Duke apart from almost every American college and university in the postwar period. The strong updraft in prosperity had spawned a great rash of fund-raising campaigns, and the Ford Foundation gave further impetus to this with its pioneering capital grants made to selected institutions during the fifties and sixties. The program was, of course, eagerly sought, not only for the dollars involved but for the prestige of the grant, and the matching

provision which encouraged future fund-raising on a more systematic pattern. (And this, of course, was exactly what the Foundation
intended.) We were fortunate to have one of these grants at Lawrence College during my years there, and it served its purpose quite
dramatically. As a result, I came to Duke with a strong, unquestioned conviction that one part of my task was to work out the same
pattern in a university context. This ambition led to a little friendly
irony from my Ford Foundation friends. "You want to be the first
president to have *two* grants in two different places?" When the
grant came to Duke it was, to some extent, because of the record
I had established. Equally it was a public recognition that Duke
needed exactly this stimulus. My successor, Terry Sanford, commented that this was the beginning of a new era of fund-raising at
Duke, and certainly the activity of the university in the last twenty
years has brilliantly borne out that fact.

For our purposes here—a view of Duke during the 1960s—two
aspects of this push for additional support should be recognized.
The turbulence of the time meant that our efforts would be flawed
and limited by the disaffection of many elements in the university's
constituency. And equally there would be suspicion and resistance
on the part of the Endowment, which saw the success at finding
new funding as a partial removal of financial responsibility from
the Endowment board to the university's authority. I never saw it
as a legitimate ground of contention, but I certainly recognized it
as a fact of life. Certain long-standing attitudes had to change if
the university was to prosper and develop the broad base of support
it deserved. There was bound to be some suspicion and discomfort
while we pushed the wall back, and it was anything but an ideal time
to seek a new level of financial support. I am glad we did.

Paul Gross: The Dilemma of Power

Before I discuss the Ford grant which gave that opportunity, I must
add one footnote to the problem of money and governance. The subject is painful for me, as it still is for many people in the university,
but it must be faced.

I have hesitated to write about Paul Gross. Under normal circumstances it would be unseemly and even irrelevant to deal with any one man in discussing a period so vibrant and ultimately creative as the sixties were at Duke. But Paul and his relationships to Duke were quite extraordinary, and a long shadow was cast across the university by both the man and his position. The antagonism between President Edens and himself was widely and publicly discussed in the late 1950s; it led to Edens's forced departure and Paul's removal from his academic vice-presidency. He remained at Duke, however, and on his retirement was named as the Endowment's educational advisor.

It is valid for us to consider the meaning and the consequences of such an appointment, because it shows as nothing else could the deep and unresolved confusion about the proper governance of the university. The Endowment had been his strong supporter during the tangle with Edens, and it did not take kindly to the fact of his removal. It was the price that had to be paid for Edens's departure. By appointing Paul as its advisor, the Endowment was in effect saying, "You may take away his title but not his influence in the university." The dual system of university policymaking was set forth for all the world to see, and as a result certain animosities were perpetuated. Indeed, it was felt that battles still had to be won and scores settled. And this tension persisted for more than ten years after the formal questions had been "settled" by the university board of trustees.

I do not mean to be melodramatic or to overstate the case. Three examples from many will show how the damage from this power struggle persisted. During the months after my election and before my arrival, I spent many days on the campus, and President Deryl Hart was deeply generous in explaining the state of affairs. Several times he identified key members of his office staff whom he had been pressured to eliminate. "I could not have gotten along for a day without them," was his final comment. Similarly, I found myself pressed to remove my senior academic colleague and put someone with other political ties in his place. (When things were at their most tense in 1968–69 I was forcefully reminded that in fact I had been given a little list of replacements and that I had acted on none of them.) Finally, Terry Sanford told me that when he arrived he was told by a senior faculty member, "I just want to let you know that

I am a *Gross* man." "I don't want you to be anyone's man," said Terry, who was well informed about this particular brand of political infighting.

It is necessary to understand these persistent attitudes and influences because they reveal a constant and unremitting effort to influence university policy. In a volatile period such divisiveness was bound to make the conduct of university business more difficult. There was always a shadow government in the wings, and I felt its presence whenever there was a crucial issue either with the faculty or with the Endowment. As a result, we had to live with one more level of disunity at a time when a united front was absolutely essential for the orderly and effective treatment of crises as they came along. If Paul did not agree with the development of an art museum or the move to develop what is now called the Central Campus, then it became measurably more difficult to accomplish these ends. If he believed in a hard line toward students, then a more flexible approach to their concerns was called into question. It was a constant presence, an interference which the university certainly did not need, and a guarantee that conflict would be even harder to manage than it should have been.

The Ford Grant

In 1952 the Ford Foundation initiated a series of college and university capital grants; before it was phased out in 1968 the program had made grants totaling $362 million to 84 institutions. (And this amount raised more than 1 billion in matching funds.) It was without doubt the most influential large program ever funded by Ford; and this was the result of the shrewdness of the concept. Put simply, the grants were made to institutions of considerable promise which had not yet reached their full fund-raising capability. They had to have worthy purposes, which were developed in elaborate proposals submitted—on invitation only—to the Foundation. The grants had to be matched, and in ratios which were difficult but not impossible for the institutions to reach.

The secret of the program's success lay in its wise use of this formula. At Lawrence College, for example, we received a grant of

$2 million to be matched two-for-one. Lawrence had done very little formal fund-raising up until that time (1955) so that the formula was demanding indeed. The publicity surrounding the grant was a great stimulus to giving, of course, and each institution was under tremendous pressure to succeed. (So far as I know, there were no failures.)

The long-term purpose of the grants was even more significant than their immediate value. The whole level of funding was supposed to rise; having learned how to do it, one was supposed to continue at a much higher level than before. This worked; none of us fell back to our pre-grant levels because we had built an organization, a large group of friends, and a pattern of stated purposes which continued to attract support. We were thoroughly invigorated, and this at a time during the 1950s and early 1960s when the postwar economy was still providing available money. The times were expansive, and we rode the elevator of rising national income.

As soon as I saw the severely limited fund-raising effort at Duke, I went to the Foundation to solicit its interest. After teasing me about my ambition to have grants in two different institutions, the program director gave us a searching look. As a result, we received an $8 million grant, to be matched on a four-to-one basis in three years. Normal grants from the Duke Endowment were not to count, since they were rightly regarded by Ford as coming from income already earmarked for the university. This formula recognized that the university had done little (hence the grant was small) but that its constituents were capable of a good deal (the ratio was high).

Reaction to the grant by the various university constituents was positive but in many ways muted. At Lawrence everyone knew the great need and was excited. At Duke there was a feeling of complacency which certainly did not contribute to our success. Then came the most turbulent period of the sixties, and we had to go to the disaffected for money. Not only was the energy of certain board members and the whole administration taken up by these crisis matters, but the world outside found it hard to concentrate on such a long-term venture as the university's first fund-raising campaign.

Almost inevitably there were board members and others of the intimate university family who found it impossible to give the university their full support. One of the effects of the Ford grant (even in tranquil times) was to put the spotlight on key members of the university constituency. If they accepted a prominent place, they found that much was expected of them, and at this time many of them did not like it. As a result, the matching of the Ford grant was not completed until after I had left, but it was ultimately a success precisely of the textbook sort described by the Foundation. New sources and levels of support were established, but (most important of all) the university learned to expect more of itself.

This last was a particularly important outcome for Duke. In my judgment Duke had suffered from that complacency which the generosity of the great Duke gifts did so much to encourage. There had to come a maturity of attitude toward funding needs, a recognition of the demands which a great university must make on its resources. Not to reach out is to fail in the essential nature of university life. Fund-raising is not often looked on as an extension of this basic character, but after seventeen years of that effort I can testify to its philosophical importance. And despite all the obstacles of the time, the Ford grant added that dimension to Duke.

Loyalty Oath in North Carolina: A Classic Issue

While we were deeply involved at Duke with a host of ventures, of which fund-raising was only one, the state had managed to sink itself in a major intellectual and social morass. In the closing days of Terry Sanford's tenure as governor, the North Carolina legislature had managed to slide through an oath of loyalty much like that which had so troubled the state of California ten years earlier.

Conventional argument for such tests is based on the assumption that no loyal American should hesitate to affirm his political position. As a result, the proponents regard with suspicion—or worse —anyone who questions either the need or the wisdom of such an affirmation. There is a murky link here with that constant fear of hidden subversives which allowed the House Committee on Un-American Activities, the witch-hunts of the forties and fifties, and finally Joseph McCarthy's rampage through the federal government.

These paranoid fears are perennial, of course. In earlier centuries they were expressed by punitive antisedition laws and more broadly by constraints of many sorts applied to minority and suspect groups within the larger society. Our own government has not been free of these, but the path chosen after World War II had a special character. The so-called cold war established a clear external target which in turn put both our State Department and our university departments of international studies thoroughly on the defensive. (Owen Lattimore was a prime victim, even though his sin involved a profound knowledge of China rather than the Soviet Union.) The notorious attacks on the motion picture industry were a logical further result; the free-thinking, often liberal and eccentric writers for the films were easy to portray as fellow travelers and corrupters of an innocent public through the seductive power of their work.

Against this background the function of loyalty oaths as a requirement for employment becomes all too clear. Those who impose the oath have it in their power to define what loyalty is, and therefore to impose on dissent—on freedom of conscience—whatever limits they choose. One may start with the most innocent-seeming requirements, but the logical end is the thought control of repressive fascism or communism. The necessity to oppose such a requirement is the duty of any responsible citizen, but for obvious reasons it falls with particular weight on the university community. The exploration of unpopular ideas or political positions is an essential university duty, and one which extends far beyond formal politics into law, theology, and the sciences. It is not an issue which can be avoided when it is raised.

So I discovered in the spring of 1965 when I was invited to give the commencement address at the University of North Carolina. Theoretically, there were many subjects available beyond the usual commencement pap—chief among them the unique opportunities for educational and social cooperation in the Research Triangle area. There was only one subject which would not seem like cowardly evasion, however, and I do not recall that I ever considered any other. (It was clear that none of the presidents of the state's universities was going to make that speech, and equally clear that they wanted me to make it. But the decision was completely my own.)

There were two negative consequences, both of them quite obvious in retrospect, and both contributed to my difficulties in the late
sixties. First, there was a considerable failure on the part of the public and of many Duke alumni to understand that the speech had to
be made. As one alumnus said to me, "Why did you feel you had to
pull Carolina's chestnuts out of the fire?" It was taken by others as
an insult to the then-current governor, Dan Moore; as an outsider I
had blundered into issues of state politics where I had no place.

Second, I had attracted the watchful attention of Jesse Helms,
at that time the ambitious station manager and editorial voice of
Raleigh's NBC television affiliate. I came soon enough to understand
not only Mr. Helms's political stance, but his political ambitions. He
was building his power base in eastern North Carolina and doing it
with his customary cleverness. I had played into his hands, and he
would make good use of me before the sixties were done. In the process, of course, he would stir up a good deal of antagonism focused
particularly on the supposed permissiveness toward undergraduate
activism at Duke. As a result, what started as a high-minded attempt
to protest a vicious law (which was struck down by the state supreme
court in due season) was turned into one more evidence of alien and
indeed subversive social thought. Conservative Duke was moving in
dangerous directions.

Jesse Helms: Politician in the Making

Jesse Helms deserves a further word. By the early sixties I am sure
that he had already targeted the eastern part of the state as his special province. In the varied political climate of North Carolina here
was a conservative electorate; one could say that it was prepackaged
for him. His invention of an avuncular persona, a voice through
which to speak to his future constituents, was a master stroke, a perfect cover for Helms's extremely shrewd and sophisticated political
sense. He was a man with the best of both worlds. He inhabited the
center of political power in the state, so that he could build his lines
throughout the state, while at the same time he could cultivate one
sector of it as his special power base.

The 1960s were a godsend for him. His constituents' sense of

order and propriety were violated often enough by events so that
he had a constant supply of news stories to view with pious alarm.
And while I was simply one sheet in his large file of material, I
turned out to be a highly visible and therefore useful one. The oath
speech was a fine beginning. From then on, every activist event on
campus could be taken as continuing proof that outsiders and alien
thinkers were trying to subvert the solid conservative positions with
which Duke was identified. In this way Helms benefited exactly as
Ronald Reagan did from the restiveness of the time. It gave him
a constant supply of provocative events; he could invoke his righteous indignation at least three times a week. Characters like myself
were bits of local color, the garnish for his major program concerns.
When I found one evening in the hospital that he was discussing
me, I was so well tranquilized that I could not turn him off; I felt
myself the bird powerless in its fascination with the serpent. He informed his audience that he had it "on very good authority": I would
never return to a full-time position at the university. Behind that
blandly assured statement (for which he had no authority at all),
there was the implied sense that justice was being done. I was clearly
on the wrong track, and his comment was well-designed to be a
self-fulfilling prophecy. Fortunately, I was a little tougher than he
wanted me to be.

Reason in Madness: The Special Case of Berkeley

Helms would certainly have felt at home in the California educational crises of the later 1960s. The political climate under then
Governor Ronald Reagan would have suited him completely—as he
proved so well in the years after 1980. And he would have found
Berkeley, of all the state universities, particularly to his liking. A
hyena cannot make the kill, but he knows where there is blood; the
California hyenas would have welcomed him to the feast, and he
would have made much of it.

Whenever we think of American universities in the years of turmoil, we think first of Berkeley. Greatest of the public universities at
that time, it partook equally of the best university traditions of intellectual freedom on the one hand, and on the other of that special

sense of golden, liberated, and yet disciplined life which seemed so special a quality of northern California. During my own brief time as a faculty member there, I felt it to be remarkable in its openness and ease, in its commitment to intellectual quality without a certain neurotic intensity with which I was well acquainted at Yale. It deserved its reputation.

And Clark Kerr was worthy of the system which included it. As president of the senior university group, he was in a unique position to use the training and experience in labor arbitration which had made him one of Berkeley's distinguished faculty. A member of the Society of Friends, he had grown up in a community of ethical as well as intellectual concern, and he would be particularly sensitive to issues of intellectual freedom, destructive war, and racial injustice. It is one of the great ironies of the period that he should be confronted with the most perverse and extreme forms of the very issues about which he held such strong convictions. He was not alone in this quandary; many of us found that our convictions were treated as nonexistent because we did not frame them in extremist ways. But Clark was in a unique position to embody this presidential heartache.

And he was so in part because Berkeley was such an astonishing town. It was a surrealist version of the classic university town, with a great variety of life-styles which ranged from the elegant to the raffish, with a climate which for much of the year allowed these to play themselves out in the open air, and an ethos which seemed to turn independence into extremism without being troubled by the distinction. It was not accidental that the first production of LSD in the United States should take place there. That psychotherapeutic drug had come from Switzerland with benign credentials; it opened the mind, it seemed to cure some of our mortal ailments, and it typified that responsive taste for the new, the untested but inviting extension of our normal awareness which seemed to fit so well into the place. The free speech movement at Berkeley hardly needed LSD to set it off; and in fact the drug world would be seen in time as an enemy to significant activism. But there was room in Berkeley for these and a host of other expressions of variance from mainstream

American society. They did not need to be imported; many of them started there.

There was a whole other dimension to the Berkeley situation, however. From what I have just said, the political magnetism of the university is clear. A long tradition of local political concern, a widely (even wildly) diverse student body, a great city just across the bay which had already by 1964 become a center for several major movements—these were among the ideal preconditions for the eruption of the free speech movement, which in turn provided the base for a complex attack on the governance, the curriculum, and the traditional academic value systems of the university. The outer political battle against the national establishment was quickly translated into an inner battle (ostensibly over many of the same issues) against the various levels of the university community.

It is particularly significant that this major trouble came early in the decade. It provided patterns of action for many other universities; it was an inspiration and also a how-to-do-it guidebook. At the same time, and quite unwittingly, it provided a far more momentous inspiration and impetus—one whose consequences we are still enduring today. A conservative coalition had been building in the state for some time. It had been outraged but not dispersed by the judicial settlement of the oath controversy.

Now the same kinds of volatile issues were being raised again, and in a way which provided a basis for conservative action without any risk of reversal by the courts. Mario Savio and the whole community around him were preparing a platform and a political career for Ronald Reagan.

The spectacle at the university provided support for conservative politicians and constant material for the conservative press. First, there was the sheer luridness, the vulgarity, the violence, and the deliberateness of the attacks on bougeois values. These attacks grew more intense and more extreme as the months went by. Their original purposes were often lost in the games of outrage which developed. Free speech became filthy speech, and dissent became overtly destructive. This had, of course, a completely predictable result: anger on the right matched outrage on the left. This was

only the visible and hysterical part of the Berkeley adventure, however. Beneath it there was a far colder, more reasoned, and more
long-standing antagonism to the university for those qualities which
many of us feel were its greatest strength. This antagonism had been
made explicit at the time of the oath controversy, of course. Now
new issues of contention could be attacked under the guise of a pious
defense of the university against its own weakness, its permissiveness, its failure to maintain order in its own house. This would be
a conservative strategy on many a campus, but it was particularly
violent at Berkeley.

Duke and the Fine Arts: More Than Meets the Eye

A true sense of the sixties is not evoked by an unrelieved ritual of its
conflicts and public outbursts, however. It was not like that, and it
did not feel like that. On every major campus there was a duality of
experience: the maintenance of a "normal" and growing life on the
one hand, and on the other the encounters with unpredictable and
often alien issues. This was particularly true of Duke because many
of our centers of growth were themselves new and untried.

Anyone reading the weekly calendar of Duke events today would
find it hard to believe the circumscribed pattern of the 1960s and
earlier. There has been a flowering—not a renaissance, since it was
never there before—but a bold, daily assertion of the importance
of artistic activity in every field. There was then something historically important, in a grotesque way, about our first moves in this
direction. I say *grotesque* because by great good fortune we had the
chance to start with the Brummer gift, a unique collection of medieval treasures which had been assembled by the distinguished col-
lectors and dealers, Joseph and Ernest Brummer. The latter's widow
made much of this collection available to Duke, and we had to de-
vise a house for it. Nothing could seemingly have been further from
the raucous uses of the arts—and especially of music—which were
so integral to the major movements of the sixties.

At a more significant level, however, there was much in common
between these two recognitions of the powers of art. It is not unfair to the early years of Duke, I believe, to say that its emphasis

was on economics and the sciences, along with medicine. It could not all happen at once, and it is easier to start with the rationalist disciplines. Many of us were conscious that a major dimension of reality was missing, however, just as the young rebels against the conventional social order were conscious of much that could be said in song and action but not so well in the endless discussions which also claimed a great share of their time and energy. In both cases, and after the fashion of the sixties, a "statement" was made which ran counter to utilitarian definitions of importance.

If the parallel seems farfetched, it is affirmed by the very opposition which was generated when we set out to create space for this new collection. Criticism of the expense incurred when we rebuilt as a museum the old science building on the Trinity campus came from many of the same folk who were most bitterly outraged by the activist interruptions of the time. The two annoyances tended to flow together, so that a necessary and vital step for the university was made more controversial than it needed to be. The central effort of the university was, in this view, distracted and deflected by an emphasis on this frivolous and peripheral interest. Students were disrupting·the even tenor of events in a dozen ways which the sixties perfected; and in the midst of that disruption the university administration was fiddling with medieval art. This stance was regarded as quite Neroesque, not "serious" enough for a serious time, perhaps, and certainly not useful or central enough for an ambitious university looking for its place in the sun.

This is not the place for an extended theoretical discussion of the role of the arts in a great university. Our attitude at the time was one of active acceptance, a thankful recognition of the golden opportunity that was offered to us. The effort to find a house was fascinating, because at first there did not seem to be anything available, and new construction would have displaced other long-delayed projects like the library and engineering additions. The space on the Trinity campus, however, was not fully utilized, and the decision to liberate some of it for a museum became a very active question of policy, with implications for some of the major social questions of the decade as well as for basic attitudes toward the future pattern of Duke —both physical and intellectual.

Among alumni and faculty there was a long-standing and deeply held affection for the Trinity campus, which led to a desire in some quarters to have it redeveloped as a separate but equal establishment—basically a coordinate woman's college with a great deal of shared teaching but at the same time a strong sense of separate identity. I had my eye so firmly on unifying the university by developing what is now called the Central Campus that I could not accept this separation even at a physical level—and I was equally opposed to it on educational grounds. Once this issue was resolved, so that we no longer thought of resuscitating the moribund science building, the way was clear to look at its other uses. There was a residue of distress, however, at the thought that the Woman's College would be more and more completely merged into the total undergraduate enterprise. More distressing, perhaps, it looked to some like an encouragement of the push for full equality on the part of several of the national women's movements. Second-rate facilities for women (no matter how sentimentally cherished) would have been hard to defend, in my judgment, but there were those who saw these moves as part of an indecent zeal for change.

Campus politics creates as many strange bedfellows as the public kind. Those who felt that money should not go to frivolous pursuits such as an art museum found themselves joining those who wanted to keep the old science building—though these same folk were pushing hard for new science facilities on the West Campus. The chief leverage for the move came from the sheer monetary value of the Brummer gift; it was the largest single gift available for matching the Ford grant, and we had to exhibit the collection. The larger value of the move emerged only with time, of course, as the building attracted other collections and became the focus for a true and substantial development in the visual arts. Perhaps the last and best word on the matter was reported to me years later by Nancy Hanks, a Duke alumna who became chairman of the National Endowment for the Arts. She was at a meeting in the museum, along with other members of the board. Just ahead of her were two of the severest critics of the project. "There's one thing still wrong with this place," said one. As Nancy (in her words) moved up to do battle, the second said, "Yes, I know. We didn't make it half large enough." This was the creative fact which remained long after the arguments of the sixties were set aside.

Two Campuses or One?

In my discussion of the art museum I alluded to a concern which many of us felt about the future of the two campuses at Duke, which were separated by an extensive greenbelt. As it happened, the first step toward a solution to this question involved the social issues of the decade much as the art museum had involved the issues of equality of education for women. (It is fascinating in retrospect to see that we were constantly moving on at least two levels in every decision we made—the first an overt pursuit of logical aims for the university, and the second a contrapuntal concern with some major issue of the time.)

From my first days at Duke I had felt strongly about the need to bring the two ends of our campus together. I have indicated some of the opposition to this move. I found that my favorable comparisons of our campus size with that of other universities fell on very deaf ears. It was the psychological distance between the men's and women's campuses which was most cherished in some quarters, and it simply had to wear itself out. The best way to move any unification ahead would be the discovery of some logical and reasonable use for space between the campuses; and at this point history came to our aid.

Housing for low-income residents of Durham had long been in very short supply, even though federal funds were now available through HUD. Then, in 1967, an apartment complex across the street from our married student housing came on the market, and the Durham Housing Authority moved to acquire it. This step caused a stir in our board executive committee, where it was felt that we might have problems with our prospective neighbors. It was strongly suggested, in fact, that we should buy the property to keep it from its proposed use. At this point I must be immodest and say that the resolution came from me. I suggested that we sell to the city instead of trying to keep something from it. There was immediate agreement; though there were later reservations (largely because we would be bringing a black population to the west side of Durham) we moved ahead, and this step in turn gave us the means to buy "Central Campus" property for housing to replace what we had sold.

This was a win-win situation, unlike so many during the period. It was part of our larger answer to the issues raised during the Vigil, though of course it was not seen that way at the time. But it was just as significantly a chance to look at the long future both of Duke and of Durham. When I see the plans now emerging for the Central Campus area, I get a good deal of pleasure from reflecting, not only that we had the right idea in the mid-1960s, but that we took hold of a problem caused by racial bias and turned it into a benefit. I will add one thing more. Because it was so successful, I suspect that it has been almost completely forgotten.

The Duke Student Body in the 1960s

It is symbolically right that discussion of the student body at Duke should stand at the center of this chapter. Essential to our understanding of the 1960s at Duke is a sympathetic awareness of their nature at the time. At one level this is an obvious statement. The urban and aggressive group at Columbia, the far-out subculture at Berkeley, the brilliant engineers at MIT—each of these helped to determine the particular pattern of the sixties for those institutions. When we look beneath the surface, however, it is harder to generalize about Duke than about most of the others. And that fact demands that we look closely at the emotional and intellectual character of the undergraduates above all. They would do more to determine the tone of the time than any other group in the university. I can speak personally as well as statistically about them, of course, not only because I saw so many of them in committees and in countless informal discussions, but because I taught them during my term as president.

Intellectually, there was no doubt of their quality. The women had on entrance a grade and SAT profile like that of Radcliffe undergraduates, and the men were not far behind, even though less dazzling. In this Duke was, of course, like most strong universities across the country. Its geographical mix set it apart, however, but again in a familiar pattern. The most cosmopolitan universities in the country were still strongly regional in student origin, no matter how national in attitude. A radius of two to three hundred miles drawn around any of them would have included a substantial percentage of the student body. Certainly this was true of Duke, yet there was at the same time a strong subgroup from the Northeast—particularly from New Jersey—and a significant number from the upper Midwest and from Florida, which as a migrant state already stood apart from its southern geography.

Duke students were economically quite well-to-do. It is not an indictment to say that Duke was socially and financially the most privileged university in the southeastern quadrant of the country. This naturally made it particularly attractive during the activist years to a great variety of "visitors" and gave its students as a group a considerable basis of security and status, a sense of ease about their individual lives. At the same time there was a considerable feeling of competition with the strongest of the Ivy universities and the best of the northeastern women's colleges. (Here we can see an important difference from the Duke undergraduates today, who know that they have fully met that competition, and are at Duke because for them it is the best place in the country.)

Even in their times of vigorous protest, they were a surprisingly polite and civilized group. I put it so because a sense of civility has not stood front and center in most descriptions of the 1960s. What *we* saw, however, is my concern here; and to us there was given a good deal of basic respect with a strong overlay of defiance, of noisy rhetoric, and of troubled activism. They had very serious purposes in mind; they were possessed at times by a good measure of hysteria; they were at one level antagonistic because they were determined to make demands which I was clear I could not meet in the ways which they urged; yet they were restrained and disciplined along with their passionate sense of outrage. In this way they managed for the most part to keep their integrity—and to allow me to keep mine. As I look at the cheap excuses, the affectations, and pretenses at seriousness which showed up on so many campuses, I have great respect for those I lived with.

Their substantial moral sense grew from several sources. First, they themselves were diverse enough to look at the issues in a complex way. No extreme groups dominated the action, as they did at Berkeley, Stanford, or Wisconsin. There was a great deal of interest in the leaders of groups from other universities, and we saw most of them at Duke. With the exception of the black students' concerted action, however, I did not see any of the coordination which grows from the pursuit of a party line. Most students were as bewildered and puzzled as the rest of us; they knew that the world was out of joint, and they debated how to set it right.

Many of them came from substantial religious backgrounds, and their ethical urgencies sprang in part from the fact that they took their faith seriously. I cannot help thinking, as I look back at the Vigil, that their elders were disturbed because they did take these concerns seriously *and put them into practice.* They were echoing Dr. King's injunction of nonviolence and at the same time of high visibility. In doing this their actions were the precursors of today's standard form of civil protest, and they set themselves apart from the activists on many other campuses. To say this is really to say that students were not the extremists in the Duke community of the late 1960s. There was extremism, certainly, but much of it came from those who were older and should have been wiser. Of those older extremists on the right I cannot, even at this distance, speak so tolerantly or with such affection.

The Silent Vigil on behalf of black employees and those events immediately before it were important enough so that they deserve our particular attention. As I have implied, they were a direct outgrowth of the particular emphasis and tone of the Duke student body. The prelude, on the evening of April 4, 1968, was routine enough at the start: a large dinner in Winston-Salem which the chairman of the Duke board of trustees and I were bidden to attend. My close friend George Gilmore drove us over and back so that we could read some papers in the backseat and have one of our customary abrasive discussions about student unrest. The chairman could not accept for a minute the fact that Duke was bound to have its share of the national ferment. "Not here and not now" was the tenor of his message to me (he tended to speak in messages).

It was late when we left him at his motel, and the car made its way home almost soundlessly through the deserted streets of the black community. Suddenly, George's gentle voice came floating back to me, under remarkable control (we were extremely close, and this discipline was quite alien from either of us when we were alone together on our trips). "I didn't want to tell you while the chairman was in the car, but Dr. King has been shot and I'm afraid." He knew the Durham black community well since he had lived in it most of his life, but his concern was for the white reaction as well. He knew better than I that, even as we drove, there were a good many white people rejoicing over that violence. My response to him was verbally routine: "We'll just have to wait and see. There's nothing we can do now." But I was as worried as he.

The next day was busy with the customary expressions of outrage. The undergraduate campus, however, was feeling a depth of guilt which no routine paragraphs of regret could satisfy. Normal student diversity of opinion was replaced by an urgent sense that something had to be done—immediately—to purge the community of the evil thing that had happened. It was taken personally by a surprising number of students; they wanted to bear witness against the murder, and they wanted the university to show its communal sense of outrage. There was a strong perception that atonement was called for, and the dean of students had a busy day trying to guide these almost evangelical emotions into some form of constructive action. There was quite a push for a march to Hope Valley, the conservative and privileged enclave several miles to the south of the university campus. Fortunately, this move was aborted; we learned later that some residents were so fearful of violence themselves that they would have shot at any marchers who seemed threatening. Instead, several hundred students came to University House, in a wing of which we lived.

They were distraught and once again looking for reasonable answers to the insane message of assassination, which had already shaken their world. The issue of race added for them a major element of guilt and anger. It is fair to say that they expected the university to set matters straight, and this expectation went beyond that communal outrage which I mentioned a moment ago. It was a burden laid on the university precisely because it claimed to be a civilized place. There was also an element of that expectation which one has of a parent. "If you know so much, why don't you do something?" This parentalism was of course anathema to the very students who were subrationally expecting parental performance from the university, but I do not mean to be critical of them when I point out that fact. They were well beyond their emotional depth, as we all were, and they responded in a direct way to the deep need to reestablish order. The disorder which they themselves created for a brief period can only be understood in this large context of civil morality, which was at the moment right at the breaking point.

Mrs. Knight and I went to the door of University House to meet them (we had had a call that they were en route). I started to try to talk with them, but it was dark outside and both of us invited them in. Like so much that happened in those hours, this was a move of instinct on our part; the house was built for university meetings, and we were its hosts. We did not see these distraught young people as demonstrators, nor did we—even at moments of great tension as the evening wore on—see them as invaders of our privacy. The general public and many of our university colleagues came to see it that way, however, because as soon as 250 or so had settled in the public spaces of the house, they presented me with the inevitable set of demands.

To catch the emotional heart of the evening as it developed, one has to picture a small group of students "negotiating" with me in my study, a large group raising their emotional temperature with song and exhortation, and the student newspaper in touch with the outside world both to announce what was being done and to feed bulletins to their peers about the disruptions around the country. I remember most vividly the explosive "All Washington's burning!" as an editor of the student-run *Chronicle* thrust his head in at the door. Those constant messages and the flickering of lights on the complex phone system set an inevitable mood of rising hysteria. Soon and inevitably there was the "Hell no, we won't go" chant, and it was clear that we had our visitors with us for the night.

I say this both because the emotional overload was so great that clearly the visit was not destined to end in a quiet departure and because the demands for specific action were well out of the arena of the possible. The chief of these demands was that I sign a document announcing that the wages of all black employees of the university would be immediately doubled. I have remarked elsewhere that a university president's position is one of authority without power; the fact was seldom so clear to me as on this particular night. My problem was twofold. I had to explain that I could not take such a step even if I would, and I had to try to explain why the option was not available to the university in any case. I can finally smile a little at my own earnest efforts to make both of these points, efforts which were guaranteed to be baffling and frustrating to the negotiators. I had to fight within myself not to be swept up in the high emotion all around me, while I knew that every effort at rational discourse was doomed to fail us, at least in the short run.

After four or five hours of this kind of exchange, we could at least agree that nothing more would be accomplished that night. There was to be a memorial service in the Duke Chapel the next day at noon, and at that time I was to address some of the issues which we had discussed so fruitlessly the night before. Meanwhile, the students would stay in the house; their future plans would depend on what they heard from me. This was a ragged solution, and clearly a face-saving one for them, but the best we could come up with at the moment. I have no idea what I said the next day, except that it was an outburst against the violence and social injustice of our society. I satisfied no one—including myself—but at least some time for reflection had been gained.

And that reflective time was not fully understood, by me or by anyone else, until many years later. Recently I had the privilege of talking in detail about the event with several of the Duke graduates who had been in the house during those days. I learned two things of great importance. First, they were very clear that the attitude which we adopted toward our guests that evening set a tone of nonconfrontation which carried through the many difficult days ahead. Second, they said that they found themselves "losing their constituent support" by the next afternoon, and then had to be helped quietly and safely out of the house. This position of ours was not appreciated at the time, incidentally. There was a sense of imposition and even outrage on the part of the elders. I have alluded to it elsewhere; it was the inevitable backlash, and it was mild in comparison with the resentment of 1969.

This encounter was a sober and even saddening event for all of us. On the student side it was a statement which at least temporarily was aborted by the unfolding of events during those twenty-four hours. On ours, there was a faint but perceptible creaking of the floor joists; it was clear to everyone that I had no Jovian power; I could take action, but I could not move my hand and make the problem disappear. At the same time I could make it much worse if I were imprudent. This limitation caused resentment among the old, and a little surprise among the young—surprise that, once reflected on, would lead to a good many test cases around the country during the next few years. The power of the undergraduate community was not what many hoped or feared it would be, but it was significant nationally in shaping the course of the immediate future.

Our students shared their moral agitation with movements as far removed as France and the Soviet Union. There was a global wave of student concern which I do not pretend to explain, except to point out that it was a deep response to confused political events in many parts of the world. Like canaries in a mine, students were telling us that there was trouble and that it was rapidly getting out of control. They did not create the trouble; they dramatized it and gave it articulate form.

The Visitors: Dissent in Many Voices

We at Duke were obviously quite capable of creating high and significant drama in response to the tragedies of the decade. But we were also a responsive community to those less than tragic figures who came to present their case, explain their ideas, and lend a hand in shaping our attitudes and actions. It is a truism that universities rejoice in their visitors—rejoice in the idea of them, at least. They are the fresh breeze, the unjaded and unfamiliar voice. I speak lyrically to suggest the special contribution which we expect, which makes the visitor at his best integral to our job, even though he stays so briefly. As I look at the 1960s, however, I see that this applause for the stranger is really a send-up on my part. I want to recognize the contributions which David Harris, Paul Goodman, and Dick

Gregory made to our community, but at the time I could have done without them and felt no pain.

Those three visitors are a suggestion of what we had with us during the period. They were the best, as well as the best-known, of those who came. But we attracted the strongest proponents of many of the major movements. We were spared the heavy drug scene, and that fact speaks for the seriousness and the integrity of the Duke undergraduate approach to these issues. (There must have been a good deal of marijuana smoked, but I never heard of any heavy LSD.) In all the other cases our students sought out the movement leaders, and Duke in turn was sought out. In this way we became a target university—in many ways *the* target university—for the Southeast. Twenty years later we should take that as a compliment to the importance of the Duke setting and the quality of our undergraduates.

There is no doubt that these visits had a substantial impact on us. If Simon and Garfunkel helped set the tone, Dick Gregory helped trigger the action (as we shall see in the discussion of the Allen Building occupation).

At the same time the preoccupations of the sixties were genuine enough, pervasive enough, that they did not need to be established by our visitors. Visitors confirmed and amplified a well-set pattern of concern, and they lent it a good deal of dramatic force. They were not the center of the action at Duke, but they did sharpen it and heighten its intensity, and in the case of Dick Gregory, a visitor defined the course of action for a group of undergraduates. Even in that case, however, the urgency of the event came from inside the university and not (as many thought) from an external rabble-rouser.

As we moved through the highly theatrical world of the sixties, we met an amazing cast of characters, many in costume and a large number masked as well. The heightened quality of events led naturally to intensified and exaggerated styles of life; it was all too easy under the impact of these exaggerations to believe that the surface was all. We could hear the shout of these styles from a great distance, but the substance which was often inside found its quiet voice drowned out in the uproar.

David Harris is a prime example. My first sense of him was so external as to be grotesque. When he came to the Duke campus to

speak he was at the height of his reputation—a cult hero in his opposition to the Vietnam War, in his leadership of student activism on
the Stanford campus, in his definite and obvious talent for projecting
his own position so that it mesmerized his audience. At a reception
which we gave for him one could sense the palpable nature of his
gifts; perhaps the fluttering girls around him confirmed it as much
as anything else. I know how hopelessly middle-aged I felt, and how
irrelevant.

He was to marry Joan Baez within fifteen months or so, and in
due time would head off to prison for his refusal to register for the
draft. These two events would certainly set him apart from most of
his peers, but I was much too busy paddling my own canoe to keep
track of his. I retained only the image of his blond assertiveness,
which seemed to be focused in an enormous belt buckle—almost
large enough to be a buckler, it seemed.

Recently I found him again, through a book he had written about
two of the explosive and tragic figures of the time: Allard Lowenstein and Dennis Sweeney who would kill Lowenstein early in the
1970s. Perhaps it would be more accurate to say that I found David
Harris for the first time. His book was a highly effective work of
self-revelation, all the more so because he was never its ostensible
subject. Instead, he shows himself moving, constantly shifting both
physical and ideological locations in a remarkable reminiscence of
the issues, blind alleys, druggy nights, and anguished decisions. The
transition from callow freshman to heroic senior was as meteoric and
breathless as cheap melodrama; what saved it was the life-changing
seriousness of the issues, not only for Harris but, tragically, for his
two protagonists.

Precisely because Harris does not present himself as a hero but
rather as a bewildered late adolescent surfing on the great rollers
of sixties' policy and debate, he emerges as a highly sensitive and
ethical figure, willing to take a position which is absolutely solid
in its integrity if not in its trappings. In the course of the growth
which prison demanded of him, he grew in a way which was not so
directly political as his stand against the war. He came to feel the
disparity between the gritty experience of living out his convictions
and the luxurious and in many ways fantastic experience of being

Joan Baez's husband. This disparity is not presented in a judgmental way. Harris was well aware that she was in full possession of her own integrity—both as an artist and a highly principled woman. But the opulent setting, which could work for her because she had earned the money that made it possible, was destructive for him. It stood in the way of his own increasingly clear sense of the way he had to live; he found himself strong enough to move away from his past, and beyond it.

As a result, when Harris says of the end of the decade, "Nothing had changed, but everything was different," he is speaking first and most centrally about himself. At the same time he reveals through himself one of the most vital aspects of the time—that the changes which counted were changes in the heart. The great movements would die or radically alter, but many of those most devoted to them would persist in their mature convictions, so that they could reaffirm singly what had seemingly vanished as a collective statement. We must respect the achievement; it is in many ways a fascinating parallel to the growth in insight of McNamara.

It is exactly this inner experience which we now tend to forget or ignore. It is sometimes said that the academic damage done in the 1960s was analogous to that achieved by Joseph McCarthy a decade earlier. The analogy is inaccurate because the interpretation of the earlier period is wrong. I happen to have had some direct encounters with McCarthyism while I was president of Lawrence College, and I can testify that it had no counterbalancing virtues as the student extremes of the 1960s had. The McCarthy push was malicious and totally unprincipled. It had strong elements of the sadistic, and it used character assassination as a means to political power. The manifestoes of SDS were certainly disturbing and at times downright ugly. The inner life of the movement had conviction a good deal of the time, however, and gave rise (as with Harris) to the most intense individual concerns.

The Road Not Taken

Charismatic figures are often like dye in the river; they color it, they may even stain the banks, but they do not determine the river's source or direction. Those are its own nature, and as we look at a variety of American universities we see that each did its own shaping to a remarkable degree. Faced with common events, the universities gave them divergent shapes; indeed, they often evoked a precise and articulated statement from movements which were somewhat incoherent in themselves. One fascinating effort was not based in a university, however, but in opposition to it. The supposed irrelevance of the established institutions led to the development of alternate courses and programs, run almost entirely by those involved and embodying a complex body of goals and convictions. The Midpeninsula Free University in Palo Alto was one of the most successful, and the self-perception which introduced its catalog in the fall of 1969 is more than a statement of purpose. It is a text—virtually a religious text—for the proper conduct of life.

Preamble

What an organization does is the best indication of what it is. And the various activities described in this catalog give, perhaps, the clearest picture of what the Midpeninsula Free University is all about. Yet since what we are doing falls short of what we hope to do, it has been felt that some statement of our intentions is necessary. We feel that the American educational establishment has proven incapable of meeting the needs of our society. It often discourages students from thinking critically, and does not afford them meaningful training to help them understand the crucial issues confronting mankind today. Bound to the existing power structure, and handicapped by modes of thought fostered by big business, by the military establishment, by consensus politics, and by the mass media, it is unable to consider freely and objectively the cultural, economic, and political forces so rapidly transforming the modern world. The present educational system in fact defends the status quo, perpetuating its evils and perils. The system has become rigid; it is no longer receptive to meaningful change. A revolution in American education is required to meet today's needs, and a new type of education—a free university—must provide the impetus for change. *Therefore we affirm:*

That freedom of inquiry is the cornerstone of education.

That each individual must generate his own most vital questions and program his own education, free from central control by administrative bureaucracies and disciplinary oligarchies.

That the class character of age in our society subverts education, and that the young are not too young to teach, nor the old too old to learn.

That education is not a commodity, and should not be measured out in units, grade points, and degrees.

That education aims at generality rather than specialization, and should supply the glue which cements together our fragmented lives.

That education is a process involving the total environment, which can only occur in a total community, in which each individual participates equally in making the decisions which importantly affect his life.

That education which has no consequences for social action or personal growth is empty.

That action which does not raise our level of consciousness is futile.

That the ultimate politics will be based on knowledge, liberty, and community, rather than on hate, fear, or guilt.

That the most revolutionary thing we can do is think for ourselves, and regain contact with our vital centers.

That the most important questions which confront us must be asked again and again and answered again and again, until the millenium comes.

That the natural state of man is ecstatic wonder.

That we should not settle for less.

Granting the pretentious quality of this, it is disturbing in quite another way. It asks many of the central questions about the purposes of education, and it does so by making one simple assumption: education is an exercise of the body, mind, and spirit designed to make us more complete, more perfect human beings, in possession of ourselves and aware of our world. It is a compelling and almost classical manifesto, quite apart from its practical realization in the courses and encounters which make up the body of the catalog.

Journeys through the catalogs of 1968, 1969, and 1970 give us a disarming, earnest, and faintly pathetic picture of much that was hoped, dreamed, and feared in the later years of the decade. They are also an instant cure for our conventionalities, our sense that knowledge not only comes in familiar boxes but is arranged and displayed in familiar ways. Here are courses 17 to 23 of the winter 1968 catalog.

17. A Food Thing—This seminar is designed for all good people who wouldn't mind getting their groceries at 25 to 50 percent off retail price.

18. Introduction to Astronomy—General survey of things extra-terrestrial, with observing sessions. Weather permitting.

19. Where Is Art At?—"Formerly we used to represent things visible on earth, things we either liked to look at or would have liked to see. Today we reveal the reality that is behind visible things." Paul Klee

"I paint to evolve a changing language of symbols, a language with which to remark upon the qualities of our mysterious capacities. . . ." Morris Graves

"There is the American fascination with disaster and grotesque happenings, in the newspapers and on TV, for instance, and it has come out in the work I've been doing." Joyce Wieland

"Now and then, in fits and starts, I do a watercolor. It comes over you like that: you feel like a watercolor and you do one." Henry Miller

"Art is anything you can get away with." Marshall McLuhan

An exploratory seminar with the visual and tactile experiences we can arrange. Museum and gallery trips as desired. Where *is* art at? Come and let's find out.

20. The Turn of the Screw: Studies in Brainwashing—Desirability, Dependency, and Dread are the three keys to successful brainwashing. They can also be used by the Police and the State, to cow the hapless population into submission. We will be studying these methods in detail. Knowledge is power.

21. An Introduction to Plato as an Introduction to Philosophy —This is the second quarter of a year-long seminar devoted to

a serious and systematic study of all the Platonic dialogues. . . . Special emphasis will be placed on the world view of Ancient Greece and how it differs from ours today. During the course of study it will become evident that the usual views of Plato put forth in American Universities are based on prejudices deeply ingrained in the post-Enlightenment character. Members will work toward a new and critical world view as an alternative to those with which they disagree.

New members joining this quarter will be asked, in addition to reading the dialogues at the rate of about 50 pgs. per week, to prepare work papers on individual dialogues; guidance and access to secondary sources will be given. Participation implies commitment to do the requisite reading and preparation.

22. The Liberation of the Legal Mind—An analysis of law as ideology—an examination of the conceptual limitations of categorical patterns of thought—a study of the extent to which the State has usurped from the Church the mantle of the Sacred with which to cloak its deception—Law as Myth.

We will invite law professors, lawyers, law school drop-outs, prospective felons, and incipient revolutionaries to ask why they are what they are.

We will read selections from Mannheim, Erickson, Marcuse, Arendt, Galbraith, Camus, Lenin, Weber, and Manning. We will do whatever else the group feels is worth the time.

Restricted to law students unless anyone else really wants to come.

For the first meeting, . . . read *The Death of Ivan Ilych*. . . .

23. Your Ecstatic Home—A courageous and realistic approach to the ordinary home, changing it into a serene, tranquil, turned-on place in which to live. A brainwashing for the Madison Avenue dicta on decorating. The student's eye will be trained to see, compare, and evaluate the possible ranges of sizes, shapes, patterns, colors, textures, etc., in relationship to their uses in solving decorating problems.

We roam freely from the domestic to the cosmic and back again. I smiled at the juxtapositions here and then realized more soberly that these were pieces of life, and that the catalogs were mosaics made up of the thought of all those who had contributed their effort, their concern. Even in the later catalogs (which are far more codified and classified), there is the same preoccupation with involvement, exploration, and self-discovery.

Perhaps the most interesting and revealing aspect of the enterprise is its reversal or inversion of the familiar university world. In their rebellion against an education which asked them to fit themselves into its boxes, walk along its predetermined pathways, the creators of a free university started with their own preoccupations, objectified and intellectualized them, and wound up with a pattern that—whatever its quirks and eccentricities—was an honest expression of themselves at a particular point in time. These courses, these catalogs are the perfect embodiments of attitudes and approaches which flashed like moonlight on the sea and were lost again, replaced by those mundane, conventional, but less alive patterns to which we quickly returned in the 1970s. Once again we saw Camelot, crazy and beautiful; once again we lost it.

Universities Under Fire: The Dancer and the Dance

We are reminded that we must be careful what we pray for: we may be burdened with it, may have to endure consequences we had not foreseen. No one can say that established American universities prayed for the adversity which broke upon them in the sixties. But that limited knowledge of future events which makes prayer so dangerous also made for special and unique difficulties on each campus as it was put under stress. The mischievous, sometimes malevolent deity of disruption sought out the characteristic patterns, the hidden weaknesses of each place. We were exploited, if you will, right at the points where our personalities and foibles showed most clearly.

One of the oldest and proudest of the universities which were to become urban, Columbia developed its unique character in many ways apart from the world city which grew around it. The very location with which it was blessed in the nineteenth century, the beauty of the high countryside along the Hudson, the sense that New York lent it a distinctive metropolitan, urbane character but without the

sour taint of the city—all of this was part of the communal personality which found itself in the early sixties faced with a restless ghetto
just down the hill, and a great city studying how to go bankrupt—
breaking down, indeed, not only in its services but in its attitudes
of civility and even of self-confidence. Beyond this, Columbia had a
corporate, almost a conglomerate quality to its organization which at
the appropriate moment invited a particularly virulent attack from
the political arm of the student left.

After all, sds had defined establishment America as a corporate society in which education had become the mere servant and
pawn of the military-industrial complex. In their eyes Columbia had
proven its vicious tendencies by the appointment of a general of the
armies as its president. The wonderful irony involved in attacking
(by implication) the man who had coined the phrase and warned us
most eloquently of the dangers of that unholy alliance—that ironic
fact was totally unknown to them, and they would not have known
how to cope with it if it had been displayed on a banner across the
face of Low Library.

The style of the university, as well as its formal organization, laid
it open to attack. Aloof and impersonal, it offered the best of all
targets—an organization which could be scorned with wonderful
and simplistic righteousness. Individuals are harder to attack than
organizations, simply because they are multifaceted. They demand
detailed treatment, even in conflict, because they are persons. In
Martin Buber's terms, the relationship has to be some version of I
and Thou. But an abstract organization invites polarization into we
and them—or even worse, we and it. The personality of the president
—Grayson Kirk in this case—is brushed aside by turning it into
gross caricature; the stage is set for a holy war, with the university as
an oppressor through its indifference to the underprivileged blacks
living on its border, and equally through the presumed support of an
unjust war suggested by its investments portfolio and the corporate
directorships of its governing bodies. Seen in this way, Columbia was
an ideal ogre. The radical left would have tried to invent it if it did
not exist, but here it was—ready to hand and ripe for the plucking.

The consequence is too notorious for my further comment, but it
leads us back to a climactic moment in the Duke experience.

A Quiet Day in Dixie

Our most difficult public event at Duke is not to be compared with Columbia's anguish and demoralization, however. The Allen Building occupation had in common with the events at Columbia only one thing—a concern for racial recognition. With us there was no confused intertwining of issues; once the occupation started, we could see clearly what we had to deal with.

The first black undergraduates had come to Duke in the fall of 1962. It had not been an easy decision for some trustees, and my own antecedents when I arrived later in the year were not encouraging, since I could not be expected to look at the change, and at the newcomers, as a native would have done. (At this time in Duke's history its student body was broader in range than its board, even without the addition of black students. There were political problems in this situation, of course, but they were not evident in 1962.) The black students were able, small in numbers but not mere tokens, and they became genuine members of the community. To say this is not to say that life was easy or even satisfactory for them at times. We were —at least many of us were—far too simplistic about their presence. We tended to feel that once we had begun to overcome the admissions hurdle, the rest would be easy. In making this assumption we were walking right toward a land mine; we were saying, "Come in, be white," and that was not what these young people wanted. They wanted opportunity, and they wanted their own proper identities. All of the later push for black dormitories, black studies, special conditions of all sorts were the expressions of this one need. The nonnegotiable demands often meant, "Hey, look at me. I want to talk as an equal, and I want to keep all my differences intact. I want to be visible to you *as myself.*" Put this basic black need into a conservative university, set it also in a context of high volatility and constant discussion of every available issue, and sooner or later the mine will be sprung. With us it was later, and we had a little help. As everyone knew at the time, Dick Gregory gave himself in 1968–69 to raising the consciousness of black students across the country. In February he came to Duke, and we invited him to dinner at University House along with sixteen black students—all that the table would hold. Armored in our white liberal innocence, we were a bit bewildered when we had no one for dinner—just a terse message saying that if all could not come, none would come. Our black servants (good friends by now) were far more outraged than we, and said so with considerable vigor. They felt the insult, and naturally we saw that we were not wanted; but we did not carry that knowledge to its logical conclusion. The speech was a rouser, of course; and two days later every black student on campus moved into the administration building. I was in New York at a breakfast meeting when the word came. I chartered a plane and was home by 11 A.M. The students were firmly in, everyone else was out, the demands were nonnegotiable in several senses of the phrase, and we had a thorough standoff on our hands.

The situation was dangerous in several ways. A great many occupations around the country had preceded this one, and both national patience and national interest had worn thin. All those in the Duke community—the broad community as well as the immediate one—who had resented the original admission of blacks but had stayed silent would now be loud in self-congratulation and hot for the severest punishment. There was a further group which cared nothing about Duke but a good deal about keeping blacks in their place. There was the inevitable inflammation of the rest of the student body, which could have uncontrolled results if a demonstration ever got loose. And there were issues of order in the university which even the most zealous friends of these students had to reckon with. Taken together, these made a tangled web of emotions, high and low rhetoric, and conflicting options for action.

As the hours went by, the options diminished alarmingly. All our attempts failed to move the students out of the building so that we could talk without pressure in some neutral place. It takes courage to do what they had done; it would have taken a good deal of maturity as well for them to walk out again. February days are short; the dark comes early. By midafternoon I was getting reports of men in pickup trucks, shotguns in the window racks, driving slowly around the outer perimeter of the West Campus, watching, waiting for dark. We had scheduled a special faculty meeting for 4 P.M.; at 3:45 I called the governor to ask for the help of a specially trained state police unit. It would take them half an hour to get into place, and the dark would come only half an hour later. We were cutting it very fine in our attempt to avoid the very step I now had to take.

When I told the faculty of my decision, there was a good deal of support. Those faculty members who had been counseling with the black students bolted out the door to warn them, but—once again —it was simply not feasible to walk out in what might be seen as capitulation. By the time they decided to move, the police were in place—largely for their protection, since I had made my fears known to the governor. By this time there were a good many other students on the open campus in front of the Chapel. From our command post on the edge of the West Campus we could hear the general noise rise to an uproar as a mass of students pushed toward the building and the first tear gas canister was rolled toward them. It sounded for a few minutes as though real violence had broken out; students took refuge in the Chapel from the tear gas; the black students were ushered out of the building and safely away from that part of the campus (none of them were detained); and the only injury, miraculously enough, was a moderate burn on two fingers of one of our familiar activists. (He tried to pick up a gas canister to throw it back at the police cordon; no one had time to tell him it was hot.)

As it turned out, of course, this turbulent half-hour was the easy part, the mere prelude to the varied action which followed. First, we had to move quickly with the legal procedure which, fortunately, we had set up months earlier for dealing with such an event. A faculty committee took on the deliberations about appropriate discipline, and I was freed to cope with the varied reactions both to the occupation and the way in which it was ended. Naturally enough, those who feared police power were highly critical of its use and had difficulty in understanding the danger to the black students in our particular location, with an enormous campus which simply could not be made secure. They had not seen the trucks, the guns, and really did not want to accept the complexity of forces at simultaneous play. If you have persuaded yourself that the police are the enemy, it is hard to accept them as the agents of peace, or to recognize that indeed they were carefully trained to play that role. (The contrast with the tragic National Guard situation at Kent State University cannot be forgotten here; it was the frightful reality which all of us feared in every mass confrontation.) This bewilderment and disagreement we were able to reckon with; in some cases we were even able to get a little education in motion.

Emotions on the other side were also predictable but far harder to deal with. There was clear understanding of what had to be done and why—this from a thoughtful minority. There was very substantial approval of my decisions—clearly for all the wrong reasons, as events unfolded. The enthusiasm was for the use of force, since the police were perceived by conservatives much as they were by liberals. Almost immediately following the incident—within a day or so—pressure began to mount for the university to take the most drastic action. "Good. Now you have them where you want them. Throw the rascals out." As I write this years later, it seems ridiculous, but at the time it was grotesque and deadly. During the following three weeks there were so many protesting—and exulting—letters from graduates that the alumni office could not reply and simply filed them by the box. I did not see them, for reasons which will soon be clear, but two or three years ago a Duke graduate doing a retrospective story told me that she had seen a good many and that she could not believe they came from the graduates of her civilized university. All the unspoken fears and resentments came into the open: these black students were intruders; they should be intruders in the dust, cast down, cast out.

And, of course, my own background cried out against me. My mother remarked later that when she saw the first news story describing me as "Yankee-born and Yale-educated," she braced herself for trouble. As I tell this difficult part of the story, I must say that I tried even then—and much more now—to understand the depth of the anger. It was everything that had happened since 1954, all concentrated in one episode. Inevitably, I was seen as the man who had somehow mysteriously caused it to happen. At the very best I had lost control of the situation; at worst I was at the heart of the problem. And indeed I was, but for a rather different set of reasons from those asserted. These external issues would normally have been my prime concern, but three other acute problems forced them to the periphery. I had to see that the disciplinary problem was solved in a fair and honorable way; I had to deal with constant threats of personal violence; and I had to make a reckoning with the internal university crisis which was building very rapidly.

The disciplinary problem would have been the easiest if it had not fed all the others. The guidelines by which the appointed committee worked led them (as did their own good sense) to a clear end. Final probation for the whole group was serious medicine; it meant that any further infractions of any kind would lead to automatic termination. At the same time every student's future was protected, and this was seen to be an equally important goal of the action taken. This was good doctrine, but obviously it was totally unsatisfactory for the external groups, of which there were several in addition to the alumni. The violence in the air could have been quieted only by some act of legal violence on the part of the university, such as the dismissal of all black students. Otherwise, the taste for violence around us was frustrated and had to express itself somehow. And segments of the university community which valued their peace and quiet—Duke as it has always been—felt that this was the last straw in a sequence of events which had kept the university on edge for several years. As a result, the decision of the committee could only feed these other difficulties.

It is painful at this distance to write about the threat of violence. There would be far more comfort in saying that we were all a little overwrought and that in fact any threats were the work of idle cranks. Unfortunately, the record is not that simple. At our 1967 commencement, when our first black undergraduates were graduating, the bomb threats were serious enough so that, after ignoring the early ones, the FBI advised us during the ceremonies that it would be better to move. The threat to our black students during their day of occupation was only too clear; if there had been any easy way to get at them, several would have been injured or killed. As a family, my wife, sons, and I were in a rather different position and yet one which shared a good deal with that of the black students. It happened that we were exposed physically as well as ideologically. University House was bordered at the rear by a large area of woodland, which in turn had easy access from a public road. It was obvious that the threats against us could easily be carried out. For three weeks after the occupation (and before I resigned) we had one of our own security guards at the house, and I will never forget (I hate to have to describe it), my "normal" 1 A.M. routine of slipping a pistol into the pocket of my dressing gown and taking a little tour with the guard. How melodramatic; but that is exactly the point. In its impact on us as individuals, the decade could force behavior that was completely out of character, could make the abnormal seem normal and even necessary.

Our youngest son was twelve at the time. When events were this heavy, we had him spend the night with friends. He was a reticent boy, outwardly cheerful, obliging to an unusual degree, but keeping his own counsel. After about ten days of this nightly commuting, he said one evening as he got into the car, "I don't like this going away from home." Just the one sentence, and away he went with no murmur. The inflection had said it all, however. We did not have any great discussion, but simply recognized that almost anything would be an improvement.

We were greatly helped to this conclusion by the multiple pressures brought to bear on us from our own community. These ranged from active (even though relatively small) student protests at the steps taken, through public letters from senior faculty calling for firm order to be reestablished, to a call for a special meeting and my forced resignation by various trustees—in particular by a former chairman and the members of the Duke Endowment board, who also served on the university's board. This is not the appropriate place to discuss Duke politics further; I mention the matter at all only because a crisis of this magnitude is an easy thing to exploit. Long-standing disagreements could be hitched to an urgent situation, and the attacks which had been covert until now went public under that wonderful umbrella phrase, "with the best interest of the university in mind."

We faced a classic case of destabilization. All of the forces which I have described—though they were not coordinated—worked together as though one master intelligence were directing them. This was, as I have said elsewhere, one of the great characteristics of the whole decade. Forces, groups, individuals might disagree, might be in conflict, but they reinforced one another in the most intense way to create the unique dynamic irrationality of the time.

And certainly we partook of the irrational ourselves, which was equally characteristic of the decade. None of us could escape the tone of events; there was a resonance which caught us up even when we wanted to stay clear. This lent a curious fatality to the action, so that we felt involved but powerless to change the conclusion which was descending on us. This meant in turn a relief and release from responsibility, which was not, of course, to be the long-term reaction but merely the eye of the storm. Afterward would come the other side of the experience, private, personal, changing one's life, but not available at all for thought in the intense period.

To put this abstract and general reality back into its concrete meaning for us, we busied ourselves with the conflicting demands from angry alumni or aggressive black leaders outside the university as well as annoyed faculty and agitated trustees within. When a special meeting of the board was called, our nonchoice became perfectly clear: to fight a motion of dismissal would simply add further confusion to the university and to our private lives. That little sign flashing *exit* (which James Conant had seen at Harvard when the call to Germany came) was target red for us, and we resigned. (And it was *we*, not *I*; no one ever worked harder for Duke than my wife.)

Duke Faculty: Where Angels Fear to Tread

This formidable sequence of events naturally provoked a many-sided response from the Duke faculty. It is no criticism to say that there was a great deal of discomfort. To chronicle it here would give a false sense of faculty attitudes during the decade as a whole. I prefer instead to consider the far more abiding and significant stresses which the sixties generated—and once again not merely because of the issues abroad but because Duke itself was in a period of rapid development. It is impossible, however, to say anything general that will hold up under scrutiny. That, after all, is the nature of a faculty; it is individual and idiosyncratic, no matter how large.

It is often radical on subjects which do not concern it directly, and highly conservative on those close to its heart. (It is, after all, a famous faculty club which has on its wall the immortal credo: "If it is not absolutely necessary to change, then it is absolutely necessary *not* to change.") And it definitely does not like to be disturbed while it is going about its own lawful pursuits.

The 1960s gave ample room for disturbance, of many sorts and at many levels. University developments—above all the merging of the Womans' College with Trinity and the first moves toward a unified campus—were disturbing to some conservatives. The thrusting vigor of the Medical Center troubled others, who failed to understand that the rising tide lifts all the boats. Some engineers were bothered because instead of a new building they had to be satisfied with a new wing to the existing building. These and a dozen other major concerns were perfectly normal; no university should be without them. The special demands of the 1960s were something else, however. Granting that fallacy of generality, the faculty members were not radical; they believed in dissent but not disruption. With the exception of a few junior faculty and certain well-known campus eccentrics, they were not likely to join any of the major movements.

There was a clear corollary to this position. The ethical soundness of the Vigil was compelling, but any sort of occupation would provoke a vigorous response. This was true not only for reasons of general disapproval but also, I believe, because most of the faculty regretted and resented the thought that they might themselves be hampered in their work. In addition, a considerable number felt that the black students had a more than ordinary duty to conform, to be good "white" students. As a result, there was a lively sense of outrage at the Allen Building occupation. This expressed itself in various ways; one of the most public was an open letter to the student newspaper, the *Chronicle*, expressing the strong conviction that the administration had lost control of the situation—and as a result that the trustees should impose order on an incoherent situation.

As I recall it, there was little wish to be involved in setting matters straight again, and the letter was certainly a vote of no confidence in the administration's efforts after the occupation. As such, I could

not avoid the sense that there was a hidden agenda in it—perhaps
only partially known to those who signed it. The occupation was
resented by the signers of the letter, and the steps taken after it were
not punitive enough. The talk about order was a smokescreen; there
was unhappiness and disagreement but in fact no lack of order. As
I see matters now, it was probably an order which the signers of the
letter did not like; we were resolving the postoccupation problems
(a very delicate process) but in ways which some faculty members
disagreed with.

It is impossible to measure the balance of faculty opinion in these
matters, because the faculty as a whole does not have to deal with
them. It seems to me that there were far more strongly held opinions
on the right than on the left, however, and that as a result it was difficult to have faculty help in building the bridges of understanding
which we so badly needed during the decade. At our flickering best
we did not have the heavy faculty involvement in handling conflict
which was true at Princeton and MIT. This is not an indictment, or if
so it cuts both ways; the administration did not succeed in attracting
heavy faculty support in resolving these major problems—or at least
in sharing them, since many were not available for solution at the
moment.

Perhaps it is accurate to say that all of us shared a position. We
were riding down the swift river of events together, and none of us
knew what was around the next bend. Then those of us in the demolition and repair squad got off and went to work, while the faculty
kept the raft going. It was a fair division of labor, even though it
made for a degree of tension whenever each group needed all the
help it could get. Exactly at this point one of the great limitations
of the decade comes clear; it was divisive quite beyond the differences of opinion and approach which I have described. There was
simply not time to deal with the crises, and the steady unrest between crises, and at the same time do justice to the total community
of relationships between faculty and administration. These relationships were one of the great casualties of the decade—not just at
Duke but on virtually every campus. As I look back, I deeply regret
all those things which could not be done to build that community

and to give it that quality of amity which it should have had under better conditions. And perhaps I felt it most keenly because I was, after all, a teaching member of the faculty. I never accepted the alienation from my peers which the sixties brought about.

Yale: Oh, Brave New World

This loss of comfortable community between the president and the faculty was broadly experienced in the sixties. If it was not as evident at Princeton as at Duke, it was probably far more so at Yale —and this despite an unusual adherence of community and a high degree of formal support for Kingman Brewster, the president. Yale provides a fascinating pattern of behavior during the 1960s. Despite its emergence as a university of world caliber, the inward and parochial quality of the university persisted, for both good and bad. Certainly there was no longer the self-satisfaction which led the senior faculty (The Fellows of Yale College in New Haven, as they were legally named) to reject the college plan when Edward Harkness first offered it to Yale in the 1920s. But without the extreme oligarchy of the Harvard governing body, the Yale Corporation was closely knit, composed solely of Yale graduates, and certainly devoted to the mystique of the place fully as much as to the wider issues of education and the national commitments which were so striking an aspect of the postwar years in the country.

Against this background the bold developments of the 1960s seem all the more striking. For they run right across the structure of the university, from a bold investments policy (doomed to disaster at the end of the decade) to a major reshaping of admissions—of what constituted a Yale man, to use one of the favorite phrases in which the mystique was embodied—to an emphasis on social preoccupations, with William Sloane Coffin, the university chaplain, as one of its main architects.

This last characteristic of the period was no sudden event, however. Built into the Yale tradition was a strong element of the Christian social gospel—far stronger than at any other of the Ivy League universities. Sidney Lovett, the university chaplain for many years and Bill Coffin's predecessor, was a man of remarkable and active piety whose influence was felt strongly by many student generations —my own included. A pacifist when it was truly uncomfortable to be one, a defender of minorities in the university before it even had a black minority, he was a stellar example of an attitude at Yale which would not be lightly set aside in a time of trouble.

At the same time—and this was equally important in the Yale pattern—Sid Lovett's connections within the university were, like Bill Coffin's, as impeccable as his moral sense. When the voices of dissent came in the sixties, then, they came from the establishment itself and would be supported by members of the Yale Corporation who might disagree profoundly with Bill Coffin or Kingman Brewster but would not turn publicly and destructively against them. It takes nothing away from the integrity of either man to say that he could maintain his opinions and survive at Yale, while this same reasoned extremism would have found few trustee defenders in most universities at the time.

This fact lent Yale a quality of daring, almost of trendiness, which was amply expressed in admissions and investments as well as in the university's policy toward black dissent, public demonstration, and violence at the Black Panther level. As a result, the turbulence at Yale worked in two quite disparate and antagonistic ways. Overt expression by the major movements on campus was guided, often co-opted, and tolerated during some very complex events by the university administration, which made its position by what it did not do quite as much as by what it did. At the same time an extremely powerful countercurrent of alumni opinion became embittered when alumni sons were passed over for admission, and angry to the point of withholding financial support as the public activities of the university became steadily more attractive to the media. Yale was on a roll, as bold in its spending of equity growth for current expenses as in its articulation of the most liberal views of social injustice. Kingman Brewster's remark that it would be impossible for the Black Panthers to get a fair trial anywhere in the United States was quite possibly true when he said it; it did not, however, suggest a fully balanced university approach to the problems of the decade.

Certainly, it *did* stand as the high water mark of self-criticism by a highly privileged university, and the rejection of what was scornfully described as establishment elitism. One could suggest that one cant phrase was replaced by another—smug elitism by radical chic.

I lay such stress on one strand in the permanent texture of Yale because it embodies a quality of mind and conscience which a great many secular-minded members of the Yale community could support. Further, the thrust of the major national movements meshed almost perfectly with this long-standing ethical bent. On many campuses the movements created the ethical structure which then supported them. At Yale it was already present. As a result, we see there, not the most violent events (though they were lurid enough), but one of the most searching considerations of the issues—and more specifically of the right of the aggressively alien members of society to a hearing and to a place within the social structure. One can question the wisdom of the extreme stance which resulted; one can doubt its long-term significance; but there is no question about the integrity of those who were so heavily involved in supporting it. And this can be said with special emphasis of the Yale Corporation, which gave unwavering support (at least in public) to an administration with which some of its members were seriously at odds during these years. Yale men have not been known over the years for their bold political positions, and many of them reacted quite resentfully to the official positions taken. There were substantial—if temporary— financial costs as graduates withheld their gifts, but the Corporation did not allow these to shape university policy. In their very firmness we see an aspect of the strength of a great private university which does not grow as much from its ethical awareness as from a profound sense of security about its own nature, its persona. If Yale chooses to espouse an unpopular cause—unpopular even with its own graduates—it is nonetheless still Yale, still the same organic institution. Many institutions tested their integrity during the decade; few of them carried the test so far; few of them had the inner cohesion which allowed it.

Administration: The Necessary Evil

The experience at Yale, Duke, Columbia, Berkeley makes clear what
was true of every major American campus. The senior administrators of those schools were called into question as never before. As
every faculty member will tell you, administrators are the hand-
maidens of the university. Most administrators would agree. But
while the faculty says it at some level of high policy, any good ad-
ministrator says it from demanding and often humbling experience.
Hard times only accentuate the limits and the importance of administrative work. Its three chief purposes must often be carried on
with flickering torches, though once in a while there are searchlights
pushing the sky.

Three chief purposes: good administration is concerned in a daily
way with keeping the enterprise afloat and moving well; in times
of crisis it is concerned with ways of meeting the unpredicted event
with vigor and understanding—involvement and yet detachment;
and at all times there shows in sound administration an overriding
sense of the place, what it is and how it might best develop. The
mix among these three changes every day, but unless all are there
the administration's work is incomplete and the university will soon
show up the weaknesses.

I speak of functions, not forms. There are many ways to put an administrative group together, and in difficult times no one can guarantee success. Beyond that truism, we found at Duke how necessary
a talent for improvisation was; but it was improvisation based on a
great deal of daily interaction among us. It is fair to say that we knew
who we were, and when we had to step into the unknown we could
do it with a good deal of confidence in one another. I will take the
observation a step further, indeed. Our administrative style was one
of constant interaction, so that we were used to working on problems
as a task force, not as a group whose diverse functions kept us apart.
We shared our turf.

To say this suggests that we were problem-solvers, rather than
academic maintenance men. None of us would claim that we were
always successful when the problems came along, but we were oriented toward them. Our success at developing the new programs and

projects of the decade shows where our hearts lay, and we brought the same attitude to the critical, unforeseen days and nights of special activity. A reading of the detailed documents which record the actions of the Vigil and the Allen Building occupation show the selfless and highly professional skill of the administrative group.

I can say this with no self-congratulation, because I was not in charge of the successful evolution of the Vigil; and during the whole Allen Building episode I was responsible only for certain major decisions, not for their weeks-long and highly effective execution. This position reflects a vital, general characteristic of the president's role during the period—and not just at Duke. He was the lightning rod and—where a decision could be made at all—he decided the path of action. Those two crucial functions kept him from almost every other role; the credit for the effective resolution of issues and situations must go to his colleagues.

There is one great danger in this relationship between the president and his close associates. When the times are rough, decisions are by no means always right; and when they come under heavy criticism, there is an unlovely but very human desire to seek shelter. Among sophisticated people this primal instinct often takes the form of "distancing," of letting it be known that one was really not in agreement but that of course one's hands were tied. We see it constantly in national politics, and it can be devastating. I am proud to say that I never saw the slightest sign of this game among my colleagues; more important than this loyalty to me was their loyalty to the university, and that is why Duke moved along so well in the interregnum after my departure. I remember clearly in those last weeks before my resignation that I warned the others to keep their distance from me, but they did not do it, nor make my role more painful by any word or action. I am proud now to pay them this highest of compliments; they richly deserve it, and the university owes them a great deal for their steadfastness.

Since I was far from alone in this dark experience, one general question deserves an answer: why did so many college and university presidents come to grief? The answer is bound up with the special nature of the position. Given the elaborate checks and balances of an academic community, the president's position is quite different from that of the chief executive in any other major organization. Put most nakedly, he has authority but not power. The board of trustees has the ultimate authority, of course; it is the incorporator and the continuing legal entity. Similarly, the senior faculty has authority over what is taught, who is to teach it, and whom it is taught to. The alumni and other major supporters of the institution may not have direct stated authority, but they have constant and profound influence on the direction which is to be taken. Students commonly exercise their influence still more indirectly, but they have seldom been the mere passive recipients of what the place has to offer. They set its tone just as surely as the faculty does, and far more visibly. The president acts in constant relation to all these groups, but he controls none of them.

He is often a voting member of the board, but not always. He often has faculty rank, if his background makes that plausible. But he serves without tenure, at the pleasure of his board, and his job is one of interpretation and mediation among the major constituents. He has as much effective authority as they choose to allow him, and no more. Autocratic university presidents are the stuff of legend, of course, but anyone who tried to imitate Eliot or Wriston in the 1950s and 1960s would have had a short and merry tenure indeed. Administrative style in colleges and universities could no longer be patterned on clerical authority, which had given a kind of crypto-sanction to the autocracy of that generation of men who succeeded the clerical generations and borrowed much of their aura and their approach to the exercise of power. By our time one had to persuade, to articulate, to attempt leadership without command.

As matters stood in 1960, this position was a very definite balancing act, but a feasible one most of the time. There was room to build a consensus, to organize the parade. The latent weaknesses of the president's office were hardly visible, in good part because the position seemed as an occupation to be highly and uncritically respected. Much of this respect was paid to the outward show of things, some to the economic power which the institutions were coming to possess, and some was a true respect for the life of the mind which the president was assumed to symbolize. I must say that I adopted this latter stance toward the job in an unskeptical and probably quite romantic way. I *believed* in it, if you will, just as many of my peers did. We took our job to be (among other duties) the articulation of the civilized life. That was the particular discipline of mind appropriate to our office and title; and if we thought too well of ourselves at times we excused it because we saw ourselves and our institutions as custodians of the great Western tradition of learning and civility. We did not settle for the genteel tradition but tried to include it in larger and deeper definitions of the educated life.

Since we saw the world in this way, we naturally operated within the collegial system of governance; and those around us certainly watched sharply to make sure that we did so. (I thought I learned some agility of mind teaching the veterans who returned to Yale in the late 1940s, but I had my graduate course in intellectual sword-play when I chaired faculty meetings at Lawrence.) The consent of one's peers was put to the test every day, and as long as external pressures on the institution were not relentless, it was a balanced system which worked remarkably well. By the very nature of its success, however, the system put the president in jeopardy. He was to be doubly vulnerable to the pressures of an unstable time, and neither he nor anyone else was aware of the fact. I say doubly vulnerable because the president, if successful, was so thoroughly a part of the mores of his institution; he partook of that openness and respect for civility which I have already described. At the same time, as we have just seen, his position itself was defined in such a way that he could not step into a new and sterner role when the times suddenly demanded it. He came up against the limits of his power, just as all the other leaders of the time did, but in a distinctive way which kept him part of the university world even while he was being pilloried for his failure to be someone else, operating with quite different sanctions and kinds of leverage.

He was neither a general nor a demagogue, but he was often expected to be both. He embodied the dilemma of unsupported authority, and virtually none of those who were pressing him this way or that recognized his position. The result for him was a high degree of bafflement and frustration, a constant sense that events were moving beyond him, and certainly out of his control. This same sense came in one form or another to all the others who tried to exercise their power during the period, but the university president was never in any doubt about it, and for one vitally important reason. The other authority figures exercised power by bringing it to bear directly on some major preoccupation of the decade. The university president had these preoccupations brought home to him as his institution became involved in them. The issues of university governance which came to take up so much of his time were an internal echo of far larger external questions. But the university president was often concerned with the impact of them on his institution rather than with their significance in themselves.

In this way he was seeing and living the issues of the time inside out, which only added to his difficulties as he tried to deal with the partisans of this issue or that. His concern had to be finally for the integrity of his university, so that each of the major issues wore a special face for him. It became the *university* black or women's movement, the *university* drug scene or new left rally. As I have pointed out, the university was the center and origin of none of these major concerns of the time. Since they were all alive in it and became aspects of it, however, they were a major part of the president's puzzle. It did not matter whether they fitted the idea of a university as he saw it; he no longer had the privilege of freedom in that or any other aspect of his professional life.

I hope that there is no retrospective self-pity involved in this brief analysis of the university president's special position of powerlessness. Whatever I felt in 1969, the dilemmas of the time are clear to me now. My chief emotion is one of great surprise that my colleagues and I managed to get any of the proper work of the place accomplished. The means of influence available to us were so transparently inadequate to the needs of the time; and, pace Mr. Hayakawa and Mr. Reagan, the techniques used at San Francisco State were not only less than adequate but in their repression were a major threat to the university they were supposed to save. We were often overwhelmed, but most of us did not betray our universities in the effort to assert power.

The San Francisco State of Mind

San Francisco State University deserves a special comment, as a mirror of the presidency, if nothing else. In the 1960s it was one of the most volatile places in the country. It shared little with Berkeley intellectually, and almost nothing in economic privilege. But it did share a region noted for its diversities of style and conviction, a sense of necessary university freedom, and after January 1, 1968, a governor who had run on a platform of "clearing up the mess in the universities." In my sketch of Berkeley I commented on the cynical politics behind this campaign. San Francisco State had the added dimension of a politically oriented chancellor of the state system. He could be counted on not only to echo the governor, but to amplify him.

Fortunately for our sense of the action and what lay behind it, John Summerskill, president from 1968 to 1970, wrote a book about his venture. He has told me that he now sees it as highly imperfect, but as an immediate record of the meaning of the action there it is superb. The very things which are undigested, which come through in their raw state, are the ones we most need to know. And Summerskill was the ideal man to be a lightning rod for the issues surrounding the San Francisco State campus. A Canadian psychologist who had worked in the Cornell administration with a responsibility for minority recruiting and programs, he came as a determined liberal with an overriding and nonbureaucratic concern for the needs of students. His tone was blithe, direct, irreverent; his approach to the problems and needs of the university was nonpolitical and often impolitic. He was, in fact, a highly unlikely president for a campus which was a political pressure cooker; and that statement is meant as a high compliment.

For political machinations descended on the state of California like a plague of locusts. There was the orthodox political struggle for control of the state government which focused on control of the universities. As this control quickly showed a taste for punitive budget-cutting, it penetrated all of the other and less orthodox political issues alive inside the universities. These issues were in part those already familiar to us, since they included those arising from the major movements of the decade. They were compounded, however, by the location of San Francisco State and the nature of its student body. It is not unfair to say that the force of these movements was squared by the high concentration in San Francisco of those who had come there precisely because they were deeply disaffected and alienated from mainstream thought on almost every subject. By and large these immigrants were not students, but they were often on campus and interacted constantly with its students.

These students were largely local and therefore urban as well as relatively underprivileged. They were several years older than the usual run of undergraduates; most had to support themselves in the community, so that they lived constantly with its tensions, its eccentricities, its extremes of behavior. As a result, the campus of the university was the city of San Francisco; there was no clear boundary between them. In more "normal" times this could be a great asset. In times of disturbance, however, this intimacy could be turned against the university; its constituents (the press and the commercial power structure, for example) would quickly become antagonistic critics. They would add still another level of political activism to what was already a witches' brew of contending issues and ideologies. Somehow in the midst of it all an educational enterprise was supposed to sustain itself.

More than that. The administration and faculty were supposed to sustain it, to have the freedom to exercise their responsibility. Instead, the administrators were subjected to constant harassment at every level, and a significant portion of the faculty joined in the attacks. If the pressure from governor, chancellor, press, and community had not existed, there would still have been the students. Given their strong and diverse allegiances, they were often at war with one another. When they and the nonstudents put on a campus spectacle, it was news right across the state. The university was obviously a scapegoat for the rest of the state university system. And, while we can say that everyone got an education of sorts out of the tumult, it was not exactly what the course of study committee had in mind.

Viewed from this distance, the chief responsibility of its officers was to keep the university alive. I cannot think of a place where the

challenges to survival took more bizarre forms. Whether it was a
sit-in, an announced nude race across the central campus (so that
the photographers would surely be present), or a demand for special
kinds of black student privilege, it was carried out with passionate
intensity and flair. This put the president in constant peril; he never
knew what was coming next (despite a surprisingly good intelligence
system) but only that it would come. And John Summerskill's particular way of dealing with this constant bombardment also put him
in peril of another kind. His operating stance was a fusion of sweet
logic and passionate conviction, presented constantly and publicly.
Nothing was hidden, and no devious administrative games were
played.

This may make him sound naive in his approach to the problems.
The conclusion would not be just; instead, one should recognize that
he was ingenuous and uncalculating to an extreme degree. We have
seen that the setting and the constituencies of the university made
for constant turmoil at one level; at another we have the fact that
the president was adding to the turmoil by the very honesty of his
attempts to deal with it. We see here in extreme form a major truism
of the decade—a major landmark in looking-glass land. Often the
steps away from the quicksand only led us deeper into it. Most of us
tried, at least, to act in a cannier way than Summerskill—not better
in any ethical sense but cannier. We did not confront the governor so
openly, we took refuge at times in a little official silence, we tried to
paper over our unpopular decisions; at times we took the mugwump
route in dealing with a particularly unpleasant issue. All to no avail.
Most of us did not have to suffer the indignity of a successor whose
chief instrument of education was a bullhorn, but we were as deep
in the quicksand as Summerskill. He simply got there with a good
deal more style and naked integrity.

Duke at the End of the Decade

There was no easy tranquility for San Francisco State after John
Summerskill resigned. The university moved on to S. I. Hayakawa's
flamboyant tenure and did not change its basic nature or maneuver past its unresolved problems. In this it followed a clear and by

now familiar pattern. American universities reacted in characteristic ways to the 1960s—ways which one might call genetically determined by their organic growth up to that time. It is also clear that they were likely to use in equally individual ways what they had learned from the period. I hope that it will not seem self-serving if I say that when I look at Duke I feel, first, that the damage done was far less than in many other places; and, second, that the gains in insight and ethical awareness were far greater.

When I say the *damage done* it is an intense relief, even after twenty years, to remember that no lives were lost, no buildings burnt, and no basic university purposes distorted beyond recovery. The damage came in a slowing of the university's educational effort, in a tone of combativeness which marred a good many individual relationships, and in the disaffection of several of Duke's outer constituencies. These were serious matters, certainly, and the damage took some little time to repair. One characteristic of the 1970s helped greatly, however. When the major movements collapsed or became heavily muted, there was such a sense of relief in many people that flagging efforts in a number of areas revived very quickly.

Inevitably, I think in this connection of the fund drive. I am sure that my own departure helped revive it, just as my presence had generated it in the first place. A year's interregnum with highly respected senior administrators in charge also did a good deal. And Terry Sanford's benign arrival helped greatly to set the tone of the campus straight again. Above all, of course, the major shift in national attitude toward the war in Vietnam eliminated a major cause of disaffection; and many of the dissident attitudes and movements no longer found shelter and support from that massive discontent. Duke benefited greatly. The new sense of ease and relief allowed the university to see itself clearly again.

As a result, it became possible to understand the sixties in a positive rather than a negative way. My concern is not with the 1970s, however, but rather with those recognitions of achievement which can now be understood and properly measured, not only by me but by all of us who are willing to look back with loving concern. To put it most bluntly, the university grew up; in several major areas of concern it became a different and far less complacent place. Even to resist one of the major movements was a great cure for comfortable inertia. (I think, for example, of a prominent alumnus with pronounced feelings about the place of black students in the university. His outrageous lobbying for his views was certainly a sign of his concern, and I hope that in the long run his loyalty to Duke may have been enhanced by his very anger.)

I see this same concern, this same loyalty, in students who disagreed almost totally with such alumni in their attitudes toward race relationships and their greatly increased social awareness. This increased sensitivity was shared, of course, by many members of the faculty, administration, and board of trustees. When you add to this the catalyst of Terry Sanford's social activism, it becomes clear that the sixties were a preparation for the policy planning groups, the bioethical controversies, the ecological puzzles, and the black women members of the security force. What might have seemed far-out, irrelevant, or downright impossible has become normal and accepted in the face of today's attitudes and major issues.

To say this is to imply that the university was in a vigorous state at the end of the sixties. The stresses of the moment tended to obscure this fact for many in each of Duke's major constituencies; the simple truth of the matter is that its critics were more agitated than the student heart of the place. By the end of the decade a large number of the elders were confused and alienated. As a result, we faced the often repeated charge that there had been too little discipline, that Duke had become permissive to a dangerous degree. This was in fact a projection onto the university of criticisms which grew from a general sense of discomfort rather than from a careful observation of what had been going on at Duke. What was taken as extreme behavior was often little more than extreme rhetoric; and the concerns of students were in any case not only genuine but rooted in the major ethical issues of the time.

As we compare Duke with the array of institutions I have briefly discussed, we can see its distinctive position. External criticism was, in the short term, as severe with us as that at Columbia or Cornell, which had in fact far more profound problems to deal with. We did not, of course, have the external political pressure which added so much to the burdens of Berkeley and San Francisco State. At the

same time we did not have the degree of inner coherence which was
evident at Princeton and MIT and contributed so much to their mas-
terful handling of issues as they emerged. Yale and Wesleyan were
special cases in many ways, of course, since they both took aggressive positions which created within them a type of submovement not
seen in the "official" position of most other institutions. We had a
position at Duke, indeed, but it was devoted rather to the most sympathetic and evenhanded treatment of issues and movements rather
than to an attempt at leading and guiding them. As a result, it is
fair to say that the issues themselves provoked extreme responses
from our constituencies, and that our own attempts to avoid these
extremes were largely misunderstood.

We were seen to be weak where in fact we were strong in maintaining the essential civility of attitude which is at the absolute center of university life. Whenever the times become strident this way
of life is challenged and put at risk. I can see in retrospect many
points at which we were not ahead of situations because we did not
anticipate their full destructive intensity. Our powers of response
were often amateurish; we did not bring a highly coordinated and
broadly based organization to bear where it might have helped us.
We never gave up our faith in students, however, nor did we feel it
appropriate to match the extremes of the young by a kind of reactive
hysteria on the part of their elders. I am proud of this fact. It was
a hard position to maintain, but it kept the scars of the time to an
absolute minimum.

The Curve of Power: University Style

The individual experience of Duke during the sixties was compounded, then, of harsh encounters and hard-won progress in the
university's central purposes. It is important to see that experience
in its context, however, a pattern which also includes the other institutions I have discussed in capsule form. In the preceding chapter
I discussed the pattern which I saw each of the major movements
follow during the 1960s, a pattern of growth, climax, and decline
with many mutations but this one great similarity. I suggested further that I saw this pattern in the prosecution of the war and in

the responsive changes of attitude in such mainstream organizations as the Episcopal church. But what of the universities? They were more heavily exposed to the major cycles of action than any other institutions. Did this create in them, almost by resonance, a similar wave pattern? And if it was there, how did it differ from the pattern of the movements?

First of all, the pattern was in good part reactive. The activist movements came on stage and almost immediately discovered that the universities were ideal theaters. The thought which initiated these movements was not university thought in any organized way; but the universities were vital both because they provided members for the movements and because their own freedom of order permitted so much room for discussion and action. As a result, we see in every university (at least in those which I know in any detail) a kind of double life. The major concerns and responsibilities continued, but they were colored, modified, and at times reshaped by the activities of a shadow university of other concerns and preoccupations which constantly penetrated the basic ongoing life of each place. The pattern is evident in each of the major events in Duke's life at the time, and a detailed look at any of the other universities would show constant analogues to our experience. It was this doubleness, this interaction, which created such seeming confusion in the daily life of the universities.

With the perspective of time, however, we can recognize that the most important single characteristic of the universities was the persistence of their basic natures in the face of so much distracting activity. As a result, their curve of action was quite unlike that of the major movements—with the exception of the women's movement. It must be seen as one segment in a far greater continuity of university purposes. Many things happened through the movements which were important for the universities, but they did not redefine the universities' central sense of purpose. Often events threw light on a weakness, but the weakness like the strength was already there —ready to be recodified by the movement but not initiated by it.

Once we recognize this characteristic, the real relation between the universities and the movements becomes clear. It was reciprocal. Just as the movements were not centered in the university world,

so the universities were never defined by the strident activity of
the movements. This distance, this tension, between university and
movement was often obscured by the fact that they inhabited one
space at one time. Its real nature was also obscured by the radical
differences of tempo. The suddenness, the constant *now*, of several
of the major movements often made the pace of university life seem
nearly static—not pace at all. One consequence was that the universities were often on the defensive; this defensiveness further blurred
the true movements of change within the universities themselves.

And so we have a complex interweaving of purposes, of curves
of growth and decline among the movements, of change and yet
persistence in the basic direction of the universities. Certainly, they
were changed by the events of the decade: in curriculum, in social
responsibility (public policy or biomedical ethics), in the recognized
place of students in university governance. As a striking proof of
their deliberate tempo, however, these changes showed themselves
over a long course of time extending into the 1980s. Educationists
who wrote about these matters were often hasty in seeing or imagin-
ing change, but the universities were far more deliberate in bringing
it about.

To Push Back the Walls

What then came of this turbulent time for the deeply involved universities? Just as each school experienced the issues and traumas of
the sixties in a way shaped by its own ethos, so the permanent contribution of the time (so far as there was one) was shaped and made
familiar by the soil of its habitat. I doubt that Harvard was moved in
any significant way; Yale took most of the next decade to recover. MIT
was not swerved from its course, while Berkeley—and even more the
city around it—would not be the same again.

And what of Duke? I am surprised at the conclusion I have
reached. Its course of development during the decade was a curious twin to the major movements and the events which flowed from
them. In both these aspects of the university's life there were new
experiences, new ways of looking, and consequences not to be re-
versed. This was as true for the individuals involved as for the uni-

versity's total organism. As a result, the 1960s were a truly creative time, even for those who most bitterly resisted the course of events. Certainly, I had no glimmer of this at the time; I was far too busy with the daily adventures to make any rational sense of the pattern. It is coming clear only now, but there is no doubt of its reality.

There were three major aspects to the growth and increasing maturity of the period. The first was individual and personal; recent conversations with students of that time indicate the illumination they found, the discovery of major issues and the thoughtful participation in their expression and resolution. And this was true, not only of the undergraduates but of certain informed trustees as well as those of us in senior administrative jobs. At times it seemed as though we were in a constant state of defense and confrontation, but that would be a false view of a complex reality. Even in times of student disagreement we were developing a sense of major national issues which we had not known at the decade's start. As I indicated in the introductory section of this book, the concerns of the sixties were all present in embryo, but invisible, unperceived.

As the movements unfolded, so did our awareness of the great issues. I can speak for myself, at least, when I say that we altered our basic mind-set during the decade. When the movements faded at the end of it, our awareness did not; we used our changed insight in less stressful times. As a result the seventies, which seem in some ways like a mere reaction of weariness, were a time of confirmation for those of us who had taken our sixties' learning seriously. The emergence of a conservative political force was only one side of reality, and one which in fact had its origins at least as far back as the 1950s. For many of us, the individual changes had consequences which were to show themselves fully only in the 1980s.

For Duke as a whole, the most important thing to recognize is the steady development of its major and legitimate concerns, the ones which were there quite apart from the special texture of the decade, while they owed certain important elements of their achievement to those years. It is clear from my discussion of individual events that we were in fact bringing together the legitimate inner purposes of the university and the outer events which at times seemed to run counter to our purposes. Even decisions as tangential as my resignation from a country club were in fact recognitions of the position which was appropriate for the "public university" as an organization whose stance was a significant witness. There was no neutral ground; to turn away from the question would make the wrong statement. We were in fact establishing a new persona for the university. It was painful, it was bitterly opposed by many, but it endured; and Duke acquired a public stature quite beyond any which it had known before. That is a large claim, but the history of the university in the succeeding years was to bear it out.

Continuums of Change: From the Sixties into the Eighties

Once we grant that the pace and stress of the sixties could not be maintained—and were not—a new issue emerges. It is an appropriate final one for this book. What did remain? What were the continuities, and how did they show themselves? How does our perception of the sixties help us understand what we are coping with now? Does our experience then make it more possible for us to define the issues of policy and purpose which lie ahead?

These are large questions, but I shall try to keep them from turning pretentious. Their very variety and oddity may help us, for we shall be looking not only at continuities of a familiar and positive sort, but at a good many which express themselves by contraries, in conflict or confrontation. Some are virtually hidden by superficial change; the old issues will wear a new cloak. Though these are large and urgent continuities, furthermore, we are in the midst of them and cannot be sure where they will take us. The most obvious skill we should have learned from the sixties, after all, is a capacity to deal with the unexpected, not only in action but in result. And there is a good deal of the unexpected in the issues of the eighties.

To speak so is already to raise an interesting question: What about the seventies? Why do I give my final attention to periods which are separated by a decade? The full answer to that question is in a sense my subject. The sixties and eighties demand discussion together because they are dynamic, question-raising, and outrageous times. It will be my purpose to show that they are also blood brothers, and the seventies were a distant cousin.

The evidence for that statement hits us at the start of the seventies and is reinforced by some of the dismal events which followed
in rapid succession. Without calling it, as Auden called the 1930s,
"a low, dishonest decade," we see all too clearly the disenchant-
ment and collapse of purpose at the beginning of the decade. A
multiyear study done by Louis Harris Associates dealing with public
confidence in major social institutions shows a sharp drop in every
category between 1966 and 1971. This is particularly important and
revealing because these are not the young radicals expressing themselves about LBJ, but a balanced range of citizens looking at the
institutions with which and in which they live (Bowen and Schus-
ter, p. 132). These figures suggest a loss of confidence across the
board, and they also imply a loss of *self*-confidence. That loss put its
stamp on the decade and was confirmed not only by Watergate and
the empty presidency which followed but by the inability of Jimmy
Carter to rouse any national interest in those questions of basic value
which were of such deep concern to him. We acknowledge all of this
and more when we speak of the self-concern, the turning away from
major issues, the acceptance of a diminished view of the possible,
and the attempt to obliterate much that was insistent and demanding in the sixties—the war, the assassinations, the efforts to remake
society. As events had conspired to heighten our experience in the
sixties, they seemed determined to dull it in the seventies. We did
not want to be fully engaged; we refused to be caught up in events
and issues. And we showed little desire for passionate public disagreements.

We gradually recovered from this "lethargy by consent." Groups
and attitudes which had quietly been building their strength showed
it publicly in the election of 1980. The tides were running hard
in some new directions—but directions with an intimate relationship in both style and substance to the major patterns of the sixties.
Superficially, the relation often looked like one of opposites, but (as
we shall see in some detail) it was and is a good deal more. This
decade, like the sixties, is given to open and often acrimonious dis-
pute. Opinion is sharply expressed and sharply countered; the fact
that we have become a far more conservative society for the moment
should not obscure the deeper similarity. Backlash, after all, has to

be related to the situation which it opposes, and when we combine this energy with the openness in discussion which the sixties almost forced upon us, we have a dynamic environment for addressing a whole range of major issues.

There is an even more striking relationship between the decades. The sixties were prophetic in their concerns. The mode of their assertion was often and obviously extreme, but they anticipated many of our unresolved issues in the eighties. This does not mean, of course, that everything we worry about now was present twenty years ago (though a great deal was) but that the encounters and disputes of the sixties prepared us to address these issues today. We were pointed toward them, though many of the issues did not loom then as they do now. The image which comes to mind is that of a distant range of mountains; they were a backdrop to immediate struggles along the road, and if we lifted up our heads we might say: "the real issues are there; the road leads us toward them." But in the heat and fever of the day we had little time to speculate until we found ourselves in that same mountain country.

A specific use of this metaphor will prove its reality. Certain issues were presented, made available to us by the sixties, often in grotesque or covert ways. The drug-use problem, for instance, showed up as a faraway province—either the domain of the beat and the hip, or the rumored escape route of the military in Vietnam. These may seem like a far cry from today's monster problem, just as in another sense they were remote from most of us in the sixties. But the line of relationship is close and inescapable. Not only were we acclimated to the drug world by the sixties, but returning veterans helped provide the underworld with a broad enough base so that the full drug culture could emerge. Vietnam even built a cadre of drug mercenaries, just as it created leadership for the private and guerrilla armies of today. At the start of the decade this incubus was barely alive in our society; by the end of the decade it was bearing down on us, and now we are deep in the country we had only glimpsed before.

At the other end of our spectrum of ethical concerns today, environmental issues are as urgent as the drug problem. Different from the drug problem in almost every way, these environmental problems too must be mastered before they master us. And the sixties gave birth to our public sense of urgency. Certainly the environment was already in trouble before 1960, but for the most part we did not know it. It is in fact fair to say that most of those causing the corrosive pollution did not think about its future hazards. If drugs were a by-product of a turbulent and violent time, pollution on a massive scale was a by-product of an affluent and product-oriented one. Our passionate, almost amorous response to the chemical wonders of the postwar period intensified and concentrated problems of very long standing. The disposal of our own waste products had never been seen as a major issue, given the great expanses of the country. As a result, we acted with real abandon even in our most densely populated state, New Jersey, while the hazardous wastes quietly took over hundreds of dumping areas in it.

The emergence of a heavy concern for this problem in the sixties is fascinating, because it came to us obliquely and as a result of the nature-oriented preoccupations of some of the alternate life-styles. The speakers for those movements set out to make a statement about the artifice and materialism of our society, and in the process they tripped over the rubbish heaps which had made the glitter possible. Starting with one cause, they found themselves inhabiting two, and the second was the more compelling. Millions of people who would never light a campfire or bake their own bread were suddenly alerted to poisoned drinking water, dying lakes and rivers, blighted forests. The voices may have been extreme, but the problem was real. And, again like the drug issue, it has grown monstrously in scope as we have moved closer to an understanding of it.

The voices of the sixties were equally prophetic when they dealt with issues of social and political debate. These voices were of two sorts: first, those concerned about particular issues—both those living them and those deeply concerned about them; and second, the voices of the issues themselves—growing inflation and chronic deficits, to name only two. In each of these cases we see that the major questions were not at all what they would become, but their tone and direction were set in the sixties. Most of all, an awareness of these issues was so firmly fixed in the general mind that it did not need to be reestablished when its underlying character became important to us in the eighties. Debate over the status of blacks and women quickly became more than debate in the sixties. Like the other major concerns of the time, it turned from argument into action, and often lost a good deal of support in the process. Important for us here is the fact that the concerns were established, legitimized if you will, by the sheer pressure of the attention they received. Those directly involved drew many of the rest of us into their arena; we did not resolve the questions then, but we were prepared to give the trials and dilemmas of these movements our attention in the eighties.

Issues as massive as inflation or chronic deficits demand from us a different, less personal sense of the word *prophetic*. The events of that time foreshadowed them, in fact created that double burden for the politics and economics of the eighties. It was a curious aspect of the sixties that we were responsive to so many issues but did not remember the obvious historical lesson that wars cost a great deal more than blood, and that the boom time was both artificial and destructive, the product of the war and not a great step forward. This relentless sequence was prophecy of the grimmest sort, the shape of things to come already present. These would become issues for social and political debate, but quite apart from that they would become brute facts of life.

Issues of foreign policy were as crucial for the future as these domestic questions. Since the Vietnam War raised almost for the first time in our history a question about the rightness of our position, it also raised major questions about our future international posture. There would be the inevitable reaction, so clear in the seventies, where one facet of the dullness of the time was a with-drawal from international involvements. (And even when such involvements were forced on us, as in Iran, they summoned up only endurance or resentment rather than any positive response.) Then would come the echoing challenge of Nicaragua, where we were forced to ask again the same questions we had not clearly answered in the sixties. The edge of our current debates is kept sharp by the whetstone of Vietnam, and no statement that the situations are different can successfully put down the fact that the motives underlying our posture and policy then and now are the same. The line of continuity between the decades is all too clear; our attempts to brush it aside merely confirm the fact.

The most personal continuum between the decades stands in bold contrast to these massive questions. It is the assertion of the person, the small group, the society redefined in ways which make it available for direct experience again. The inward-turning quality of the seventies was in this way not a break with the sixties but an emphasis on one aspect of the many-sided assertiveness that preceded it. It was a mere interval between the outbursts of the sixties and the group conflicts which—as we can now begin to see—are making the eighties as contentious and divided a time as the earlier decade. This quality in our present will be discussed in more detail shortly. Here, we should simply recognize that we are now living in an atmosphere of divisiveness at the personal and small-group levels. I suspect, indeed, that we see this decade as being much less unruly and disrupted than it really is, for the simple reason that so many of us have been there before. (There are more political reasons, of course; if you are constantly told that you have returned to the old-fashioned America of peace and plenty, it may take a few years to recognize that what is really going on is quite different.)

This quality of foreshadowing which I call prophetic is, of course, only one aspect of the continuum of concerns which flows from the sixties into our present decade. In the sections which follow I shall be concerned first with continuity and change in social groups and organizations, then with the foci of continuing debate which interact with the major social organizations to create a pattern for our social structure. Out of that analysis will come my concluding section, which considers the questions of value animating us now—and in their stubborn importance likely to be with us for years to come.

The current positions of the major groups and movements of the sixties are striking for the changes which have taken place in them. The women's movement, for example, is—as it has been for 150 years—too strong to put down; but there have been major shifts of emphasis if not of direction. As we saw in the 1970s, success brought with it a certain turning away from the intensity which put such a stamp on the sixties. This deflation was intensified, of course, by the reactionary backlash which led to the defeat of the ERA. A weak movement would have felt that as a major setback; to the tough-minded women of NOW it seemed to provide a rallying cry.

And in any case the intensity of the women's movement is not the heart of the matter today. It is rash for a man to say this, but it seems to me that the solid accomplishments of the women's movement are so many, and the acceptance of them so matter-of-fact, that they constitute a major rebuke to the right-wing attempts at demolition. I do not want to make progress seem easy; in contrast to the sixties it sometimes seems pedestrian and painfully slow. In pay scales and in access to senior positions, there is still a good deal to accomplish. At the same time the success of women in major political contests has been enhanced by the fact that in most cases they succeed without a major emphasis on gender; there is in almost every case a balance of women and men who vote them into office. That one fact is perhaps more significant than any formal cause or public affirmation.

Further, most of the women voted into office are not political monsters, careerists who have sacrificed everything to their calling. Married and with a statistically average number of children, they are a remarkable testimony to second careers in today's society. We are keeping our vigor longer, and it is becoming clear that this makes major new achievements possible, together with a family, for women in their fifties and sixties. (This seems to be one viable alternative to the career woman who today marries and has children much later than twenty or thirty years ago.) The whole pattern of these lives is a clear extension and exploration of the convictions so passionately asserted during the sixties. If the tempo is down, the affirmation is not, and the achievements are clearer by the year. Women are penalized unfairly by the slow career advancement of the whole generation now moving into middle age, and they have not yet established themselves in the academic world (for one) as their talent and numbers demand. Despite these shortfalls, however, the achievements of the sixties are certainly an integral part of the improved position of women today.

The same cannot be said—at least in any clear-cut way—about the current position of blacks. The efforts of the sixties, for all their passionate and often tragic affirmations, have not issued in any full continuity of accomplishment—or even opportunity. The educational collapse which in fact we now see is obscured by the brilliant athletes, the compelling and perceptive news people, the bright minds in business school and beyond, the powerful place occupied by blacks in urban politics. The recognition they receive is real, remarkable, and long overdue. Yet the larger reality is somber, and it shows up most clearly once we get away from the privileged and gifted few. Unemployment rates for young blacks are disturbingly high, and they are matched by the declining numbers going to college. The single-parent family, which came to us straight from the social arrangements of slavery, is still a major pattern and a major problem. These are the intractable black realities of the eighties, as they were of the sixties. Why has improvement been so difficult?

An answer may lie in the emphasis and direction given to these issues during the 1960s. They may have been major problems, but they were not central to the rhetoric of the time, and the rhetoric set much of the agenda. It pointed us to issues of identity—political, personal, social. Of all the dreams of the decade this was the most poignant; it was also doomed to failure by the extremes of its own expression. Much more profoundly, however, it was doomed because these questions of place and identity were not the central ones. Black power was an understandable rallying cry, but the separation it implied gave support to the very people opposed to the mainstream integration of blacks. Many of the difficulties being put in the way of black opportunity today result directly from the opening given to bigots by the excesses of black activism. To say this takes nothing from the vital purposes of that black assertion; it merely points up the difficulty faced in solving the savage puzzle of blacks in American society.

As a prime example of that puzzle, take the place of blacks in predominantly white colleges and universities. Once the decision had been made and implemented that blacks should be actively recruited, there was a considerable feeling of relief. We were making progress, we felt; it might be slow, but for blacks with those degrees in hand society would open up and the rest would follow. The racial problem would gradually diminish and dissolve away to a memory. In fact, for an extremely limited number of blacks this solution worked. But it had two corollaries which we did not think about—and I speak quite personally when I say so.

First, this limited progress separated highly mobile blacks from their less fortunate fellows, and therefore it did virtually nothing to change the range of opportunity for the great mass of black society. Second, the chance for success is complicated by the persistent nature of that push for black identity which marked the sixties. There is a worldwide hunger for small-group identity today, and it is as strong as ever in the black society of the United States. Those fortunate few who have broken free are really living in two worlds— that of highly privileged white society and that of a questing, questioning black subculture. The black subculture maintains that quest with great style and flair; it does not have to settle for imitations of white success. But a profound dilemma remains for most blacks. They cannot use the standard American route of assimilation, at which we have done so well, nor are they one of those closely knit societies within our larger social fabric which sustain themselves by the strength of their inner cohesiveness. Black society does not have what the Chinese or Hassidic cultures have; its origins in this country have precluded that possibility. Even the tardy recognition of the great contributions to the larger life of the country which have always been made by blacks does not give us a remedy. It does point up the problem, however. The achievements against great odds tell us how much is wasted, and tell us also that the solution to the problem must be as indigenous as the difficulty itself.

We must recognize the essential difference between the issues raised by and for blacks and those which seem helpful—and have been for 150 years—in assimilating waves of white immigrants to the complex structure of American society. We have learned how to accommodate even those elements of the immigrant cultures which do not want to be assimilated—or should not be since they grow from the personal and religious core of those groups.

Our black citizens, on the other hand, are as old an immigrant group as the first white settlers. They came in bondage, however, leaving their own traditions and cultures behind; indeed, they were tumbled together from many diverse cultures. As a result, their own "American" culture has had to be built up, almost like a coral reef, from the millions of small and unknown contributions to self-awareness, to pride in accomplishment, to the beginnings of true self-esteem. That the assertion of these qualities in the 1960s could not accomplish miracles should surprise no one. That the failure of those assertions left a good deal of discouragement is equally clear, but it means that in the 1980s we must again address the questions of equity that have been raised so often. Recent attempts at denial by the Reagan administration seemed only to make more obvious the need for a wise attack on these bewildering issues. In this as in so much else the present decade has shown an antiphonal quality, resonating to the issues articulated twenty years ago without moving ahead with an effective response to them.

This lack of creative response is linked in turn to certain problems in our larger society which echo much that I have said about the position of blacks. The 1960s articulated some very substantial dreams of justice in the social order; the 1980s have given an odd shape to those dreams. As a society we seem less concerned now with social equity than with financial success. We have interests and standards which are expressed by a range of activities running from Lotto and the weekly numbers' drawing to the salaries in major athletics, entertainment, and business. All of these result from a particular quality in our social life which is not necessarily sinister in itself, but which has developed some disquieting overtones and implications. Money has become the focus of our attention in a new way and shows a much more abstract or symbolic emphasis than ever before. It is used to quantify one's luck, talent, or acumen; the amount is not necessarily related in a rational way to those qualities, however. It seems almost to work in reverse. If one hits a big jackpot, negotiates a huge contract, is paid a seven-figure salary, he is by definition worthy of our attention and often our adulation. The individual is still valued, but the individual is valued in this curious new way which depends on an enormous mass market—that is, on the contributions of an enormous number of other individuals.

It would be good socialist doctrine to suggest that these astonishing peaks of income—and the valleys of poverty which exist below them—are the clear result of a social order whose injustice is proven by the very fact that these gross inequities can exist at all. My own concern is quite different. These superstar incomes by themselves are only a small part of the problem, but our attitude of grudging adulation toward them may very well be the wrong way to go. I sus-

pect that it keeps us from thinking as critically as we should about
the basic structure of society, and this indifference is reinforced by
the huge publics which make these enormous rewards available. We
gain great individual pleasure from our part in these mass events,
but we may be dulled to deeper human and social needs which are
not reached by our current versions of bread and circuses.

One economic phenomenon of the eighties suggests all too clearly
how confused our patterns of value have become. The great game
of merger and acquisition being played at the moment by American
business is a remarkable spectacle. Seen from a distance, it creates
a picture of giants tossing mountains about. Looked at more closely,
it is a largely nonproductive enterprise which moves great amounts
of money into the hands of those who play the game most skillfully.
There is ample evidence that it has weakened a great many of the
industries which are chips in the pot, and so it has a damaging impact on society at large. Capitalism has betrayed itself here. The
purpose of capital acquisition ceases to be productivity and becomes
an end in itself. This destructive aspect of forced acquisition and
takeover is now seen quite clearly, but the remedies are themselves
often destructive, so that we have the dismal spectacle of American
industry, already under serious challenge from many other parts of
the world, busily tearing itself to pieces. And if we ask what attitudes and opportunities allow this to happen, we find that we are
right back with the major questions which the 1960s were asking. It
is curious indeed that we should now find in the most laissez-faire
aspects of our society these same issues of social health or infirmity
that the young radicals of the sixties were espousing. Yet the short-
sighted rapacity of the financial high rollers forces us to ask whether
anyone has a right to destroy the social structure—and in this case
the industrial structure—for private gain. That the new left scorned
that industrial structure is not the issue; the question of morality in
the workings of a capitalist society definitely is.

These questions of equity are garishly lit at the moment by a conservative thrust in politics which was carefully and quietly nurtured
during the seventies and—as all the world knows—has tried in the
last eight years to make the world safe for every kind of deregulated
activity. Mr. Reagan's sweeping move to the right, and the bold steps

taken to implement it, can be seen as a reaction to the extremes of
the sixties. More significantly, however, this rightward shift stands
as a major aspect of that continuity of extremes which binds the
two decades together. Just as the genuine issues of human rights
and individual hopes were forced upon us even in the most hysterical movements of that earlier time, so now these major questions
of economic health are forced upon us, even in the most naive extremes of supply-side optimism and blindness to the deficit burden.
The similarity with the sixties is one of tempo, and signs are beginning to appear that the same pattern of dream, explosive action, and
disillusion is about to be reenacted by the supply-siders and the anti-
tax-increase fanatics. The basic centrism—and common sense—of
American society asserted itself at the end of the sixties; it is now
showing itself again in the complex result of our recent elections.
This rhythm is only one aspect of social continuity between the decades, but it is striking that it should appear again in the political
ferment of these last years.

Perhaps the only other "continuity of extremes" to compare with
this political ferment is found in the Pentecostal religious movements. It is obviously no coincidence that these sects should largely
and intensively support the conservative political positions which
have recently been presented. The Reagan brand of politics seems to
be strongly populist (at least until one looks at the benefits flowing to
a privileged minority). Further, it preaches in secular idiom a strong
born-again gospel. The country is to be converted back to its own innocent days which the president invokes so amiably. Political oppor-
tunism brings the two movements together, but the rhetoric creates
a bond of familiarity, hope, and expectation between a small and
extremely powerful political group at the apex and a large cluster of
congregations throughout the country. The relationship constantly
threatens to get out of hand, but its power is undeniable.

Most fascinating and significant for my analysis, however, is the
parallel of expectations between these religious movements in the
eighties and several of the major cults of the sixties. Everything on
the surface is different: the communicants, the language, the deity
—or deities—worshiped. When we look beneath these obvious contrasts, however, we find a shared hope of redemption, a sense of

revelation which can come only with some sudden change, a conversion. We find a strong sense of separation from those who are not saved, and above all we find a great impatience—and sometimes a good deal of fear as well as scorn—for the intense or devoted use of the intellect. This general pattern, of course, is in the familiar tradition of American popular religious life; the great revivals have always shared many of these qualities. To my knowledge, however, there has not been in a thirty-year period a double revival, in the course of which the established denominations have been thrown on the defensive, caught between the eccentric but enthralling cults of the sixties and the compelling simplicities of the gospel cults of the eighties.

What links them together despite their monumental differences is the depth of the human yearning which they embody, and the equal depth of impatience with the familiar or traditional ways in which that religious concern was supposedly being satisfied. Though the overt movements of the sixties faded, the need to which they spoke remained in our society, and remained unsatisfied. Saying this, we can begin to see why the sixties will not down. The inner questions and searchings of those years are central, no matter how far-out their form.

This has been true of the continuing changes in the university world. These changes reflect a fascinating continuity of concern, and once again they show the same superficial break with the sixties which we have seen in other major social structures. The universities were badly bruised by the events of that decade. (I mention the obvious because in this case the eventual results were not quite as obvious as the initiating causes had been.) Certainly, it was predictable that after the strenuous confusions of 1963–70 there would be a push on everyone's part into some setting free from storms. The vocational and utilitarian character of higher education in the seventies was a refuge for the universities as well as for those who went there as students.

The sixties had managed to raise a large number of uncomfortable and indeed "unsafe" questions about the importance of education, calling into question many of the great conventions of liberal education. The battle cry of relevance received its ironic fulfillment in the seventies with curricula which were relevant indeed—to those goals of business, profit, and short-term vocationalism which were absolute anathema to the relevance hunters of the late sixties. It was a time of exhaustion but also of self-criticism and an inner, unpublicized regrouping of purposes and priorities in higher education.

Of course, there were some urgent practical reasons for this emphasis. The universities had to recover not only their own self-esteem, but the confidence of the society around them. As we saw earlier, a good deal of public skepticism had developed about university effectiveness as well as basic direction. What better way to prove one's stability than to demonstrate a good deal of immediate usefulness? Here was a cause that students, faculty, and administrators could agree on. It was a fine corollary to the more penetrating concerns of the inner councils, and it was the precursor as well to one of the great cyclical affirmations of educational importance.

Every generation or so there is a rediscovery of the importance of liberal studies, which include both the great traditions of knowledge and the great means of sharpening and enlivening the mind without some immediate "useful" end. Such a reaffirmation is well under way, but it is strengthened and to a degree guided by the preoccupations of the sixties. It is, in short, more than the usual rediscovery; it has been invigorated and reenforced by the questions which were asked twenty years ago both by undergraduates and by certain of their far-out gurus. This reenforcement is built into today's academic community, for many of its brightest young tenured faculty were the activist students of the sixties. The normal cycle would have moved from the early fifties to the early eighties. Indeed, it has. The language of today's major statements about liberal learning bear the strongest family resemblance to those manifestoes which my peers and I were issuing in 1951 and 1952. But today there is an added wave in the sequence, an added push. It shows itself not only in the intensity of today's documents—much more urgent and less genteel than those of a generation ago—but in the issues which are assumed to be the proper province of college and university education.

The extracurricular life of universities has often been issue-oriented. But the presence of major issues on and within the college campus today is substantial enough to show itself in the curriculum and in the basic concepts of education as they involve the whole community. Extremely complex ethical issues, for example, have become not only acceptable but essential subjects of concern between lawyers and medical men, or among political scientists, economists, and philosophers, or between historians and theologians. We shall consider further these major subjects of mutual concern and debate. Here, it is chiefly important to note that they are now integral aspects of the formal academic life of the institution. Further, they have two other characteristics. They are among the very issues which were most actively debated during the sixties, and they are also the issues which draw heavily—and indeed inevitably—on the patterns of knowledge and skill which stand at the heart of liberal education. The career-oriented narrowness of the 1970s is seen now to be inadequate for the very careers it was supposed to advance. We see again that the power to think broadly, to relate varied kinds of knowledge to one another, the power to ask the difficult questions and look for creative answers—all of this is essential for the development of a significant career. The sixties and eighties draw together in the complexity of their view of "success," of "significant" living. The sixties did it through a critique of conventional learning, while the eighties have continued that critique with a return to the essentials of liberal learning. The continuity of concern is striking.

And this continuity is equally evident in a rather different aspect of society—in the varieties of work and life-style which are available today. We saw patterns of living in the sixties which were often eccentric and sometimes bizarre. Like Robert Frost's road not taken, they seemed sometimes to be chosen because they were less traveled. But there was a good deal more to it than that. These variations from the norm often represented honest variations in talent and temperament, variations not always honored by society. We brought into the sixties strong patterns of conformity for the successful children of successful parents. It went without saying that the paths to be followed led through college and into business or one of the great professions. And these were arrayed in an order which had a great deal to do with expected income. This was almost the gospel; it was endless upward mobility. But there were a good many sons and daughters who did not resonate to this pattern. They had hand skills, artistic skills, perhaps a talent for the art of living itself, so that money earned was only a means for building a highly independent social pattern. The sixties articulated these alternate paths as part of a far broader questioning and rebellion.

The sharp edge of that rebellion did not persist, but the alternatives did—and, as we shall see, so did the questioning and debate. The adolescents of the 1960s, like those who have come to maturity since, show a much higher percentage of career choices based on aptitude and social taste than their parents did. We see many cabinetmakers, skilled mechanics, farmers, and woodsmen whose parents are professionals in the conventional sense of the word. Like styles of dress, hair, or beards, we are far more comfortable in our cultural variety than we were before the sixties. Until that decade the great melting pot had been at work, not only on our ethnic variations but on the norms of acceptable social position. This new assertiveness is in its largest aspect part of a world resistance to the homogeneous. Within our own country it is striking to see that the return of the seventies and eighties to certain conservative styles and patterns of thought has not dampened this social diversity.

Quite the opposite, in fact. Even the tiresome and overpublicized yuppie phenomenon of the seventies and early eighties was really only one among many examples of the freedom to set individual goals and directions. It got a great deal of attention, but in large part this attention came because of the economic impact and the consumer styles which the phenomenon fostered. The yuppies kept a good many advertising firms healthy, but they did not define our society. No one group or style does that in the 1980s. As we turn now to the debates over the unresolved issues of our own decade, it is important to remember that we are comfortable in these adversary relationships because we have learned to be at home with great social diversity. We live it day by day as a legacy from the sixties, and it allows us to approach with sharpness and indeed aggressiveness those other legacies of the earlier time—a whole galaxy of unresolved social, economic, and political issues of the greatest importance for the collective future of our culture.

In any attempt to understand these current issues we must start with one basic characteristic of the 1980s. The decade has turned out to be a time in which the social texture is established not by debate pointed in any one particular direction but by the very insistence of debate itself. We are not only litigious over personal issues but over the great issues of public policy as well. The presence of argument is our hallmark; the class action lawsuit is our chosen weapon. The Reagan administration talked of a new consensus, but the facts are quite otherwise. We are insisting, instead, on a new openness, a deep-seated criticism of society by its members which shows itself—among a hundred other ways—in the fact that we are voting for people rather than parties or platforms. (The widespread personal popularity of Ronald Reagan is a prime example of this fact; disagreement and a major shift of national position back to the center did nothing to alter his personal acceptance, but at the same time there was broad disagreement with his policy pronouncements and actions.)

If this is the basic stance of society, it has a plethora of issues available to keep its critical powers in fit condition. These specific foci of debate are in turn the most visible evidence of the substantial questions of value which face us now. These questions are indeed a legacy from the 1960s, and not merely because they are abiding and concern thoughtful people at any time. They are a legacy because these issues are now at the cutting edge of our daily reality. The sixties raised them by insisting on the examined life, and this even though the examinations were often uncritical and misinformed. We have to do with patterns of thought and action created both by changing social groups and the issues laid upon these groups by the brute facts of physical environment, forces of international upheaval, maldistributions of wealth and opportunity, and certain choices of final value for our country and our world. These are large words, but the facts will bear them out.

As we look at the major issues created by the present state of our physical environment, it is clear that they were articulated in the sixties by the prophetic groups which seemed—and often were —fringe elements in society. Now these issues are concerns of the establishment in the world of the 1980s. New Jersey's seven hundred toxic waste sites have been developing for at least fifty years, and the mountains of rubbish which are forcing Philadelphia to consider an incinerator/steam plant were filling up the available space twenty-five years ago. Low-level nuclear waste was an inescapable problem as soon as the first plant was fired up. When these questions were discussed in the sixties there seemed to be ways around them. No one today (except a few members of the White House staff) thinks we have options. Acid rain and massive water pollution are here; they are no longer the rallying cry of the young cause-mongers, but of governors and senators.

The most complex and difficult example of environmental crisis is, of course, that of nuclear power generation. The spectacular disasters of the last few years have obscured what—for the United States at least—is an equally important part of the puzzle: the cost of this power. If we could obtain nuclear power at the costs that were projected, it is reasonable to assume that we would invest in the heavy expense of adequate training and fully developed safeguards. As it is, the program has been flawed both by its expense and by its own inadequate controls and procedures. We cannot do without it, given the number of plants already in operation; we must now perfect our handling of them, and once again there is no option. Rather, there *should* be no option, and whenever there is a major breakdown the wave of protest is strong. Like many other issues of the sixties now transposed into the eighties, we are "in transit," however. The magic is flawed, but we have not yet made a real reckoning with that fact in order to shape new directions.

The military-industrial complex is more than a disturbing legacy from the sixties, of course. The fact that Dwight Eisenhower gave that relationship its enduring name should have lent more credibility to the problem than it received at first. The puzzles of this relationship have been sharpened and deepened in our own decade by the policies of the Reagan administration, which combined enormous military expenditures with a laissez-faire attitude toward their administration. The resulting abuses, which have come to light in companies as respected as General Electric and General Dynamics, force on us criticisms of the relation between government and industry which do not need the new left politics of the sixties to spur them on. One of the most interesting aspects of the relationship between the two decades, indeed, is this shifting of the ground for criticism, so that the reason for it becomes central rather than fringe radical, while the necessary remedies are far more extreme than those proposed earlier.

We are facing two issues: the use, and direction of use, of finite resources for military purposes; and the invitations to corruption to which I have just alluded. Public awareness of these issues has grown very rapidly in the past few years, fueled by major analyses which show that from the most hawkish perspective we have failed, with all our money, to accomplish the ends for which it was spent—and which were claimed for it by the Reagan administration. (See A.T. Hadley's *The Straw Giant*.) We are as uncoordinated and confused as we were when the Rockefeller Report was issued in 1960. The continuity here is all too evident. Vast amounts of money have managed to create equally vast problems, both for national defense and for national standards of ethical conduct. Twenty years ago those who raised these identical questions would have scorned the establishment concern for them. Today they are issues at the center of our social fabric. We have combined the radical and conservative views in a centrist concern—still developing—to set these two issues straight again before they damage us beyond repair.

In another and quite different arena we have issues which are equally massive. The puzzles of American agriculture are not as direct a legacy from the sixties as those of the military, but they are clearly related to basic issues of the use of the land that were first articulated in a substantial way by the environmental groups which began to build their strength in that decade. In the process they have absorbed the agricultural question into the more fundamental question of the use and abuse of natural resources. This is not to say that the immediate tragedy of an Iowa family farm is identical with the continuing battle to keep public lands from private exploitation. But the two have a great deal in common as soon as we begin to ask the basic questions. These questions are both extremely conservative and boldly radical. How do we protect the rights—indeed, the existence—of private property on the one hand and the public good on the other? The uncontrolled market forces of the day seem often to do violence to both. But at the same time the entrenched subsidy programs lead to overproduction and thus to the abuse of the land, while the public lands suffer from overuse by the very citizens who pay for them. And constantly prowling around the edges are exploiters, the public-be-damned types, who pushed James Watt forward as a willing agent for their depredations.

This is a fascinating mix of forces, and it shows clearly the contribution of the sixties to these current confrontations. That contribution is seldom as overt as in this debate: the sacredness of the land on the one hand, and its neutral existence as a source for extracting wealth on the other. This issue was posed in dogmatic, almost theoretical terms in the 1960s. Now it is immediate and pragmatic since the lives of families and communities are at stake. To that immediacy the earlier decade has contributed its atmosphere of questioning; without its often simplistic dogmatism we are restating many of the questions it posed. We have taken its insights and matured them. The issues are now seen in full color, where the sixties posed them in black and white.

Much the same can be said of a whole range of social problems which occupy us—indeed, preoccupy us—and call for resolutions that the sixties did not succeed in bringing about. The social legacy of that time shows itself in the continuing conflict over minority discrimination, the place of working women at every level, the singularly difficult position of gays now that AIDS has become so sinister a presence, and in the increasing disparity between the poor and the rich, which twenty years ago was an exaggerated cause for the left and is an ugly reality in the glitzy 1980s. In each case there was an articulation of the problem, a statement of possibilities which are now being realized in their full urgency. In each of these areas there is implied a continuing question of place, of legitimacy. We noted it as one of the major thrusts of the questions asked by the noisy social critics of the sixties; now we are being asked what we plan to do about the issues so long articulated and ignored. This is a highly significant shift in expectation. It is as if the sixties had grown up, so that the brave new world of those bold pronouncements is now the everyday when we must make them work or repudiate them as viable aspects of our society.

There have been a good many recent attempts to do the second, to deny that the pronouncements of the sixties have any continuing validity, and one way or another to strike them from the record. The virulently successful attack on the ERA was a striking example of this counterreformation. So are the many official attacks on busing or minority quotas for hiring in public agencies. We are not concerned at this point to judge these attacks, simply to make clear that they represent a small part of the massive recent attempt to rewrite most of the social history of the country during the last half-century. These particular issues were more urgent for the sixties than for any earlier decades (though the 1930s first set the social agenda for our time), and the same can be said for abortion rights and gay rights, which after their passionate affirmation in the sixties have been in many quarters put heavily on the defensive.

It is important to realize, however, that these denials, these loudly trumpeted attempts to rewrite history, have not been generally accepted. The bumper stickers which remind us that the moral majority is neither moral nor a majority have a good deal of statistical validity. Recent samplings of public opinion show that the great conservative shift is really something quite different—a major reaffirmation of the centrist position in political allegiances. And that reaffirmation leaves room for—indeed, demands that we *make* room for—a careful appraisal of the unfinished business of the 1960s. We are now in a position to face these issues in the only way that makes sense for the long future: through an assessment of their basic ethical implications. A good deal of the conservative push has been legal and technical rather than fundamental and ethical; it has been dedicated to forcing regressive change, and that has been one of its great limitations. The centrist questions on the other hand are also central; they accept the questions posed by recent history and cast them in ethical form. These questions and the tentative conclusions, or at least directions, which result are my final concern.

As I consider them, I am well aware that many did not emerge first in the 1960s. We have seen in some detail the causes of that decade which had long histories. But the sixties gave them a particular shape and urgency; those qualities and characteristics can now lend added force to the efforts of our own turbulent time. Perhaps we can understand them more clearly if we accept the fact that we are living, not with the stand-tall, peace-and-plenty time of Reagan administration mythology, but with a time when many of the animals are out of their cages. The disturbed sixties are prophetic of the uneasy eighties.

Three major areas of concern have been sharply defined by the questions which the 1960s passed to us. First, there have been crucial world realignments of power and attitude which make demands far different from those we faced in the 1960s. Second, a pattern of national priorities has changed in eccentric, often extreme ways and still waits for some stability at the end of the 1980s. And third, there is a need for a vision of purpose which can speak coherently to both our national and our personal needs. Each of these questions is complex and crucial, and none can be set aside for another day.

World realignments are of two kinds: those which resulted directly from the Second World War, and those continuing shifts which received their greatest impetus from the end of colonial relationships in Asia and Africa. The first change fed the second, of course. The leaders of the colonial power groups clearly saw the disarray even of those who had "won" the war. Britain, France, Belgium, and the Netherlands were in no condition for a massive defense of their holdings, while the colonials (many of whom had been educated in exile for their future roles at home) were extremely well informed about the weaknesses in their masters' governments. This general loosening of the control lines was, of course, viewed with anger and resentment by many conservatives in the home governments and with wide-eyed approval by many in the United States, which saw clearly enough that its own empire was financial, not territorial. We could well afford to take higher ground by taking no ground. We rejoiced in the virtue of our position and tried to persuade ourselves that nothing but good would come of these massive postcolonial changes. Our own political philosophy was being triumphantly vindicated; we were realizing one goal of the war, and we rejoiced to see the new nations springing up.

What did we forget or fail to recognize in this time of euphoria? Quite a bit. First, for every educated leader there were several whose power came from tribal or familial authority. Second, much of the education for those who had it was theoretical, often radical, and had little specifically to do with the problems of governing a new country. Third, an educated citizenry was unavailable to the new leaders to help sustain their new governments. Fourth, and in some ways most devastating of all, these new countries had no guarantee that their economies were viable; they had worked more or less well under a colonial system which was exploitative but usually gave some return to help sustain the colony. The degree of responsibility varied, of course, from Belgium at one end to England at the other. Now virtually all responsibility was removed, and new relationships had to be developed, not only with the former colonial powers but with the Eastern bloc countries which saw a whole new world of opportunity for trade and influence.

Right at that point the postcolonial world became complex and indeed bewildering for our own foreign policy. The clear articulations of the cold war were applied in unmodified form to the world of these new and often doctrinaire Marxist countries. We saw the theoretical Marxism and forgot the passionate nationalism. Cuba and Vietnam were the direct result, and today we are tangled in the murky conflicts of Southern Africa, where American oil fields are guarded by groups to which we are loudly and officially opposed. We are still unsure how our ideas of freedom should apply to the new nations as well as the small ones. We have found it all too easy as a result to maintain that anticommunist governments are automatically good ones. Every dictator of the right knows our party line, and matches it with one of his own to guarantee him our support.

I have rehearsed this pattern of attitudes and events, in part, because it contributed so heavily to the Vietnam tragedy and thus to a network of other events in the sixties which depended on Vietnam. Beyond that, however, the confusion of attitude is still part of our official thinking. President Reagan calls the Contras "freedom fighters" and suggests that they are like the heroes of the American Revolution; he is revisiting Vietnam when he says this, and the analogy is chilling to many of us. It is a terrible legacy from the sixties, often embodied in phrases like "the war we weren't allowed to win," which flex our macho muscle but fail to address the urgent issues of a new world with new alignments. We have had twenty-five years since the Rockefeller Report and still cannot manage a position complex enough and constructive enough to meet the needs of the new countries and the new governments in older countries. The emphasis of the sixties on independence and individuality is important here. It still offers us a path out of our constantly embattled foreign policy. So does the lesson of Vietnam, if we are willing to learn from it.

The realignments of wealth pose major questions of national priority, which (like those of social or personal independence) were posed by the sixties in a philosophical mode and must now be addressed as urgent and factual. The new left movement spoke constantly and vehemently about the disparities in our society (which, as we have seen, have been further aggravated over the last fifteen years). Now the issues are equally seen as worldwide, and they take two major forms. The less-privileged nations have become steadily deeper in debt to the more-privileged ones, so that economic colonialism has become as common a charge as political colonialism once was. (There is the same ironic twist, of course. The debtor country has the lender country in its power once the debt gets large enough so that it can neither be paid nor written off. In colonial days the economic muscle supplied by the colonies was essential to the affluence of the parents.)

Meanwhile, the most-privileged nations are involved in their own realignment, which makes a debtor nation out of the United States, a highly uneasy creditor nation out of Japan, and a tangled multinational market out of Western Europe. In many ways this is the most radical development of the 1980s; the ethical/economic discussions of the sixties have become the political/economic negotiations of our decade. The same major questions can be asked in the language of either decade, however. For the sixties it was, "What is the ethical basis for economic development? How do we relate social and economic responsibility?" For the eighties it becomes, "How do we control the wild swings of the world economy? How can we balance national and international economic forces so that we do a minimum of violence to these multiple goals and needs?" And for us at the moment the ethical, the social, and the economic have fused in the issues of protectionism and the balance of trade.

The sixties did not have an answer, but they posed exactly this question of balancing the various "goods" in a complex situation.

Their position often seemed extreme because they were (as they saw it) redressing a balance in ethical concern. The land and those who worked it, for instance, had lost the regard they deserved. Now in the eighties we see a desperate struggle to affirm that regard by our attempts to save the traditional American farm. None of us predicted that the question would become so acute. But those who were pondering social issues in the sixties put this and several others before us for our concern and action. Now, however, the action must be taken in the context of continuing world realignments.

The reorientation of governments is inseparable, then, from economic shifts of the most dramatic sort. Virtually no economy in the world functions as it did in 1940; the interrelated world economy has no parallel in history. My concern with it here is, first, a recognition of its sheer magnitude and, second, even more centrally an understanding that the perception of its overwhelming importance is a product of that intense awareness of issues which the 1960s have passed along to us. Each of the great movements had as an important part of its gospel a claim that the economic structure of life— for blacks, for women, for the disinherited or powerless—was seriously awry. This stance was directed primarily toward conditions in the United States. But as we take the movements together we find in them a microcosm of world economic unrest and dislocation. When historians look at us a hundred years from now I suspect that these issues will loom even larger for the last forty years of the century than they do at the moment. There will be a clear continuum, and the ferment of the sixties will be the time of its first identification —often by those who had little grasp of the inner or theoretical dynamics of the issues to which they pointed. And yet their innocent assertions were closer to the truth than the highly knowledgeable analyses of the Rockefeller Report, to say nothing of the naive economic philosophy (if one may dignify it with that word) of the Reagan administration. To use the old image, many of the thinkers of the sixties were describing an elephant by feel and in the dark. Now we can see that they identified the beast with a fair degree of accuracy.

These are continuities which can be argued, since our current perception of major economic shifts is still murky. There is little

ambiguity, however, in the terrible continuities of force and violence which received so great an impetus from the major events and
emergent attitudes of the 1960s. This presence of violence in our
world exists across a very wide spectrum of activity, from mercenary
ventures directly related to the education provided by Vietnam (as
magazines like *Soldier of Fortune* make all too clear) to the nihil-
ism and violent anarchism which are equally cynical attacks on the
civil order. Between these extremes we can see several subcultures:
the terrorists who profess to support a cause but wind up making a
cause out of their violence; the drug rings which make a high art of
both smuggling and murder; the groups which (out of hopelessness)
turn to violence as the most visible way of making a statement about
their position; and the mythic celebrations of violence which half-
dominate motion pictures and television. Pornography has in it a
heavy element of violence, of course; it seems to stand as a final symbol of our confusion of values. But the confusion exists everywhere.
Each of the major foci of violence has come into being through a
bewilderment over the meaning of individuals as they face societies
which themselves hold out no hope of positive or creative human
relationships.

To say this is not to excuse violence, but to expose it, and equally
to suggest why it exists in a clear continuity from the 1960s. Early
in this book I mentioned a particular inheritance from the Second
World War: the ethical decision that all means were justified in destroying the German grip on Europe. This moved very easily into an
ethic of amorality in which the techniques of violence were steadily
elaborated. In a confused and fractured world they could even be
a substitute for civilized action, justified by situations and societies
already in chaos. The end result was the official brutality of Vietnam, and from that a dispersion of violence worldwide. This is not to
say that Vietnam was the causative agent; but techniques, weapons,
and attitudes were perfected there and made ready for wider use.

They found a world ready to receive them, and for one reason
beyond all others. The most striking feature of international society
today is its balkanization. We are hopelessly intertwined, but at the
same time we have a profound and nonrational desire to break apart
into ethnic groups, subnational groups, alignments that will give

some immediately available meaning to our lives. The one world of 1945 is still one, but in a sense not envisioned then. We are one in our common desire to find separate identities, and the most modern modes of violence are the instruments of that pulling apart. It is all too clear that the techniques of terrorism are shared. Equally clear is the fact that many of the motives of terrorism are also shared. "I will have my way, or I will destroy the society that opposes me." Tribal savageries are not new, but until the last twenty-five years we thought we had put them behind us. Quite the opposite turns out to be the case. The end of colonial control was only one cause of that violent loosening of structure which asserted itself forcibly in the sixties and has now become a world revolution. Since we are living so intimately with it, we may misapprehend the full implications of what we are seeing day by day. If we step back and ask how many societies have been forcibly altered in the last quarter century, however, my statement will no longer seem so farfetched—disturbing in the extreme but undeniable.

And the clearest proof of this revolution does not lie merely in the violence of its worldwide expression. It is seen most sharply in the religious commitments which are driving the revolution in many different cultural forms but with one central purpose. The search for local order and identity which we see in a hundred subnational and tribal movements is equally (and often identically) at work in the reassertions of religious dogmatism. Obviously, this sense of revival has a great deal to do with the removal of external cultural and religious standards in the postcolonial world, but it runs deeper into the spiritual dark of the late twentieth century.

As we look back at the religious history of the last 250 years in Western Europe and the United States, we see a double pattern: on the one hand a steadily increasing rationalism in thought *about* religious issues, and on the other a remarkable sequence of outbreaks of religious enthusiasm—often seemingly spontaneous, anticlerical, and even revolutionary. Both of these major elements of religious experience were under pressure from emergent patterns of scientific and philosophic thought; these in turn increasingly claimed final validity for themselves through the supposedly verifiable nature of their statements about the universe. The conflicts which resulted

have been many-sided, complex, confused, and the begetters of confusion. Seen against such a background, the explosion of fundamentalist thought in Christian and Islamic affirmations is almost as
predictable as the lifting of a lid when the pot starts to boil.

To say this implies certain basic assumptions about the nature of
individual religious desire. The evidence of history is paradoxical in
the extreme. All of the great religions are, in one form or another,
religions of love and respect—for oneself, for one's fellows, and for
the deity. And virtually all have stimulated devastating and barbaric
wars in the name of that deity. I mention this obvious and deeply
painful fact both because it is relevant to us in daily ways (it is part
of the texture of the 1980s) and because the basic human reason for
these appalling events is even more deeply of our time. The fundamentalist religious resurgences, the ethnic and tribal reassertions,
the antigovernment, terrorist, anarchic outbursts, the world drug
outbreak, the arts of violence and the violence of much art have a
vital center.

All of them symbolize and yet embody an escape from the
disturbed inner lives of countless millions of individual men and
women. If we look soberly at our century, we see that it has been
a time of massive uprooting, worldwide murderous wars, genocide
in the name of purification. We have managed to tear our world
apart in a hundred cunning and sophisticated ways; now we are at
a time of reckoning. The reassertion of religious concern today is
often crude, narrow, violent toward those who do not agree, who
are not of the group; and that is exactly the point. The inclusive-
ness of nineteenth-century religious thought was in a way like the
generalities of science and the supposed "laws" of social behavior.
It constantly implied the diminution of the individual, of the small
cohesive group, and we have carried that implication to an extreme
in our own mobile and mass society. The violence done to the coherence of individual lives creates a counterforce. A person may be
born again or lost in the drug world, but by one means or another
he will break out of this constant flux of events whose meaning he
cannot control or understand.

That this reaction is irrational does not argue against its reality.
Quite the opposite. We have in our society a profound division be-

tween the rationalist procedures and assumptions of our pervasive technologies and our personal desires and yearnings, which are for the most part deeply nonrational. The reaction against Western influence which we see in Asia Minor and Africa is only in part a reaction against the domination of alien governments. It is even more violently a reaction against Western cultural styles, so heavily based on material goods and services, so restless in their productivity and their passion for constant change. And the same challenge to our accepted norms is coming from within, and often in the most perverse and destructive ways. The fundamentalist upsurge has turned against scientific thought, mistaking it as the enemy, while in fact the misapplications of scientific insight are the real culprits. Similarly, the appalling increase in drug use is evidently based very largely on feelings of inability to face our society's pressures and inhumanities. Both these extreme manifestations of discomfort tell us that something is profoundly out of order in Western society itself.

These two reactions to our society's current structure and emphasis have one common attitude or stance. They differ as much as any two positions could, and yet they both express a desire to find quick but absolute resolutions for the profoundly complex problems which face us all. Without accepting either approach, one can understand the driving forces which lead to both; only an unthinking person would brush off either the forces or the reactions. The misfortune of our society resides in the fact that one approach is physically destructive and one emotionally delusive. The quick fix of the born-again movement brings great comfort to its members, but it "solves" the great problems by brushing them aside or by trivializing them so that they are apparently easy to handle. (Drugs, of course, work even more directly; they obliterate the possibility of dealing with external problems at all by rapidly becoming themselves the all-consuming problem.)

The techniques used by many of the fundamentalist sects bear out my judgment. Put most simply, their religious statement is enmeshed in a network of all that is most seductive and diverting in secular society. This synthetic environment reaches its apogee in the PTL's Heritage USA theme park developed on the border of the Carolinas, but we see it in the glossy pop-rock singing groups on

evangelical TV shows, or in the remarkable trappings of Dr. Schuller's Glass Cathedral. The gloss and glitter are a spectacular substitute for thought, and equally a substitute for the mysteries which
stand at the heart of all the great religions. In these treatments of
religion, gratification is increased to a maximum, and serious demand is diminished accordingly.

To say this is to shift our attention from world realignments to the
state of our own country where these drug and religious involvements are more enveloping than those in other major societies. I
take them to be symbols and indicators of our profound uncertainty
about our national direction. The political bewilderments and forays
of the last twenty years tell the same story: a loss of direction and
high purpose at the end of the sixties, the petty and yet monstrous
dishonesty of Watergate, the nondirection of the Ford and Carter
administrations, and the eight years in which we have experienced a
massive and deliberate attempt to untie, reverse, or eliminate many
of the most carefully developed structures of government. This process was advertised as a return to the basic American verities; it
begins now to show its truer nature as a perversion and exploitation
of those verities.

All of us like to invoke the Declaration of Independence and the
Constitution. We have not for many years, however—if ever—been
treated to the spectacle of an attorney general who would atomize
our judicial system, or a much-honored military officer who uses the
Fifth Amendment to conceal the facts of a foreign policy disaster
from his commander in chief. That commander calls his insubordi-
nate officer a national hero and refuses to ask the essential question
of him: where is the high responsibility to law by which we were
established? It is easy to get hysterical about these grotesque events
but hard to exaggerate them. Life is stranger than art in these cases,
and we are dealing in sober fact with one of the major good/evil
forces of our time—the power and reach of television to create the
image of a president while in fact we have only the wizard of Oz.

The real issue behind these events of the moment is not political
alignment but intellectual and moral integrity. When the president's
former chief of staff trivializes his own job he, like the president,
turns the authority of the White House toward image and effect. The

power of the medium and what can be shaped by it is a substitute for hard thought and firm standards. When the real world breaks in and refuses to be manipulated, we find ourselves with totally unnecessary crises in government. We have always known that a preoccupation with outer and seeming reality—the fictions of leadership, for instance—is often the enemy of inner and enduring leadership. We now have the technical means of persuading by image which the weak Roman emperors lacked; otherwise, nothing has changed very much. We are, however, faced constantly with challenges to our judgment, with a pressure for instant and mass reaction to events *as presented* which has never been the case before.

This is only one of the forces which heighten the daily demands on us as citizens. The extremes of the 1960s were a decade-long testament to this fact, both in what concerned us and in the means by which we expressed our concern. Now the issues are even more urgent because unresolved for so long. Put simply, we have to decide what we want our society to be. We cannot drift any longer. This was the state of affairs when we declared our independence; it was the harsh reality when the southern states seceded from the Union; and, with a set of issues different but yet similar, it is our position today.

The chief questions which we must answer may be subject to conservative or liberal interpretation, but in themselves they are neither. They belong to no party. They are the inescapable national problems to which the sixties introduced us: the distractions and corruptions of power, economic as well as political; the fragility of our economic structure; the tangled problem of social justice in the face of bankrupt past policies; the passion for destruction on the part of those who live without hope or direction; inept and often unprincipled foreign policy; threats to the rule of law; the challenges of finding unity in our remarkable social diversity. There are many other issues— the protection of our environment chief among them—but those I have mentioned are major for anyone who tries to see our society as a whole.

Men have commented almost forever that power often seems to change those who hold it for the worse. We have given some massive recent expression to the general doctrine, however, and when the master of great political power is frustrated in his purposes—

as LBJ was and as Ronald Reagan increasingly became—there are manipulations for which all of us pay heavily. In the heady world of corporate finance we see almost the opposite problem. Lacking restraint, the merger marauders have made move after move to the enrichment of a few and the weakening of almost every corporation caught in the game. In finance as in government, the rest of us will be powerless to fend off these evils until we call them by their right names—fraud, deception, larceny on an amazing scale. The many examples must be faced, not as individual events but as patterns of exploitation in which the institutions of political and economic life are dangerously weakened.

This occurs at a time when world pressures from both the most-developed and least-developed nations are putting our own economic order under the greatest stress it has endured since the 1930s. We are subverting ourselves from within precisely when it is essential for us to build our external economic strength. (There is an analogy with seventeenth-century Spain, so confident of its flow of wealth and yet deeper and deeper in debt, so blind to the real forces which would make for the health or disease of its future economy.) In the 1960s many groups were concerned about the inequities and misdirections of society, and the military-industrial complex was seized upon by the new left as an evil force. Now its demands on our resources are matters of the greatest public urgency, since they play so heavy a part in the great deficit puzzle.

More profoundly, these demands are basic to our philosophical priority-setting. Is our combination of high-technology, military construction, and service-oriented business an adequate base for our economic future? The question has not yet been seriously addressed. We are beginning to learn where we are weak, and we have begun to decide on an ad hoc basis which types of industry we shall try to rescue and which we shall let go. Yet we still have not taken the question of the sixties fully to heart: what is worth pursuing and why? Many of the sixties' answers to the question were obviously naive since they did not take seriously the absolute necessity of a strong economy. On the other hand, the radicals of the sixties (young and old) were wiser in one way than most of the professional economists at this moment; they asked economic questions in a full social context. They did so because they took the situation around them to be serious in the extreme, and they knew that economic resources misdirected would pull the rest of society down. This radical gospel of the sixties should be (as it is not) the conservative dogma of the eighties. Our recovery from the inflation/recession of the early eighties seems to have blinded us to the need for a firm basis of economic thought and action.

To say this is also to imply the opposite situation. We have no more found an effective response to our social problems than to our economic ones. There has been a good deal of talk in the last eight or ten years about the death of liberalism. Some of this is thoughtful regret that in the sixties and early seventies so many public programs failed to achieve their ends. Some comment has been gleeful almost to the point of obscenity, however. Confusing failed programs with invalidated needs, some have asserted that since the programs did not do what was expected, it is obvious that nothing can—or should —be done in these areas; the need was, in fact, grossly overstated from the start.

This is an arena in which the initial perceptions of the 1960s are particularly important for an understanding of our current problems of social equity. The frontier thinkers of that decade certainly found the standard liberal programs and attitudes inadequate; these programs and attitudes did not really speak to the basic issues of social justice and equal opportunity (despite the best rhetoric of LBJ and his staff). Here we must recognize that the scorn of the radicals was directed against the easy solutions of the establishment; the basic questions were not ones of program and money but of attitude toward social change. That distinction is precisely what we need today, what we have still not recognized clearly enough to move effectively with new programs. A return to old programs is not the answer. But if we recognize that this judgment is in itself only a further refinement of the question, we are ready to respond to the real issues which the sixties raised about people and their needs. The critics in those years saw, as we should see even more clearly today, that our society tends to chew up—and at times demolish— the lives of those who have not managed to compete, are unlucky, uneducated, feckless, or lazy—though there are fewer of these last than our complacent critics would have us believe. The puzzle of matching competence to opportunity was often viewed romantically —even naively—by the social theorists of that time. Now we deal with realities far harsher than they imagined, and yet of the same family. The homeless in our streets are certainly the invisible people of the 1960s, but no longer hidden.

Our answers must be as practical and substantial as the problem. And while this is not primarily a book of solutions, I feel strongly that in this most painful area as in the others I discuss, the sixties taught us where to look for answers. The problem, they said, was that people and organizations did not match. We must change the relationship in this as in so many other areas of social life by finding the points at which the individual and his society can relate to one another again. From this insight came the great cry for relevance and many of the criticisms of education. In areas of basic human need the relevance must—then and now—be more than a handout. Above all, it must involve significant work. And when we look at our cities we see an enormous amount of work that needs to be done. Certainly, we are imaginative and energetic enough to relate the needs of the city and its least privileged citizens to one another. And if we are not, we can take lessons from some of our friends in Europe and Asia where successful models are available.

By doing this we might begin to deal with a special aspect of the social collapse which was just beginning to show itself in the sixties —the senseless violence and destructiveness which we see acutely in many parts of the world but which also seem endemic in our own cities. Its causes go far deeper than social inequity, however, or I would not mention the subject at this point. The use of the most violent means of attack on village and civilian populations during the Vietnam years provided a pattern still acceptable in many quarters and often carried out in Africa and Latin America by those who got their on-the-job training in Southeast Asia. That *attitude* of violence is a terrible legacy for us; it has its parallels in the religiously motivated violence of the Middle East or the nationalist/religious hatreds of Northern Ireland. But it is a dimension of our society which did not exist in these pervasive and sophisticated forms until the underground ventures of World War II and the military-political activities of the CIA in the sixties. Vietnam confirmed these and added its own far more persuasive commitment to mass violence as an instrument of national policy.

To say this is certainly not to say that we were without violence before 1940. Our whole history has been intimately involved with it. But the violence of the frontier had a clear and positive purpose, as did the long agony of the Civil War. What sets our time apart is its *acceptance* of violence. In earlier times we moved from violence to the arts of peace. We were not callous. In many ways we have become so, and that callousness—coupled with the drug horror among other major aspects of a disrupted society—gives a special quality of barely submerged violence to our general and also intimate daily perception of our world. It is both an external and an internal presence for us; it is a subliminal fact of life as we walk in any great city. I cannot say how to get away from it, but it is clearly part of that gift of death which the sixties handed on to us. The answers will come only as we revisit the patterns behind the terrible gift and change them. Anything less is a mere treatment of the symptoms.

That last medical metaphor is relevant not only to our struggle with domestic violence but to our ineptitude and confusion in the conduct of our international relationships. The Vietnam defeat caused such a revulsion in national feeling that for some years we certainly floundered as we tried to distance ourselves from international commitments. This first legacy from the 1960s was followed by a far more damaging one—the attempt to revise the facts of that time and to replace them with a reassertion of American interventionist policy which has in fact resulted in an unholy tangle of confused and often failed programs. We have come perilously close to that doom of repeating Vietnam history in Central America. We may have been saved from it by the incredible irony of the events revealed in the Iran-Contra hearings—events in themselves the most extreme expressions of our interventionism.

This series of events taken simply as examples of foreign policy are deeply disturbing because they seem to imply that major decisions can now be made by subordinates in the cellars of government. The real warning, the real lesson, we should have learned from the sixties (and have not) goes a good deal further, however. The extremes

of the sixties were at many points (not just in foreign policy) a testing
of the rule of law. The bitterness of that time, and the failure of its
strongest movements to sustain themselves, were directly related to
positions and actions which went beyond the boundaries of order as
American society conceived of them. Twenty years later the conservative expounders of law-and-order doctrines are caught in a web
of duplicity and illegality. One of the great triumphs of the 1970s
was, of course, a ringing reaffirmation of law at its best and highest.
Among the most somber aspects of our own decade is that we seem
to have forgotten so soon and so disastrously what that affirmation
meant. We see it now subverted by the very men who have sworn to
uphold it and draw their power from it.

It would be hard to overstate the importance of this issue in our
society. For the last twenty years it has been constantly challenged,
and as a result it is present today in our thought and debate. Under
the slogan of "law and order" it has been a rallying cry for the right;
as a perceived threat to individual freedom and racial equality it has
been a shibboleth for the new left. In fact, of course, the real issues
of the rule of law have been challenged over and over again. The
dissenters from Puritan orthodoxy, the Virginia planters and Boston
merchants who challenged royal prerogative, the Confederate states
which confronted the Union, at these and a hundred other points we
have asked one extremely difficult question of ourselves—a question
of law which is not merely one of legality but something far more
fundamental. How far is it possible to go in maintaining a structure
for society on the one hand, and providing on the other adequate
space for dissent, for alternate life-styles, and for the progress of
those who do not yet have a secure place in our society? This, in an
extreme form, is what the sixties were asking. On a more familiar
and limited scale it is the question posed by the new right and by the
many dubious uses of power in the seventies and eighties.

The issues of our environment—its proper management and its
protection against biochemical pollution and resource exploitation
—are as central to this question of law as the more flamboyant
examples posed by our elected officials. Who has a right to the country's resources, and who is to be held responsible when they are

abused? James Watt and the deregulators obviously had one answer; the bureaucracies of the major government agencies clearly have another. The paradox, of course, is that the supposed apostles of law on the right are desperately eager to eliminate all controls in society, while the apostles of freedom are just as eager to wrap us in procedures, penalties, and all the cumbersome machinery of government administration. We are left asking, "Whose law? Whose freedom?" More significantly, we are forced to turn once again to ends rather than means and to ask how the greatest good of the greatest number is to be reestablished, if indeed it is to stand as one of our articles of faith.

These articles of faith continually demand that we recognize once again the nature of the affirmation so carefully and yet boldly crafted by the founding fathers in the Declaration of Independence and the Constitution. When we reflect, it seems clear that this serene, reasonable, and generally applicable pair of documents may be the one force that has held us together during two centuries of increasing diversity and often divisiveness. More aggressive documents, or more highly specific ones, would have magnified those disagreements beyond the point of easy return. The very fact that interpretation is essential at many points has given us great flexibility in meeting social questions and in modifying our political structure to meet changed needs and conditions. It is now clear that we have had in the last twenty-five years a crucial opportunity to test that flexibility.

As the Rockefeller Report revealed—both through its insight and very substantially through its limitations—there was a watershed of change in social attitudes and interests which was about to show itself even without the climactic events of the early 1960s. As we have seen, it was radically enhanced by all that fueled the great movements of the decade, so that we have experienced one of the great "revisitings" of our culture and way of life. That revisiting has taken us through excesses of the left and the right; it now seems to be bringing us back to some center, some balance of attitudes which is not yet an answer to the major issues I have just described. Those issues must be resolved by our vision of the good society. That

vision has been displayed in several partial ways between 1962 and
the present. Now we need to articulate it in a form comprehensive
enough so that we can print it with a capital V.

We are most aware of such a need in times of loss, of failure. The
watershed which we experienced in the 1960s has often been commented on as a loss of innocence resulting from the experiences of
the Vietnam War, which in turn gave us a new and more mature
view of ourselves. As I have shown in the course of this book, that
change was only one among many—an important part of the whole
cluster of shifts which together make up nothing less than a revisiting of the American Dream. For the dreams of individuals and
groups which provided a metaphor for the body of this book are also
the most accurate expression of the country's need at this moment to
find its high dreams again. The 1960s destroyed many dreams, or at
least modified them heavily; others were initiated; others still were
sustained despite the conflict over their meaning (for example, in the
women's movement and the rejection of the ERA). And it seems to
me that in these last eight years we have tried another and nostalgic
national dream; the experience has been a bit like putting on an old
suit only to find that it no longer fits.

Now we have before us the perpetual task which is also perpetu-
ally new—that of defining our dreams so that they can play a shaping and creative part in moving our present reality toward our best
hope for ourselves. The 1960s taken as a whole were one crucial step
in that unending process; and it should always be remembered that
one of the most remarkable things about our society is its ability to
go through that process over and over again, building new kinds of
unity from its diversity of cultures, attitudes, and convictions. The
old and in many ways seemingly romantic dream which our society
holds of itself is not dead. It has not been destroyed by the traumas of
the last twenty years any more than truly liberal sensibility to social
need has been destroyed. We have been shaken by many distresses.
Let us hope that we can put them to good use now.

To do this we must accomplish what both the sixties and the
eighties have so far failed to do. We must create a dynamic balance
between our large vision and our specific actions. Our great leaders
of the past have always had this creative power. What we need now

is some sense of it in society at large. It must be understood again through a recognition that our leaders may be ahead of us but not separate from us; at their best they see what we do not yet understand and help us realize it. We come alive in common purpose and together accomplish what they set forth as the goal. Lincoln's grasp of the terrible necessities of the Civil War is a major example; or Washington's strategy for the defeat of the British, so long thwarted, so little understood; or FDR's attack on the desperate dilemmas of the Great Depression.

This type of vision leading to effective action has been in short supply for the last twenty years and more. We cannot know whether JFK could have avoided the Vietnam trap which destroyed LBJ's presidency; there are bits of disturbing evidence that Kennedy was already heading down that dark road, and certainly many of his key advisors carried on what he and they had already articulated. The result of their persistence was of course that complex alienation from our political leadership which all of the major movements demonstrated. Each in turn tried to accomplish purposes so massive that they called for some national consensus. Those purposes seem so flawed in retrospect because even when they were reinforcing one another they could seldom bring the vision and the action together in any enduring way.

The problem of the Reagan administration and the 1980s is strikingly different, but just as destructive of any national unity of purpose. Obviously—all too obviously, it now seems—Ronald Reagan and his partisans set out to articulate objectives designed to return the country to what they saw as its old purposes, its basic Americanism. This was to be accomplished by presenting an image of these values—at which the president was often remarkably effective —in the full expectation that events would then turn the image into reality. Many of the so-called policies of the Reagan administration were in fact just images; they were stage sets, and when they were taken to be something more their weaknesses soon showed. Supply-side economics, unfettered deregulation, unguided military buildup, SDI, all have been advanced as major solutions to national problems. The problems are undeniably real, but the solutions are not. They do not come to grips with the issues they claim to resolve, and as a result they are dreams more delusive and more destructive than those which foundered at the end of the 1960s.

Most striking of all is the fact that the litany of discarded programs and downplayed concerns put forth by the Reagan administration in its budget planning and its bureaucratic guidelines were virtually a mirror image of the causes and proposals held high by major groups in the 1960s. To carry matters one long step further, the major programs put forth were precisely those which created some of the gravest antagonisms of that former decade—a great military machine and belligerent intrusion in the affairs of small countries. One does not have to believe that we are about to send troops to Nicaragua to recognize that we are in a looking-glass land relationship to the 1960s. There is one absolutely major difference, however: the opposition and resistance which were the province of the young and the offbeat are now mainstream. (It is respectable to oppose military action in Nicaragua, even if the Reagan administration maintained that only the ignorant and the misguided were in opposition.)

The urgency of our present situation is heightened by these relationships to the 1960s. They may not tell us how to move, but surely they do two things. First, they tell us how *not* to move; and it is one of the minor tragedies of the moment that we are still busy trying to rewrite the lessons of the sixties so that we will not have to accept and apply them in dealing with our current massive problems. Second, they do tell us what to take seriously, what to grapple with. The continuity between the sixties and the present is a great and sobering gift of understanding if we choose to take it so. Otherwise, we are condemned to walk the street of dreams again.

Index

Abolition movement. *See* Movements: abolition

Abortion rights. *See* Women: abortion rights

Academic community, 18. *See also* Universities

Activism. *See* Movements: activism

Adams, Abigail, 28

Adams, John, 28

Adams, Samuel, 62

Africa, 5, 6, 9, 10, 182, 189, 194; postcolonial, 41; "return to Africa," 84

Agriculture, United States, 179–80, 185

AIDS, 180

Alice in Wonderland, 95, 96

Allen Building occupation. *See* Duke University: Allen Building occupation

Alternate life-style groups. *See* Countercultures: alternate life-style groups

Altizer, Thomas J. J., 99

American Dream, 198

American Revolution, 30, 62, 183, 199

Aquarians. *See* Countercultures: Aquarians

Are You Running With Me, Jesus?, 86

Art: as criticism of society, 77; at Duke, 114–15; in the 1960s, 48, 70–77. *See also* Film; Music; Popular Culture

Asia, 182, 189, 194

Assassinations, 41, 58, 62, 68, 89, 91; John F. Kennedy, 38, 68; Martin Luther King, 68, 69, 122; Allard Lowenstein, 126; Malcolm X, 68

Association of American Universities, 64

Axis powers, 9

Auden, Wystan Hugh (W. H.), 73, 74, 162

Baez, Joan, 126, 127

Batista, Fulgencio, 41

Beat Generation, 19

Beatles, 70

Belgium, 182, 183

Berkeley, Calif., 112. *See also* University of California at Berkeley

Blacks: black American culture, 1920s and 1930s, 25; black nationalists, 68, 84; "black power" movement, 78, 79; black

Blacks (*continued*)
  women, 27; as Duke employees,
  as Duke students, 97, 99, 101,
  102, 134, 138, 141, 155; as immigrant population, 169; integration, 7; migration to urban areas,
  20, 21, 22, 24, 27, 32, 33, 43; in
  the 1980s, 167–69; on Rockefeller
  Report Panel, 7. *See also* Civil
  rights: black educational and
  social rights; Movements: black
  movement
Black Panther Party, 90, 144
Blake, William, 70
Board of trustees. *See* Duke University: board of trustees; Universities: committees and boards
"Bonds of conflict": among movements, 45–53, 54, 58, 59, 60;
  generational, 53, 54; sexual, 62;
  women's movement, 54
Brewster, Kingman, 143
Brummer, Ernest, 114
Brummer, Joseph, 114
Bryn Mawr College, 30
Buber, Martin, 133

California, 108, 151; educational
  crises, 111
Cambridge University, 30
"Camelot" speech/metaphor. *See*
  Kennedy, John F.: inaugural
  speech
Cannon, Charles, 103
Capital grants. *See* Ford Founda-
  tion capital grants
Capitalism. *See* Economic issues:
  capitalism
Carroll, Lewis. *See* Dodgson,
  Charles Lutwidge
Carter, James Earl, 162, 190
Castro, Fidel, 4
Catalyst, 38, 39

Cater, Douglas, 66, 67
Central America, 195
Central Intelligence Agency, 195
Chaucer, Geoffrey, 72
China, 4, 59, 84, 92, 109; in French
  Indochina, 3
Christianity. *See* Religion: Chris-
  tianity
Civil rights, 11, 37; black educa-
  tional and social rights, 18, 22,
  25, 62, 167, 168. *See also* Move-
  ments
Civil War, 18, 62, 191, 195, 196, 199
Cleaver, Eldridge, 60, 61
Clifford, Clark, 66, 67
Coffin, William Sloane, 86, 143–44
Cold war, 4, 30, 109
College presidents. *See* Duke Uni-
  versity: presidents; Universities:
  presidents
Colleges. *See* Universities
College students. *See* Duke Uni-
  versity: students; Universities:
  students
Colonialism, 9, 182, 184, 187. *See
  also* Economic Issues: postcolo-
  nial world; Postcolonial world
Columbia University, 59, 118, 132–
  33, 134, 146, 155
Communes. *See* Countercultures:
  communes
Conant, James, 140
Congress, United States, 37, 60. *See
  also* Political issues: United States
  government
Constitution, United States, 190,
  197
Consumer culture, 14, 15
Contras, 183
Co-optation, 44, 50, 55, 83, 95
Cornell University, 151, 155
Countercultures: alternate life-
  style groups, 51, 52, 84, 164,

176; Aquarians, 47, 48, 75, 93; communes, 51, 52; drug cults, 11, 44, 47, 48, 51, 52, 78, 81, 82; drug culture, 112, 125, 150, 165, 186, 188, 189, 195; flower children, 44, 78, 82; in 1960s, 17, 19, 48, 172, 173; religious cults, 11, 82, 86, 94; subcultures, 25, 27, 84. *See also* Movements; Religion

Cuba, 5, 9, 59, 84, 183; Bay of Pigs, 41; Cuban missile crisis, 37

Cult figures, 47. *See also* Countercultures

Cults. *See* Countercultures

"Curve of action." *See* Patterns: change in 1960s

Dante, 6

de Beauvoir, Simone, 40, 55

Declaration of Independence, United States, 190, 197

Depression. *See* Great Depression

Deregulation. *See* Political issues: deregulation

Dirksen, Everett, 67

Dissent, 141, 196; forms of, 9. *See also* Movements; Political issues

Dodgson, Charles Lutwidge, 95

Donne, John, 71

Drugs. *See* Countercultures: drug cults; Countercultures: drug culture

Du Bois, William Edward Burghardt (W. E. B.), 26

Duke, James Buchanan, 102

Duke Endowment, 96, 100, 101, 102–4, 105, 106, 107, 139

Duke Power Company, 102–3

Duke University: Allen Building occupation, 125, 134–36, 137, 140, 141, 147; alumni, 74, 110, 123, 137, 140, 155; art museum, 106, 115, 116; board of trustees, 96, 97, 99, 101, 120, 134, 139, 159; Central Campus, 106, 116, 118; Chapel, 123, 136; *Chronicle*, 122, 141; Divinity School, 99; East Campus, 115, 116, 141; as employer, 97, 120, 122; Engineering School, 141; faculty, 140–42, 146; financial foundation, 102–4; and fine arts, 114–15; fundraising, 104, 107–8; gifts, 114, 116, 117; governance (administration and boards), 96, 100, 101, 105, 106, 108, 116, 121, 146–48, 159; grants, 104, 107, 108; Martin Luther King, Jr., memorial service, 123; Medical Center, 141; in 1950s, 105; in 1960s, 96–102, 104, 105, 120–24, 125, 133, 134–36, 137–40, 141–42, 143, 146, 154–56; after 1960s, 158–60, 173; presidency, 24, 29, 64, 78, 80, 100, 102; Silent Vigil, 101, 120–24, 141, 147; southern heritage, 98, 100; speakers, 120, 124; students, 118–24, 159; University House, 120–24, 134, 138; West Campus, 116, 117, 134, 136. *See also* Ford Foundation capital grants

Durham, N.C., 97, 117, 118, 121

Durham Housing Authority, 117

Dylan, Bob, 8, 70–75, 77, 83; compared to Cole Porter, 72. *See also* Music

Eastern Bloc countries, 183

Economic issues: capitalism, 33, 171; corporate finance, 192; deficit, 164, 165; economic disorder in 1960s, 6; economic growth in 1880s, 32; economic power centers, 5, 6; effect on uni-

Economic Issues (*continued*)
versities, 107; inflation, 5, 164,
165, 195; in 1980s, 170–71, 176,
180, 184, 191; postcolonial eco-
nomics, 5, 184; Reagan budget,
200; world economic order, 4, 5.
See also Great Depression
Edens, Hollis, 97, 105
Education, 6, 13, 14, 62, 88; history
in United States, 29, 30; theorists,
85, 87. *See also* Civil rights: black
educational and social rights;
Movements; Political issues;
Universities
1870s–1880s, 32–33
Eisenhower, Dwight, 11, 12, 178
Eliot, Charles William, 148
Eliot, Thomas Stearns (T. S.), 23,
71
Employment, 33. *See also* Duke
University; Social issues
Environmental issues, 51, 163, 164;
natural resources, 179; in 1980s,
177, 191; toxic waste, 177
Establishment America, 33, 133;
antiestablishment groups, 62;
liberal establishment, 36, 47. *See
also* Movements; Political issues
Europe, 9, 10, 43, 184, 194; in
1940s, 31
Extremist groups. *See* Movements

The Faerie Queene, 77
Faulkner, William, 26
Federal Bureau of Investigation,
138
The Feminine Mystique, 38, 39
Film, 70, 75–77, 186; motion pic-
ture industry, 109
Folk music. *See* Music: folk
Ford, Gerald, 190
Ford Foundation capital grants,
103, 104, 106–8, 116

Foundations, 15, 16. *See also* Duke
University; Universities
Free love movement. *See* Move-
ments
"Free-speech" movement. *See*
Movements
France, 46, 124, 182; French Revo-
lution, 31, 93; in Vietnam, 3, 12,
40
"Freedom fighters," (contras), 183
Friedan, Betty, 15, 26, 39, 40, 56
Frontier mentality, 34
Frost, Robert, 36, 175
Fundraising, 96. *See also* Duke
University: fundraising; Ford
Foundation capital grants; Law-
rence College; Universities

Garfunkel, Art, 125
Gay rights. *See* Movements: gay
rights
General Electric, 178
General Motors, 51
Generation gap, 52, 53; in *The
Graduate*, 75
GI Bill, 14
Gigi, 72
Gilmore, George, 120–21
Glass Cathedral, 190
Goldwater, Barry, 61, 83
Goodman, Paul, 43, 53, 68, 83, 124
Government. *See* Political issues:
United States government
The Graduate, 53, 70, 75
Grants, 15. *See also* Duke Univer-
sity: grants; Ford Foundation
capital grants; Foundations
Great Britain, 182, 183
Great Depression, 16, 22, 199
Great Society. *See* Johnson, Lyndon
Baines
Greensboro, N.C., 97
Gregory, Dick, 124, 125, 134

Gross, Paul, 97, 104–6
Guerrilla warfare, 12, 13, 80, 163.
    See also Political issues; Violence
Guevara, Che, 92
Guthrie, Arlo, 71
Guthrie, Woody, 71

Hadley, A. T., 179
Hair, 11, 70, 75, 81
Hanks, Nancy, 116
Harkness, Edward, 143
Harlem in 1930s, 25
Harris, David, 83, 124, 125–27
Hart, Deryl, 105
Harvard University, 140, 143, 158
Hayakawa, Samuel Ichiye (S. I.),
    150, 153
Helms, Jesse, 110–11
Heritage U.S.A. theme park, 188
Hickey, Marguerite, 7
Higher education. See Duke Uni-
    versity; Universities
Hinduism. See Religions: Hinduism
Hitler, Adolf, 43
Ho Chi Min, 4
Holly, Buddy, 19, 70
Homeless. See Social issues: home-
    less
Hope Valley (Durham), 121
House Committee on Un-American
    Activities, 108
Housing and Urban Development,
    117
Hudson River, 132
Humanities: vs. sciences, 16, 17
Human rights. See Civil rights;
    Social issues

Immigration, 32. See also Blacks: as
    immigrant population
Industrialization, 6, 15, 171; in-
    dustrial labor, 33, 34. See also
    Economic issues

Inflation. See Economic issues:
    inflation
Innocence: in Dylan's music, 73; in
    Hair, 75; loss of in 1960s, 78–82,
    198
Integration. See Blacks: integration
Iran-Contra hearings, 190, 195. See
    also Political issues
Ivy League universities, 143. See
    also Columbia University; Cor-
    nell University; Harvard Univer-
    sity; Princeton University; Yale
    University

Jackson, Andrew, 67
Japan, 5, 184
Jazz. See Music
Jefferson, Thomas, 32, 62
Johnson, Howard, 64, 65
Johnson, Lady Bird, 63
Johnson, Lyndon Baines: Great
    Society, 12, 50, 63; meeting with
    Douglas Knight, 66–67; and
    public opinion, 37, 38, 49, 63, 64,
    68, 81, 162, 193, 199
Johnson, Samuel, 28
Joyce, James, 19, 73, 90. See also
    Ulysses

Kannapolis, N.C., 103
Keats, John, 70
Kennedy, John F., 36, 78, 199;
    "Camelot" inaugural speech, 13,
    36, 93, 132. See also Assassina-
    tions: John F. Kennedy
Kent State University, 136
Kerouac, Jack, 19
Kerr, Clark, 112
Killian, James, 1
King, Martin Luther, Jr., 43, 47,
    50, 61, 120, 121. See also Assas-
    sinations: Martin Luther King;
    Duke University: Martin Luther
    King, Jr., memorial service

Kirk, Grayson, 133
Kissinger, Henry, 1, 4
Knight, Grace, 24, 122
Korea, 1; Korean War, 8, 9

Ladies' Home Journal, 7
Latin America, 6, 194. See also
    Political issues
"Law and order" doctrines, 196,
    197. See also Political issues
Lawrence College (University), 18,
    97, 104, 106–7, 127, 149
Leary, Timothy, 45, 51, 81, 82
Left-wing politics. See Political
    issues: left-wing politics
"Lesbian sisterhood." See Move-
    ments: "Lesbian sisterhood"
Liberalism. See Establishment
    America; Political issues
Libraries. See National Commis-
    sion on Libraries and Informa-
    tion Handling Resources
Lincoln, Abraham, 62, 66, 69, 199
Literature in the 1960s, 7. See also
    Popular culture
"Looking glass" metaphor, 95–96,
    200; and the paranoid mind, 96;
    San Francisco State University,
    155; in universities, 95, 96
Louis Harris Associates study, 162
Lovett, Sidney, 143, 144
Lowenstein, Allard, 49, 50, 126.
    See also Assassinations: Allard
    Lowenstein
Luce, Henry, 1

McCarthy, Joseph, 108, 127
McNamara, Robert, 62, 63, 64, 66,
    69, 127
Malcolm X, 43, 45; "bullets or
    ballots" speech, 46, 78. See also
    Assassinations: Malcolm X
Marcuse, Herbert, 43

Marriage: bonds of, 57; as nine-
    teenth-century institution, 34.
    See also Women
Marshall Plan, 8
Marxism, 84, 185
Massachusetts Institute of Tech-
    nology, 64, 98, 101–18, 142, 155,
    158
Media: portrayal of women, 26;
    saturation, 20. See also Popular
    culture; Television
Middle East, 194
Midpeninsula Free University,
    128–32
Military: spending, 4, 11, 15, 178,
    179, 192, 199. See also Political
    issues; Violence
Military-industrial complex, 11, 12,
    178, 192, 200
Moore, Dan, 110
Moral Majority, 181
Movements: abolition, 28, 34,
    55; activism, 6, 28, 47, 48, 53,
    83, 157; black, 9, 20, 22–30,
    43, 44, 46, 47, 48, 49, 50, 57,
    58, 120, 134–36, 140, 144, 150,
    168, 185; bonds of conflict, 45–
    53; extremist, 62; free love, 34;
    "free-speech," 58, 112, 113; gay
    rights, 52, 56, 180, 181; "Lesbian
    sisterhood," 52, 56; of 1960s,
    7, 16, 26, 29, 30, 41, 78, 90, 94,
    152, 156, 159, 164, 172, 173,
    185; in 1970s, 162; peace, 42,
    58; student, 20, 42, 43, 48, 57,
    58, 59, 64, 79, 85, 126; utopian,
    11, 58, 75, 82, 84; women's, 9,
    20, 22–30, 34, 44, 48, 53–58,
    79, 116, 150, 157, 166–67, 185;
    World Federalist, 13; young
    radicals, 44, 49, 53, 59, 84. See
    also Blacks; Countercultures;
    Political issues; Students for a

Democratic Society; Universities;
   Women
Music, 20, 50, 70–75; blues tradition, 71; folk, 70; jazz, 25;
   vocabulary, 92

National Association for the Ad-
   vancement of Colored People
   (NAACP), 25, 50
National Commission on Libraries
   and Information Services, 66, 67
National Endowment for the Arts,
   116
National Guard, 136
National Organization for Women,
   166
Netherlands, 182
Neutral scholarship. See Universi-
   ties: neutral scholarship
Newark, N. J., 22, 46, 78
New Frontier, 12
New Haven, Conn., 23, 42
New Jersey, 164, 177
New left. See Political issues: new
   left
New Orleans, 25
New York City, 132. See also
   Columbia University; Harlem in
   1930s
Nicaragua, 200
Niebuhr, Rheinhold, 13
1920s, 25, 26, 30, 31
1930s, 48
1940s, 9, 149
1950s: Duke, 105, 159; economics,
   107; political situation, 6, 10, 11,
   12; witch hunts, 108
1960s: antecedents, 1–35; higher
   education, 153–56, 156–68; his-
   toricism, 83, 84; "nodal points,"
   38; as a "nova" period, 31; outcome, 88–89, 93, 158–60; pace,
   20; paranoid decade, 96; relation

to 1870s–1880s, 32, 34, 35; relation to 1980s, 161–200; rhetoric
   of 1960s, 9, 10, 91, 92; surrealistic
   quality, 83, 90, 91. See also Duke
   University: in 1960s; Movements:
   of 1960s
1970s, 57, 173, 174, 176; decade
   of self-interest, 76, 90, 166, 175;
   transition decade, 6, 93, 159, 161,
   162, 196
1980s, 4, 7, 57, 98, 158, 166; relation to 1960s, 161–200; social
   apathy, 21. See also Political
   issues: Reagan administration;
   Religion
North Carolina, 97, 108, 110. See
   also Duke University; Helms,
   Jesse; Political issues
Northern Ireland, 194
"Nova" periods of history, 30, 32,
   33

Oh! Calcutta!, 75
Oklahoma, 72
On the Road, 19
Oxford University, 30

Palo Alto, Calif., 128
Patterns: of change in 1960s, 45–
   53, 78, 156–57; historical, 10, 11;
   of social change, 30, 35, 197
Peace Corps, 36
Peace movement. See Movements:
   peace movement
Percy, Charles, 1
Philadelphia, 177
The Pilgrim's Progress, 77
Plato, 36, 77
Political issues: balkanization in
   the 1980s, 186; conservativism,
   31, 113, 159, 171, 181, 191, 192;
   deregulation, 197, 199; domino
   effect theory, 41; foreign policy, 2,

Political Issues (*continued*)
4, 9, 89, 165, 191, 195, 196; left-wing politics, 43, 58, 59, 68, 69; liberalism, 21, 36, 49, 50, 68; new left, 44, 47, 48, 78, 150, 171, 184, 192, 196; in 1960s, 4–6, 8–13, 41; in 1980s, 176–79, 184; political activism, 47–53; protectionism, 184; radical political thought, 31, 33, 44, 49, 53, 59, 84; Reagan administration, 170, 171, 177, 178, 179, 181, 182, 185, 190, 199, 200; right-wing politics, 183; social/political issues in 1960s, 164–65; in Victorian America, 32; United States government, 17, 196, 197; United States presidency, 36, 60, 63, 67. *See also* Establishment America; Movements; Vietnam: Vietnam War

Popular culture, 19, 26, 39, 43, 58, 70–77, 186

Populism: of the frontier, 34; Reagan, 172

Pornography, 186

Porter, Cole, 72, 73

Postcolonial world, 5, 9, 10, 182, 183. *See also* Africa: postcolonial; Economic issues: postcolonial economics

Postwar period, 20, 22, 25. *See also* Cold war

Power and authority: acquisitiveness, 22, 60, 69, 89; economic, 191; industrial power, 17; police, 136; university presidents, 123, 148; whites, 26; world realignments, 182. *See also* Duke University: governance; Duke University: presidency; Universities: governance; Violence: and force

"Power elite," 14

Presidencies. *See* Duke University: presidency; Political issues: United States presidency; Universities: governance

Presley, Elvis, 19, 70

Princeton University, 98, 101, 142, 143, 155

Prospect for America. See Rockefeller Brothers Fund Panel reports

Racism, 18. *See also* Blacks; Civil rights

Radcliffe College, 118. *See also* Harvard University

Radical political thought. *See* Political issues: radical political thought

Raleigh, N.C., 110

Reagan, Ronald, 111, 113, 150, 151, 152, 183, 192, 199. *See also* Political issues: Reagan administration

Religion: Buddhism, 71; Christian fundamentalist revival, 187–90; Christianity, 13, 28, 77, 143; clergy, 88; at Duke, 120; Eastern religions, 82, 94; in 1880s, 34; Hinduism, 77; Islam, 188; Methodist church, 99; Pentecostal religious movements, 172–73; Roman Catholic church, 86; on television, 190; university-related, 13–14; women and religion, 28. *See also* Countercultures: religious cults

Research, 15. *See also* Technology

Research Triangle area, 109

Right-wing politics. *See* Political issues: right-wing politics

Ripley, Dillon, 66

Rockefeller, Nelson, 1

Rockefeller Brothers Fund Panel reports, 1–8, 11, 40, 89, 179, 183, 188, 197; I: *Mid-Century*

Challenge to American Foreign Policy, 2–3; II: *International Security: Military Aspects*, 2, 4, 5; III: *Foreign Economic Policy for the Twentieth Century*, 2, 4, 5; IV: *Challenge to America: Economic and Social Aspects*, 2, 4; V: *Pursuit of Excellence: Education and the Future of America*, 2; VI: *The Power of the Democratic Idea*, 2

Roosevelt, Franklin Delano, 41, 67, 69, 199

Rudd, Mark, 78

Rusk, Dean, 1, 64–65, 68, 81

Sanford, Terry, 104, 105–6, 154–55; as North Carolina governor, 108

San Francisco, 152

San Francisco State University, 150, 151–52, 155

Sarnoff, David, 1

Savio, Mario, 78, 113

Schuller, Robert, 190

Schwartz, Felice, 39

Sciences: vs. humanities, 16, 17

The Second Sex, 40

Sexual mores, 52, 53. *See also* Countercultures; Movements; Women

Silent Vigil. *See* Duke University: Silent Vigil

Simon, Paul, 125

Slavery, 25. *See also* Movements: abolition

Smith, Page, 32

Smith College, 30, 39

Social issues: homeless, 194; in 1980s, 176, 180, 184; public programs and social assistance, 21, 25, 195; social diversity, 176, 191; social equity, 164, 192, 194, 197; social revolutions, 17; social theorists, 194; upward mobility, 175; world social order, 9. *See also* Blacks; Civil rights; Movements; Patterns: of social change; Women

Society of Friends, 112

Soldier of Fortune, 186

Soul City, 91

South (American), 22, 24. *See also* Duke University: southern heritage

South Africa, 183

Southeast Asia, 3, 10, 12, 40, 41, 194. *See also* Vietnam

Soviet Union, 4, 5, 43, 59, 109, 124; with China a military threat, 4, 5, 6, 9; in Europe, 9; in French Indochina, 3

Spain, 9, 192

Spenser, Edmund, 77

Stanford University, 120, 126

State Department, United States, 41, 109. *See also* Political issues: United States government

Stevenson, Adlai, 13

The Straw Giant, 179

Students. *See* Duke University: students; Universities: students

Students for a Democratic Society (SDS), 83, 127, 133; Weathermen, 59, 61, 90

Style, 93. *See also* Art; 1960s: rhetoric of 1960s; Popular culture

Subcultures. *See* Countercultures: subcultures

Summerskill, John, 151–53

Supreme Court, United States, 18. *See also* Political issues: United States government

Sweeney, Dennis, 126

Switzerland, 112

Technology, 32, 51. *See also* Research

Television, 186, 190, 191. *See also*
    Media; Popular culture
Teller, Edward, 1
Terrorism. *See* Violence: terrorism
Third World, 5, 11
Tommy, 70, 76, 77
Toxic waste. *See* Environmental
    issues: toxic waste
Trinity College (Durham). *See*
    Duke University: East Campus
Truman, Harry, 12
Trustees. *See* Duke University:
    board of trustees; Universities:
    committees and boards

Ulysses (James Joyce), 19, 77, 79, 90
Undergraduate colleges. *See* Uni-
    versities
United Nations, 8, 10, 11
Universities: academic life, 175;
    committees and boards, 96, 148;
    deans, 29; enrollment, 14, 24;
    governance, 58, 69, 80, 96, 148,
    150, 158, 174; "neutral scholar-
    ship," 17; presidents, 24, 29, 64,
    78, 80, 95, 97, 109, 123, 147–50;
    and religion, 13, 14, 78; students,
    15, 20, 21, 25, 40, 42, 43, 88,
    148, 158, 174; unrest, 85, 87,
    93. *See also* Academic commu-
    nity; Blacks; Bryn Mawr College;
    Cambridge University; Civil
    rights; Columbia University;
    Cornell University; Harvard Uni-
    versity; Ivy League universities;
    Kent State University; Lawrence
    College; Massachusetts Institute
    of Technology; Midpeninsula
    Free University; Movements;
    Princeton University; Radcliffe
    College; San Francisco State
    University; Smith College; Stan-
    ford University; University of

California at Berkeley; University
    of North Carolina at Chapel Hill;
    University of Wisconsin; Wes-
    leyan University; Women; Yale
    University
University of California at Berkeley,
    111–14, 118, 120, 146, 151, 155,
    158
University of North Carolina at
    Chapel Hill, 109–10
University of Wisconsin, 59, 120
Upward mobility. *See* Social issues:
    upward mobility
Urban areas, 194. *See also* Blacks:
    migration to urban areas; Harlem
    in 1930s; New York City
Urban League, 7
Utopian movements. *See* Move-
    ments: utopian

Vatican II, 86
Victorian era in America, 32
Vietnam, 3; North Vietnam, 65;
    South Vietnam, 40; Vietnam
    War, 6, 9, 12, 37, 45, 49, 58,
    60, 62, 66, 79, 80, 89, 165, 183,
    184, 185, 186, 194, 195, 198,
    199; criticism of/opposition to
    Vietnam War, 45, 46, 60, 64, 65,
    78, 89, 90, 91, 126, 155, 156, 165;
    veterans, 163. *See also* Violence:
    in Vietnam War
Violence, 188, 195; at Duke, 138;
    and force, 45, 61, 91; nonvio-
    lence, 120; terrorism, 10, 186,
    187, 188; in Vietnam War, 12,
    45, 62; World War II legacy of
    violence, 10. *See also* Guerrilla
    warfare; Movements; Power and
    authority

Washington, Booker T., 26
Washington, D.C., 4, 15, 36

Washington, George, 62, 199
Watergate hearings, 162, 190
Watt, James, 180, 197
Weathermen. *See* Students for
    a Democratic Society (SDS):
    Weathermen
Wesleyan University, 156
Westmoreland, William, 45, 60, 61,
    83
White House, 178, 190
Wilson, Woodrow, 67
Winston-Salem, N.C., 120
Women: abortion rights, 181; em-
    ployed outside home, 20, 55;
    and family, 55; and religion, 54;
    on Rockefeller panel, 5, 7, 24;
    sexual morality, 52; in society,
    22, 23, 24, 26, 30, 39, 164, 166,
    167; in Victorian America, 32.
    See also Blacks: black women;
    Movements: women's; National
    Organization for Women; Social
    issues
Women's College (Duke Univer-
    sity). *See* Duke University: East
    Campus
Women's College (Greensboro,
    N.C.), 97
Wordsworth, William, 73
World Federalist movement. *See*
    Movements: World Federalist
World War I, 25, 61, 62
World War II, 4, 5, 8, 9, 10, 14, 15,
    16, 22, 23, 40, 43, 61, 62, 103,
    109, 140, 182, 186, 194

Yale University, 23, 42, 101, 112,
    143–45, 146, 149, 156, 158
Young radicals. *See* Movements:
    young radicals
"Yuppie" phenomenon, 73